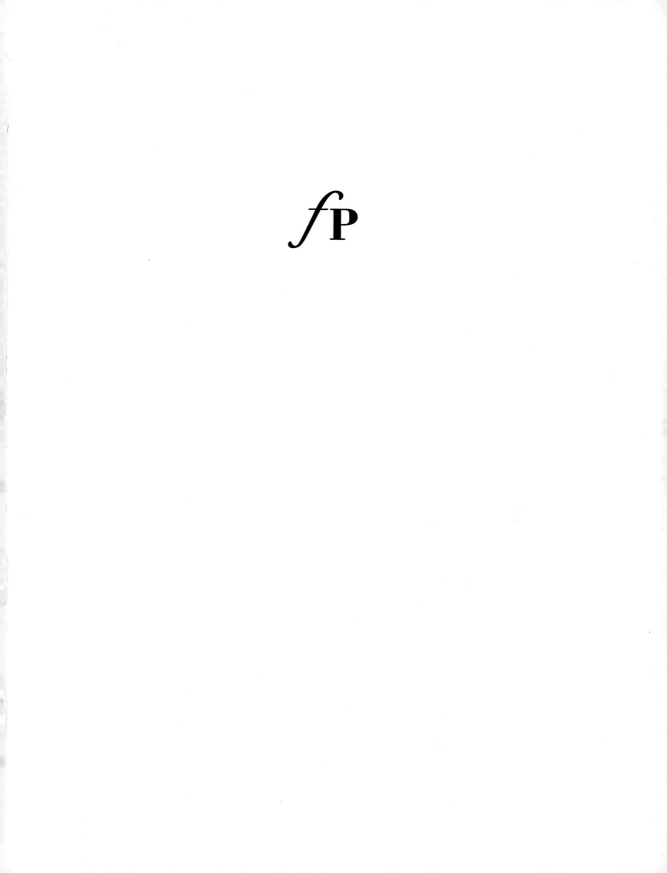

Also by Buddy Valastro

Cake Boss
Baking with the Cake Boss

Cooking Italian

WITH THE

Family Favorites as
Only Buddy Can Serve Them Up

Buddy Valastro

Photography by Miki Duisterhof

FREE PRESS

New York   London   Toronto   Sydney   New Delhi

FREE PRESS
A Division of Simon & Schuster, Inc.
1230 Avenue of the Americas
New York, NY 10020

First Free Press hardcover edition November 2012

FREE PRESS and colophon are trademarks of Simon & Schuster, Inc.
TLC, Cake Boss and their logos are trademarks of Discovery Communications, LLC,
used under license. All rights reserved. tlc.com.

For information about special discounts for bulk purchases,
please contact Simon & Schuster Special Sales at 1-866-506-1949
or business@simonandschuster.com.

The Simon & Schuster Speakers Bureau can bring authors to your live event.
For more information or to book an event, contact the Simon & Schuster Speakers Bureau
at 1-866-248-3049 or visit our website at www.simonspeakers.com.

DESIGNED BY ERICH HOBBING

Manufactured in the United States of America

1 3 5 7 9 10 8 6 4 2

Library of Congress Cataloging-in-Publication Data
Valastro, Buddy
Cooking Italian with the Cake Boss : family favorites as only Buddy can serve them up /
Buddy Valastro.
page cm.
Includes index.
Summary: "100 delicious, essential Italian-American recipes." —Provided by publisher.
1. Cooking, Italian.   I. Title
TX723. V35 2012
641.5945—dc23
2012021667

ISBN 978-1-4516-7430-9
ISBN 978-1-4516-7432-3 (ebook)

I dedicate this book to my wife, Lisa.
I may sometimes steal your recipes, but you've always been my soul mate,
in the kitchen and in life. You're my rock and my best friend,
and I'll always love you.

Contents

Breads, Pizzas, and Sandwiches

Soups

Pasta and Risotto

Main Courses

Sides

Buddy Basics

Desserts

Author's Note

In August 2009, a violent storm ripped through New York and New Jersey. The weather reports focused on how the storms uprooted a number of trees in Central Park, but for my family, the most noteworthy and heartbreaking damage occurred in New Jersey, where the extreme wind and rain devastated the local tomato crops.

I know what you're probably thinking: "Buddy, you're in the baking business, not the tomato business."

That's true. My family, the Valastros, makes its living by baking and selling just about anything you can think of: cookies, pastries, pies, and—of course—our incredible theme cakes, at Carlo's Bake Shop. It's what we're known for. What put us on the map.

But there's another side to our family and its relationship with food, and it's just as personal, maybe even *more* personal, than what we do at the bakery. I'm talking about the recipes and dishes, meals and traditions that nourish our bodies and souls when we go home. There's no more important recipe or dish in our lives than Sunday gravy, sometimes known as Sunday sauce, the pasta sauce we gather to eat together at the end of every weekend. We eat it so regularly that a few years back my family began our own tradition, one that we borrowed from my wife, Lisa's, family: making huge batches of sauce at the end of the summer and canning it for each household, based on how many bushels of tomatoes each family orders. To give you a sense of how much Sunday gravy we go through in a year at my house, Lisa orders twenty bushels of tomatoes, and each bushel yields twelve large jars!

Lisa and I began doing this after we were married, then we expanded the tradition to include our extended families at Carlo's Bake Shop on Washington Street in Hoboken. Today we do it at our new, nearby factory. This is how it works: One team of relatives is on cleaning duty, scrubbing the tomatoes in the industrial sinks; another team quarters the tomatoes and gets them into the huge forty-, sixty-, and eighty-gallon steam kettles, along with olive oil, onions, and salt. The tomatoes are cooked until they break down, then we allow them to simmer for an hour. Another team processes the fruit through a machine that removes the skin and seeds, leaving us with a sauce. That sauce goes back into the kettle and is brought to a boil, then transferred to jars that have been sterilized in the dishwasher. We add basil and the jar is vacuum sealed, locking in all that incredible, just-cooked flavor until we're ready to call on it throughout the year.

In 2009, those storms wreaked havoc with our sauce making. Rather than just placing a huge order for tomatoes from one source, we had to scrounge around, securing a bushel here and there from area farms. Because tomatoes were so scarce, some family members had to drive out to farms in person and beg for a few bushels. But we were that determined to stick to our tradition and make our Sunday gravy!

I'm not going to lie: What we ended up with after all that work and the cooking that followed wasn't exactly world-class: The tomatoes had survived the storm, but they had a lot of scars and bruises. As a result, the sauce was runny and, even after all our patient simmering, the flavor wasn't as intense as it usually was.

But I'll tell you something: We didn't get upset. To us, the Sunday gravy of 2009 was a metaphor for life itself, especially life in a big, tight-knit family like ours. There will always be ups and downs, but we worked together to make the best of it, we were all there for our annual cooking and jarring ritual, and we left with those jars of sauce we treasured so much. It may not have been the best, but it was good enough, and next year, we knew, we'd have better luck.

For me, that story is and always will be a gentle reminder of my family's priorities and how far we'll go to adhere to them: Even with all the fame we've enjoyed as a result of *Cake Boss,* when we're away from the lights and cameras, live shows, and book signings, we're just like any other family. We enjoy chilling out and spending time together, and there's no way we'd rather do that than around a table, a place that keeps us grounded and connected to each other, as well as to the relatives who came before us. As proud as I am of our professional success, I'm just as proud that we've been able to continue making time for our family and extended family, and we're talking *a lot* of people, to meet several times a week and eat together. And, as busy as we are at the bakery and filming our television show, we'll still make time to hunt down bushels of tomatoes if we need to, in order to keep our traditions alive and well.

Of course, Sunday gravy is just one thing that we eat. We also have lots of other family dishes—appetizers and salads, soups and pastas, main courses and desserts—that have become part of our repertoire over the years. In this book, I'm honored to share with you my family's favorite recipes, and tell you the stories of what makes them so near and dear to our hearts. I hope they might become favorites for your family as well, and that they help you create memories to last a lifetime, the same way they've done for us Valastros.

Buon appetito,
Buddy Valastro
Hoboken, New Jersey
April 2012

Nothing Brings Families
Together Like Food

Long before my sisters and I were born, there was a table at the heart of the Valastro family.

I don't mean an actual, physical table. Or at least not a *single* actual, physical table. I mean that the act of gathering around a table has been at the center of our lives and traditions for generations, whether for a nightly dinner with one's immediate family, a larger gathering around the tradition of Sunday gravy, or a holiday when more people than you could possibly imagine would fill a relative's modest house to overflowing.

When I was a kid, my maternal grandmother, Madeline, hosted countless family meals, including holiday dinners, in the basement of her house in Hoboken. It wasn't a big house; in fact, the basement measured just about fifty feet by twenty-five feet. It was an open space with a kitchenette in the corner, a couch area with a television, and a bathroom with the littlest shower you ever saw: Only my diminutive grandfather and the youngest of the grandchildren could even fit in there.

Because she hosted so many family dinners, Grandma Madeline kept a number of folding tables set up end to end at all times to make one long table. She'd cook for days, preparing so many dishes that it seemed her tiny, old, white oven could not have produced that much food without breaking down. But somehow she and it always got the job done.

When family arrived, Grandma Madeline would already have put out a huge spread of antipasti, or appetizers, and the adults would wash them down with my grandfather's homemade wine, which he made in his garden and stored in whatever bottles he could get his hands on, everything from actual wine jugs to soda bottles. There'd be pasta (either lasagna or ziti), then a main course, often determined by the occasion: We'd have lamb for Easter and turkey for Thanksgiving. Sometimes, Grandma Madeline would prep those meats at home except for the roasting, then bring them to the bakery and cook them in our big ovens, a very common practice back in Italy.

After dinner, the men would congregate in that little loungelike area: They'd eat oranges and walnuts and drink my grandfather's homemade grappa. I can still see them there, talking and laughing.

Those were special times, precious times, and they were the kind of moments that were the cornerstone not just of our family, but of most families. However, times are changing. People work longer hours than they used to, and parents and kids alike spend more time punching buttons and touch pads on their smart phones and tablets than they do talking to each other. That makes me sad, but I'm not going to lie: Our family has experienced a little of that as well. Nevertheless, we've managed to maintain our traditions. We were raised to believe that nothing brings a family together like food, and those are words we live by. Always have, and always will.

Of course, my family existed long before my sisters and I did, and long before there was a Carlo's Bake Shop, so the traditions that we carry on in our homes today aren't just a part of our personal past, but also of family legend and lore. Many of the dishes we eat go all the way back to our ancestral towns and villages in Italy, where our parents and grandparents first ate or cooked them. Some of the first stories I ever heard about Lipari, where my paternal Grandma Grace was from, or Altamura, where my maternal Grandma Madeline was raised, were told as those wonderful, loving women stirred a pot of soup or stuck a tray of lasagna in the oven. When I eat those dishes today, I don't just remember my time with those family matriarchs; I also imagine myself standing on the streets of those villages, surrounded by craggy cliffs and old stone houses, the roar of Vespas in the air, enjoying the illusion that I was there with them back in those olden days.

As I said, nothing brings families together like food, and not just around a table. It also connects one generation to another and helps keep alive our memory of relatives who have left this world, their recipe cards more valuable than the other material possessions they might have left behind.

Most of my immediate family's recipes come from my mother, although my father was a brilliant improviser in his own right. Before I was born, my parents and sisters lived above the original Carlo's Bake Shop on Adams Street in Hoboken. Mom cooked dinner for the family seven nights a week, and continued to do so when I was born and the family moved to the nearby town of Little Ferry. Dad was off to work before the rest of us were awake, so dinner was a sacred time, the only meal for which we were all together and could share what was going on in our lives. And so, we were trained to treat dinner with respect: There were no distractions like television; I can only imagine what Dad would have done if I'd whipped out a mobile device at the table. Fortunately, we didn't have cell phones back then, so I never found out. (He would make an exception if the bakery called, but even then, he'd be aggravated. I can still hear him barking "Hello!" into the receiver when he answered it, to make clear to whoever was calling that they'd better keep it quick.)

Food is so central to our lives that you could mark time with it, both on a daily basis and throughout the year: Back when my sisters all lived at home, Mama had a roster of dinners that were as regular as the nightly specials in a restaurant, or the shows on a television schedule. It changed according to the season, but a sample lineup, from the winter, might go like this: The week started with Sunday Gravy. (There's much more about this, starting on page 179.) Monday was chicken cutlets with vegetables;

Tuesday was pasta with leftover Sunday Gravy and its meats; Wednesday was a soup such as *pasta e fagioli* (pasta and bean soup); Thursday was chicken and potatoes baked together in the oven; Friday was fish, such as broiled porgy (bream) or fried flounder; and Saturday was steak with peas and onions. The only time Mama deviated from her batting order was when my father decided to whip something up for the family.

Our annual rituals were, and remain, just as dependable: *pasta e lenticchie,* a soupy dish of pasta and lentils, on New Year's Eve, the legumes an Italian superstition promising good luck for the coming twelve months; on Valentine's Day, Lisa and I always have linguine with clams and lobster because that's what she made for me on our first Valentine's Day together (although these days our celebration is trumped by our son Carlo's birthday, which falls on February 14); we eat lamb on Easter Sunday; go out to an early dinner on Mother's Day; barbecue shrimp, lobster, hamburgers, kabobs, and sausages on Father's Day, Memorial Day, and the Fourth of July; and on Thanksgiving we go all-American, eating turkey and stuffing, cranberries, and sweet potatoes.

On Christmas Eve, we have the traditional Italian feast of the seven fishes, although that's a relatively new development: For our entire lives, the holidays were different for us than for most people, because the bakery was open. When we were kids, our father wasn't around until dinner, and as we got older, we all began working at the bakery as well—including on holidays. When we were all grown, we didn't have any daytime celebrations of Christmas; instead, after we closed the doors of the shop, we'd all end up at somebody's house, improvising a dinner.

In 2010, I decided to close the bakery for Christmas. We try to provide everything for our customers, but anything picked up on Christmas Eve will still be delicious on Christmas Day, so I decided to give the whole family, and other employees, the holiday off. Inspired by memories of my father and his spontaneous cooking binges, as we were closing the shop that December 24, I invited everybody to our house for a feast of the seven fishes and hit a fish market in Hoboken for some last-minute shopping.

Next thing you know, all of my sisters and brothers-in-law and their kids were at Lisa's and my home, and we all cooked together: we made calamari, shrimp cocktail, fried flounder, Aunt Nina's mussels (page 49), linguine with clams, seared scallops in cream sauce, and a quick baccala (salt cod) and tomato stew.

That dinner wasn't planned, but it's already become a tradition, yet another way to bring us all together and set the stage for our kids to stay connected for years to come.

FOOD AND ME: A LOVE STORY

Did you ever wonder what makes food so important in all cultures? I think it's because it engages so many of our senses that it triggers memories like nothing else: The smell of frying garlic brings me back to our family home, and my mother starting her Sunday gravy early in the morning (if you think bacon is the best smell on a Sunday morning, you didn't grow up in a house with Sunday gravy); the sweet, fennel-tinged scent of frying sausage takes me back to the block parties and street fairs of my youth, and the sausage and pepper sandwiches I loved so much; and Grandma Madeline's baked ziti with creamy mortadella sauce brings me back to her finished basement and all the family gatherings she hosted.

My own relationship with food has grown and deepened over the years. When I was a kid, I could take it or leave it. It was like fuel to me, something to keep me going as I biked around town, played touch football with my friends, and (when I got older) went out on the town. But, as I matured into an adult, my palate, which is a fancy way of saying *my taste buds,* matured as well. I developed some real taste and a true appreciation for good food. There are milestones in my eating life that I can point to and say, "*There!* That's when I became a more serious eater!" For instance, I had an aversion to ketchup when I was very young (as I said, I was finicky), but in time grew to love it, and the same was true of sushi or the Italian equivalent, *crudo,* which at first grossed me out, but which I came to not only enjoy but appreciate, because of the quality and technique involved. Another example would be the octopus I had on my first trip to Sicily. When I was a kid, the tentacles and suckers skeeved me so much I couldn't even bring myself to try it, but once I had a bite of octopus in Sicily, fresh from the sea and grilled to a char, its toothsome flesh revealing a pleasure I'd never imagined, I had yet another favorite added to my rapidly growing list.

Food has also been a way for the family elders to teach my generation about the past, about our history and heritage back in Italy. For example, once in a while, my father's mother, Grandma Grace, would get a craving for a favorite dish from the old country, like a fish soup she served with toast smeared with aioli, which is a garlic mayonnaise. When that moment came, my father would clear a space for her in the kitchen at Carlo's, and she'd cook the dish, the oceanic aroma duking it out with the sugar and flour, until, inevitably, the savory scents won out and we'd all follow our noses to the stove, forming a chow line.

Grace wasn't the only one who sometimes cooked at the bakery. Once in a while, my dad would take a big spider, the webbed strainer we used to fish zeppole and other pastries out of hot frying oil, stick a steak or lamb chop on it, and grill it in the open flame of a candy stove; one day, my Uncle Mario came by with a side of beef he'd been gifted by a business acquaintance in the Bronx and I grilled steaks that way for the whole crew. It took a while, but it was worth it!

Which brings me to my real cooking hero: my father. Just as he taught me everything there was to know about baking, Dad taught me all I needed to know about cooking. He didn't show me many specifics; mostly I learned by his example, and sometimes by helping my mother cook things like meatballs and watching how she made them. My father was a self-taught home cook who simply had a knack for throwing food together and having it come out terrific, and one of his great pleasures was interrupting Mama's weekly meal lineup to cook something spur of the moment for the family. I remember going to Chinese restaurants with him, like The Jade in Lyndhurst, New Jersey, or Chan's Dragon Inn in Richfield, and loving the fried rice. Sometimes, the day after, he'd decided to whip up fried rice at home, without using a cookbook or asking anybody how to do it. And it always came out perfect. That was my father: Nobody taught him or me how to cook. I'm sure it must have had something to do with how much time he spent baking, but I believe he simply had a gift and that he passed it on to me.

I still remember the first thing I ever cooked. In junior high school, I took a home economics class, and we learned how to make pepper steak. I decided to try it myself and make dinner for the family, interrupting the nightly schedule the way my father sometimes did. The dinner was a smashing success, and I was on my way. Before you knew it, I was trying a lot of pasta dishes; a very successful early one had a simple cream sauce. I also loved the grill. I was a gym rat in my teens, and would often come home from working out, famished, help myself to one of the steaks Mom always had in the refrigerator for Saturday night, and throw it on the barbecue out back.

In time, as I grew up and had my own children, I became a good home cook myself and, like my father, developed the ability to experiment successfully, whether whipping up dinner for Lisa and me or inviting all my sisters and brothers-in-law over for a dinner of anything from fajitas to a pasta put together from whatever happened to be in the pantry.

Food is also one of the things that initially drew me to my wife, Lisa, who grew up with many of the same traditions and rituals that I did. When we were first falling in love, I was struck that we had this shared value, a mutual understanding of and appreciation for the foundation created by spending time around a table with your family.

Lisa is an amazing and passionate home cook who takes great pleasure in cooking not only for me and our kids, but also for as many relatives as feel like coming over. Some of her specialties include linguine with shrimp and roasted tomatoes, and her version of my grandmother's eggplant parmesan.

Lisa and I also try to involve the kids in our cooking whenever possible. She and the kids have a tradition of making a tiered cake for me on my birthday. And, on a daily basis, the kids enjoy helping out in the kitchen. Buddy, Jr., loves to clean garlic and does a proud and perfect job of it; Sofia and Marco love to peel potatoes, carrots, and anything else they can get their hands on; and they all love to bake at home, helping me out by cracking eggs, measuring flour and sugar, and mixing ingredients. Sometimes, we'll take a whole Sunday and bake cookies from morning until it's time to dig into that precious Sunday Gravy, when all of our traditions come together.

Why I Wrote This Book

First of all, I love food, and I've also seen throughout my life that food doesn't have to be complicated to be delicious. When I think of all the different things that my relatives could do with garlic and onions, canned tomatoes and parmesan cheese, sausage and veal, it never fails to amaze me. So, when I see restaurant chefs on television talking about ingredients I can't pronounce that come from places I've never heard of, and telling me to follow their instructions to the letter, I sometimes feel like the cooking and the food have gotten a little too serious—even soulless. If I want to eat restaurant food, I'll go to a restaurant!

It sounds like a cliché but, as a self-taught cook, I know firsthand that great food can be made by somebody who keeps it simple and cooks with love. The recipes in this book are simple recipes, for a lot of reasons: Some of them were first cooked by my relatives back in Italy when they were poor and couldn't afford many different foods. Other recipes are meant to showcase a great ingredient or two, so family cooks know enough not to get in their way. Almost all these recipes are prepared with other people around, and while gabbing with friends and relatives while preparing the meal, if you don't keep things nice and easy you could get distracted and make a mistake!

The other reason I wrote this book was to share the family stories and recipes behind the dishes that my relatives and I grew up on, and still cook and eat today. I'll be honest: I'm doing this as much for myself and my family as I am for you; before I wrote this book, these recipes weren't collected in one place. Many of them weren't even typed—they were scribbled on grease-stained recipe cards, or scraps of paper, or lived only in the memory of the person whose specialty they were. Now, we have them all typed between two covers. In other words, I'll be using this book as much as you will!

MAKE IT YOUR OWN

I'll let you in on a little secret: I'm a great professional baker, but as a home cook, I'm nothing special. I can turn out some pretty delicious dinners, but I don't think that my recipes, or even my relatives' sacred recipes, as delicious as they are, are written in stone: You can replace dried oregano with fresh, substitute one shape of pasta for another, or leave out something you just plain don't like. Who knows? You may even come up with something better than the original!

The main thing I want to say about the recipes in the book—again—is that you don't have to follow most of them to the letter. Many of them are dishes that were first made by one of my relatives or discovered in a restaurant and adapted by somebody else. In particular, if you don't have the exact ingredient I recommend, don't worry: if you don't have one vinegar, try another; if you don't have the same pasta, use another; if a recipe has three kinds of cheese, but you happen to have two on hand and feel like trying it *right now,* then go for it. (I point out some possible adjustments in the head notes and ingredients lists for a lot of the recipes.) That's how I learned to cook. You might discover a better way to make a dish, or you might make a terrible mistake and learn what *doesn't* work. That's okay.

How to Use This Book

This book is organized like most other cookbooks. After this introduction, you'll find some general notes about your pantry and cooking equipment, then we'll get right into the recipes, which are organized the same way in which a meal is organized: Appetizers, Finger Foods, and Snacks; Salads; Breads, Pizzas, and Sandwiches; Soups; Pasta and Risotto; Main Courses; Sides; and Desserts.

Just as I encourage you to play around with the recipes in this book, don't feel as though you have to serve the dishes for the part of the meal I've suggested. I say it up front in the very first recipe: Bruschetta is usually served as a starter, but it makes a great snack on its own at any time of day and would even be delicious alongside eggs for breakfast.

Along the same lines, soups and salads can often be meals on their own, especially at lunch, and pasta can be a starter, a main course, a side dish, or (shhh, don't tell anybody) a midnight snack, eaten cold, or nuked in the microwave.

I want you to play with your food, in the best possible way: break the rules a little, have fun with it, and don't take it too seriously. Even if you make a mistake, there's always another meal just a few hours away.

RECIPES

Each recipe in this book comes with a headnote, a little introduction in which I tell you about the dish, perhaps why it's important to my family, a tip on how to cook it, or both.

After that, you'll find the ingredients, then the instructions as to how to prepare and cook the dish.

INGREDIENTS

When recording ingredients for the recipes in this book, I tried to be as casual as possible while still being responsible.

- In cases when I feel an exact amount of an ingredient is called for, I give you the amount in spoon or cup measurements, such as "1 tablespoon minced garlic."

- In cases where the amount doesn't need to be quite as exact, I don't make you break out the measuring vessels, instead calling for, say, "1 large garlic clove, minced."
- As far as how much of an ingredient you need to buy to get a chopped or diced amount, if you need less than a cup of chopped or cut ingredients, I don't spell it out for you because most fruits and vegetables will give you at least a cup. If you need more than a cup, I get more specific.

Here are some notes on ingredients used in many of the recipes, and what I mean when I call for them.

- Butter is unsalted (sweet or sweet cream) butter, because salted butter doesn't allow you to control the amount of salt in a recipe.
- Cream is heavy cream, also called whipping cream.
- Herbs are fresh herbs unless otherwise indicated, except for bay leaves, which are dried. (I also usually call for dried oregano, but specify it in the recipes.)
- Eggs are large eggs, preferably free range or organic. Why? Because they taste better!
- Milk is whole milk; I don't recommend substituting low-fat or fat-free milk in my recipes.
- Salt is coarse or kosher salt, unless otherwise indicated.
- Sugar is granulated sugar, unless otherwise indicated.

DIRECTIONS

Before getting down to the fun part—the cooking—read the recipe all the way through. Then read it again! Visualize the steps so that you know exactly what you have to do.

Then, get all the ingredients prepared and ready to go. I also suggest that you arrange them in the order in which you'll be using them, which will help guarantee that you don't leave anything out.

If there are people around who know how to cook, deputize one of them to be your *sous* (assistant) chef. I find that a spouse is a perfect choice for this important role: You get to spend a little time together doing something fun; what could be better than that?

This might be a good place for me to mention that each recipe has prep time and cook time indicated. These times are approximate: They will be influenced by how many people are cooking, how quickly you're able to work, and how long things take to finish on the stove or grill or in the oven. But you should find the times helpful in planning what to cook and when to begin.

Finally, have all the various cooking vessels you'll need ready, as well as a serving dish or individual plates. I'd even recommend that you take charge and enlist some-body to make sure the table is set, everybody's ready to eat, and drinks are poured when the cooking is done so that the food doesn't get cold: There's nothing worse than making a big meal, then watching it cool off while all that other stuff goes on.

If you do all these things, it will help you relax and enjoy the fun part: the cooking!

Seasoning with Salt and Pepper

Most of the recipes in this book do not list an exact quantity of salt and pepper. The reason is that you need to season to taste. The easiest way to do this is to season a little bit, then taste and add more salt and/or pepper if necessary. (In recipes with raw eggs or poultry, I give an exact amount so you that don't have to taste those ingredients, which can be dangerous.) Everybody has their own sense of how much salt and pepper they like. Of course, some people have to curb the salt due to dietary restrictions for themselves, a family member, or a guest, so I leave this one in your hands, which is how it's done in most recipes.

The Pantry

There's nothing like having a well-stocked pantry to be sure you'll cook as often as possible. When you have all the necessary basics, such as spices, oils and vinegars, flour and sugar, canned tomatoes and pasta, it makes it that much easier to cook. It also makes dishes seem less expensive because, if you have all the basics on hand, you don't need to spend a fortune, either in time or money, when you hit the market; you might only need to buy three or four things to make a lot of the dishes in the book!

Here are some key items that I suggest you have on hand at all times.

SALTS
Coarse, kosher salt for all-purpose seasoning and a fine sea salt as an occasional finishing agent or for preparations in which coarse salt might not dissolve properly.

BLACK PEPPERCORNS
I don't recommend buying or using commercially ground pepper. Keep black peppercorns in a mill and grind it as you use it, for the freshest, most potent flavor.

OILS
The three oils I recommend you keep in your pantry are olive oil for dishes in which you desire its distinct flavor; canola oil or another neutral oil such as grapeseed, for dishes when you don't; and extra-virgin olive oil for use in salad dressings, as a finishing agent, and, occasionally, for cooking. I also sometimes like to drizzle intense white-truffle oil over dishes, especially mushroom dishes, for an aromatic flourish. However, only buy it if you plan to use it a lot; it's expensive and will go rancid more quickly than most oils.

VINEGARS
For me, the essential must-have vinegars are red wine, white wine, and balsamic. Other vinegars called for in this book are sherry, champagne, and apple cider, but whether you make them part of your regular inventory is really up to you and how much cooking you do; you can always buy these as you need them, or substitute one of the other vinegars for these.

SUGAR
I sometimes use white, granulated sugar to cut the acidity of tomatoes in sauces. It's also, obviously, essential in dessert making.

CANNED TOMATOES AND TOMATO PASTE

If you're going to cook Italian food, it won't be long before you reach for a can of tomatoes. Whole, peeled tomatoes, diced tomatoes, and crushed tomatoes are all well worth keeping in the cupboard, as are a can or two (or a tube) of tomato paste.

WINE

This is one of the few places where I'm going to put my foot down and insist on something: Don't buy or use anything that goes by the name *cooking wine*. Even the most unremarkable wine is better for cooking. Keep a bottle of inexpensive red, such as Chianti, and a bottle of inexpensive white, such as Pinot Grigio, for cooking.

DRIED PASTA

I suggest having at least one box of each of the various pasta categories such as long (spaghetti), short (ziti, penne), small (ditalini or tubettini), lasagna, and orzo, on hand at all times.

ARBORIO RICE

This is the most popular risotto rice; you should always have a small bag or box of it.

JARRED AND CANNED VEGETABLES AND CANNED AND DRIED LEGUMES

Most vegetables and beans should be purchased fresh, but I call for jarred roasted red peppers; marinated artichoke hearts; brined black olives; canned white beans (or a bag of dried white beans), such as cannellini; and dried brown lentils pretty often. While more a condiment than a vegetable, I also like to keep some sun-dried tomato pesto on hand because it packs such a punch; if nothing else, you can use it as a sandwich spread.

DRIED HERBS AND SPICES

Crushed red-pepper flakes, those confettilike bits that you see in pizza parlors, come up a lot in Italian-American cooking, because they're such a quick and easy way to add a little heat. While I usually prefer fresh herbs to dried, every cook should have dried bay leaves on hand, and I usually go for dried oregano over fresh because fresh oregano can be a little intense. I also sometimes call for dried basil, parsley, and Italian seasoning. Saffron is expensive, but you'll probably use it often enough to make it worth having at least a small container of it. For dessert making, and occasional use in savory cooking, ground cinnamon, nutmeg, and allspice also come up fairly often, although whether you should always stock them is a judgment call. Here's a good rule of thumb for deciding what to make part of your pantry: You should throw out all dried herbs and spices that you've had for a year or more because their flavor dims; if you don't think you'll go through a particular ingredient in that time, buy it only as needed.

CAPERS
It doesn't matter if they're packed in salt or brine; capers add a salinity and gentle crunch to sauces and such, so keep a small jar on hand.

ANCHOVIES
Anchovies are rarely the center of attention, but they have an intensity of flavor that can add a boost to a lot of dishes, and not necessarily seafood. Whether they're packed in salt or brine doesn't matter. If you can find it, a tube of anchovy paste is also worth having around for punching up sauces and other dishes.

ALL-PURPOSE FLOUR
I use a lot of flour in my cooking, for everything from breading ingredients before frying to thickening braising bases. As its name suggests, all-purpose flour works for just about everything.

WONDRA FLOUR
If you don't already use this mix of wheat and barley flour, you may not believe how much it improves the crunch in fried foods.

CORNMEAL
I don't use cornmeal a lot in actual cooking, but it's the best thing to sprinkle on a pizza peel to keep the dough from sticking, so it makes my pantry list.

CORNSTARCH
Flour thickens sauces when you add it at the beginning of a recipe; cornstarch does the same thing at the end of a recipe. I also sometimes use it as part of the breading mix for fried foods.

WORCESTERSHIRE SAUCE
This inimitable sauce doesn't come up often, but when it does, it's one of the few ingredients that can't quite be replaced. Keep a bottle on hand; if nothing else, you can always drizzle it on grilled steaks.

MUSTARDS
You might be surprised how often Dijon mustard and Colman's mustard powder come up; you rarely perceive a mustard flavor in the dishes I use them in, but they add a distinct zing to salad dressings, breading, and other preparations.

STOCK

Either make and freeze your own (pages 301-303) or buy a good-quality chicken and/or fish stock or broth; pick a low-sodium recipe so you can control the amount of salt. There is one recipe in the book that calls for beef bouillon, but that's a more and more rare ingredient these days, so it's not an essential item. A bottle or two of clam juice can also come in handy, especially if you cook a lot of shellfish.

ACTIVE DRY YEAST

If you plan to make pizza, you'll need active dry yeast, so you might as well keep a small packet or three on hand; they don't take up much room so there's no reason not to.

DESSERT ESSENTIALS

In addition to some of the ingredients named above (flour, sugar, spices), if you make a lot of desserts, you should probably have the following on hand.

Vanilla (bean and pure vanilla extract)
Bittersweet chocolate (in chip or block form) and cocoa powder (a good brand such as Callebaut)
Nutella (optional)

FRESH AND PERISHABLE INGREDIENTS

While not pantry items, these perishable items come up a lot in my recipes, and in most cooking, so are always good to have around:

Unsalted butter
Often-used vegetables (garlic, Spanish onions, carrots, celery)
Bacon and/or pancetta (Italian bacon)
Bread
Cheeses (hard, aged cheeses like Parmigiano-Reggiano and pecorino Romano will last a long time; fresh ricotta and mozzarella won't, so only keep those on hand if you'll go through them on a weekly basis)
Eggs
Lemons
Milk

Appetizers, Finger Foods, and Snacks

Picture a dining table so packed with food that you can't see an inch of the table's surface itself: platters of cured meats, such as rosy pink prosciutto di Parma, waxy red discs of salami, floppy slices of mortadella, and beside it, assorted cheeses: cubes of pecorino Romano and fontina, little balls of mozzarella called *bocconcini* ("small mouthfuls"), and a Mount Everest–sized hunk of the mother of all cheeses: Parmigiano-Reggiano, with a small carving knife plunged into it like Excalibur, so everybody can break off the piece just right for them.

There's a basket of bread, and little plates of marinated mushrooms, hot cherry peppers with morsels of prosciutto and provolone tucked inside, sun-dried tomatoes, roasted red peppers, Roman-style artichokes, and whatever else anybody brought along that day.

When families like mine get together, the appetizers, or *antipasti,* alone would be enough to serve as a meal for families from most other cultures. There are all kinds of reasons that this part of our gatherings is almost a lunch or dinner unto itself. Mostly, there's the tradition. Going to a Valastro dinner without appetizers would be like going to the movies and skipping the popcorn; it's part of the tradition that simply can't be removed.

It's also a time to mingle. Once you're plopped down in your chair for dinner, you can't move about freely, going from conversation to conversation like a trapeze artist. Even when it's just a few relatives meeting for a weeknight dinner, antipasti time always has a buzz and energy all its own.

Antipasti also infuse any gathering with the charm of the familiar. It's like a ritual: There will always be those meats and those cheeses, those little snacks. In my family, every house has its own specialties that we look forward to whenever we go there, or when the main cook (usually the wife) brings that dish along to larger events. Each one calls to mind certain people, places, and events that my relatives and I remember fondly.

Here are a few notes about the recipes in this chapter:

- My family is huge but, since I don't know how big yours is, I've scaled most of the recipes in this chapter down to feed four or four to six people, which wasn't easy. If you're serving a large group, most of these recipes multiply well, so just increase the quantities accordingly.

- Be strategic. If cooking a number of dishes for, say, ten people, you don't need ten true servings of everything because everybody will eat less of each item. For example, my recipe for rice balls, *Arancini* alla Buddy (page 56), will feed way more than ten to twelve people if those people are also sampling Gloria's Fried Artichokes (page 35), and the Baked Chicken Fingers (page 54). So, the more dishes you're serving, the less you will need of each one.

- Don't feel bound by the fact that these recipes are located in this chapter. You can serve many of them as a snack at any time of day and some of them, such as the rice balls and chicken fingers, could even make a small meal, especially if paired with a simple salad.

- If you're planning an entire meal, don't make the same mistake a lot of home cooks make and think of appetizers and the meal as two separate things. Try to consider them together and not repeat too many ingredients, especially fish, poultry, or meats: For example, if you're serving Mama's Chicken and Potatoes (page 228) as a main course, then save the Baked Chicken Fingers (page 54) for another time. Same thing with the style of the food: if you're making Stuffed Mushrooms (page 33) as an appetizer, maybe don't make the Stuffed Jumbo Shrimp (page 208) on the same day. The one area where I think it's okay, even good, to be repetitive, is with the grill: If you're grilling outdoors, nobody will mind having that wonderful, smoky, charred flavor touch just about everything you're serving.

- The first rule of entertaining is to have fun at your own parties: Do as much of the prep work as you can before guests arrive, so you don't have to be away from the table long to get things ready to serve. If you have a large enough kitchen, you can have people hang out right there, so you can visit with them while you cook, or maybe even get them to help out. Like I said, nothing brings a family together like food, and that goes for making it as well as eating it!

BRUSCHETTA

Bruschetta is a popular and irresistible Italian hors d'oeuvre that is like a two- or three-bite open-faced sandwich.

The classic bruschetta is topped with tomatoes and basil, but you can make it with just about anything—usually people use the word bruschetta to refer to the tomato topping and crostini to refer to other variations, but I call them all bruschetta: Why get complicated?

I was first introduced to bruschetta by my maternal grandmother, Madeline, who also taught me about its origins and a little about the resourcefulness and grit of my ancestors and the Italian people in general. Like so many Italian staples, bruschetta is a poor person's food: My grandmother grew up poor, in Altamura, Italy, in the mountains of the Puglia region, where tomatoes were plentiful, practically free, since everybody did their own farming. As if that weren't enough, the bread—considered by most to be the best bread in Italy—was cheap, as bread usually is. The amazing thing about bruschetta was that it was made to get the absolute most out of those ingredients, giving them a second life by using day-old bread and tomatoes that were past their prime and almost falling apart: Dicing the tomatoes hid their condition, and toasting the bread concealed its staleness, although that staleness was also a benefit: The firm interior helped keep it from getting soggy when piled high with juicy chopped tomatoes. Clever people, my ancestors.

Bruschetta

Bruschetta is usually served as an appetizer, but can also be a stand-alone snack at any time. Don't rule it out at breakfast; the classic tomato version makes a wonderful sidecar to egg dishes.

Don't feel confined by my bruschetta recipes. There are almost no limits to what you can top toasted bread slices with to make your own versions. Another terrific possibility is caponata (page 300).

Bruschetta with Tomatoes, Olives, and Capers

SERVES 4 TO 6
PREP TIME: 15 MINUTES
COOK TIME: 5 MINUTES

I didn't understand any of the rich history of bruschetta when I was a kid. All I knew was that when I went to my Grandmother Madeline's house, "Grandma's gonna make bruschetta!"

Grandma Madeline lived in a row house in Hoboken—the footprint of the structure was about twenty-five feet across by 100 feet from front to back. The gathering place was actually down in the finished basement and when the family got together it would be packed: my parents and grandparents, aunts and uncles, sisters and cousins. It didn't matter how many of us there were; we always managed to fit into that little basement.

Bruschetta provided a real connection between the Valastro ancestral home, Italy, and our family's adopted home in America, because if there's one thing that New Jersey is proud of, it's tomatoes. My father always kept a little vegetable garden at our house, and sometimes brought tomatoes over for Madeline to use in her bruschetta. To my delight, my oldest son, Buddy, Jr., loves gardening: In 2011, with the help of my mother-in-law, Gloria, herself an avid gardener, I set up a big garden in our backyard and Buddy, Jr., tends it, growing his own tomatoes and zucchini, as well as herbs, including basil, rosemary, and parsley. He takes care of it every day and, when he lets us use his tomatoes and herbs for bruschetta, the family's deep history with this humble appetizer comes full circle in a way that never fails to move me.

6-inch piece baguette, excluding ends, sliced crosswise into twelve
  ½-inch slices
¼ cup plus 1 tablespoon olive oil
½ large garlic clove, cut in half crosswise
1 cup ¼-inch diced Roma tomato
¼ cup drained, finely diced roasted red peppers
¼ cup pitted, coarsely chopped black olives
3 tablespoons finely diced red onion
1 tablespoon capers, soaked for 10 minutes in warm water,
  drained, and rinsed

Kosher salt
Freshly ground black pepper
3 tablespoons red wine vinegar
3 tablespoons finely grated Parmigiano-Reggiano

1. Position a rack in the center of the oven. Preheat to 350°F.
2. Arrange the baguette slices in a single layer on a baking sheet and drizzle with 2 tablespoons olive oil. Toast until golden brown, 2 to 3 minutes. Remove from the oven and rub the slices with the garlic clove (see note). Let the slices cool.
3. While the bread is toasting, put the tomatoes, peppers, olives, onions, and capers in a medium mixing bowl. Season with salt and pepper, bearing in mind that olives and capers are salty. Drizzle the vinegar and remaining 3 tablespoons of olive oil over the mixture and toss gently, taking care to not bust up the other ingredients. Let marinate for 15 to 20 minutes at room temperature to let flavors develop.
4. Arrange the baguette slices on a platter. Use a slotted spoon to spoon equal amounts of the mixture over each baguette slice. Sprinkle some cheese over each one, and serve.

Note: To rub garlic over hot, just-cooked food, cut a clove in half, then impale the uncut side of the clove on a fork and use it like a brush to apply the cut side of the garlic to the food and impart a gentle garlic flavor. This also works great on grilled meats, especially pork chops and steaks.

Fresh Bread?

Although bruschetta is classically made with day-old bread, you don't need to use stale bread to make it; just be sure to toast the bread enough that it becomes crispy and firm and can carry a generous heaping of juicy tomatoes without them soaking through.

Madeline's White Bean
and Tomato Bruschetta

SERVES 4 TO 6

PREP TIME: 5 MINUTES

(NOT INCLUDING PREHEATING OR PREPPING GRILL)

COOK TIME: 10 MINUTES

My grandmother wasn't the only Madeline in the family who loved bruschetta. My sister Madeline adores it, too, and has even developed her own twist on it: This is her house bruschetta, with white beans and celery added, and balsamic vinegar in place of plain old red wine vinegar. Those easy changes really take this humble appetizer to a new level. The biggest difference is texture: The beans add a nice, toothsome quality that gives way to their one-of-a-kind creaminess, and the celery adds crunch and color. The beans are also wonderful absorbers of flavor, soaking up the sweet acidity of the tomatoes and vinegar and helping all the ingredients come together.

I like to serve this on grilled bread because of the way the charred flavor offsets the balsamic vinegar, but if you don't have the grill fired up, it's fine to use a grill pan, or even to toast the bread in the oven as in the previous bruschetta recipe (page 26).

To add another element to this bruschetta, rub garlic on the bread slices as in the previous recipe.

3 medium vine-ripened tomatoes, seeded (see note) and coarsely chopped
½ small red onion, minced
1 large celery stalk, end trimmed, coarsely chopped
Kosher salt
Freshly ground black pepper
1 can (15 ounces) white beans, such as cannellini, drained and rinsed
2 tablespoons extra-virgin olive oil
About 1 tablespoon balsamic vinegar, plus more to taste
Olive oil, for greasing the grill
6-inch piece, excluding ends, crusty Italian bread, sliced crosswise into
    twelve ½-inch slices

1. If using a charcoal grill, light and let it burn until the charcoal is covered with white ash, about 45 minutes. (I do not suggest going to the trouble of lighting a charcoal

grill for this recipe.) If using a gas grill, preheat it. If using a grill pan, proceed with the recipe.

2. Put the tomatoes, onion, and celery in a medium mixing bowl. Add a generous pinch of salt and a few grinds of pepper. Stir gently to avoid breaking up the tomatoes. Cover loosely with plastic wrap and let rest for 15 minutes at room temperature to give the mixture time to release its juices. Remove plastic wrap and gently stir in the beans. Drizzle the extra-virgin olive oil and vinegar over the mixture and gently stir to combine. Taste and, if necessary, adjust the seasoning with salt, pepper, and a few more drops more of vinegar, if desired.

3. If using a grill pan, heat over medium heat.

4. Brush the grill or grill pan with olive oil. (A good way to do this on a grill is to pour some oil into a shallow bowl, then grab a kitchen towel with long tongs and dampen it in the oil. Use the tongs to brush the grill with oil from a safe distance, being careful to work quickly to avoid a flare-up.)

5. Grill the bread slices over indirect heat (not directly over the coals or flame), turning once with tongs, until golden brown on both sides, 1 to 2 minutes per side.

6. Use the tongs to transfer the grilled slices to a platter. Use a slotted spoon to spoon some of the bean mixture over each slice. Serve at once.

Note: To remove seeds from tomatoes, cut the tomato in half through the stem (I like to use a serrated knife for this because it goes through the sometimes tough skin more easily). Working with one half at a time, hold it cut side down over the sink or a garbage can and gently squeeze out the seeds. To get any lingering seeds out, rinse the cavity out under cold, running water and loosen any especially tenacious seeds with your fingers.

Tapenade Bruschetta

SERVES 4 TO 6
PREP TIME: 10 MINUTES
COOK TIME: 10 MINUTES

As I have said, you can make bruschetta with just about anything, and one of my favorite variations is to top the toasted bread with tapenade. Although it's pretty common these days to see tapenade served alongside bread in Italian restaurants here in America, tapenade actually comes from the French region of Provence. (Here's another interesting detail: Everybody thinks of it as a black olive spread, but its name comes from the Provençal dialect word for caper, *tapeno*. I think the capers got the nod because they add such wonderful and distinct flavor.) I don't know if it's because of my seaside Sicilian heritage, but I love the unique saltiness of olives, especially kalamata olives, which are used in this recipe. Tapenade is an especially useful recipe for entertaining because it can be made up to 1 day in advance.

3-inch portion, not including the ends, of baguette,
   sliced crosswise into twelve ¼-inch slices
2 tablespoons olive oil
½ cup (4 ounces) goat cheese, at room temperature
¾ cup Tapenade (recipe follows)

1. Position a rack in the center of the oven. Preheat to 350°F.
2. Arrange the baguette slices in a single layer on a baking sheet and drizzle with the olive oil. Toast until golden brown, about 2 minutes. Remove from the oven and let the slices cool.
3. Use a rubber spatula to spread each baguette slice with goat cheese, then arrange them on a platter. Mound 1 tablespoon of tapenade atop the cheese on each baguette slice. Serve.

Tapenade

MAKES 1 GENEROUS CUP
PREP TIME: 5 MINUTES

When making tapenade, adjust it to suit your own taste, making sure that you have the right balance of sweet and savory flavors, adding some additional olives, capers, or raisins after first processing it.

In addition to spreading it on bread, I love using tapenade as a sandwich spread (it takes chicken sandwiches to new heights), spooning it over cooked white-fleshed fish, such as halibut or cod, sautéed or roasted chicken breasts, and pork chops.

*¼ cup golden raisins, soaked for 10 minutes in warm water
    and drained, plus more if necessary*
*½ cup whole, pitted kalamata olives or other black olives,
    plus more if necessary*
*2 tablespoons capers, soaked in warm water for 10 minutes,
    drained, and rinsed, plus more if necessary*
2 tablespoons flat-leaf parsley leaves
1 teaspoon chopped fresh thyme leaves
*1 medium orange, zest finely grated, juice squeezed and reserved
    (be sure to catch the seeds and discard them)*
1 tablespoon olive oil
Kosher salt

1. Put the raisins, olives, capers, parsley, thyme, orange juice and zest, olive oil, and a pinch of salt in the bowl of a food processor fitted with the steel blade. Pulse just until the ingredients come together in a coarse mixture. Unplug the processor, remove the lid, and use a spoon to taste the tapenade. If necessary, add more olives, capers, or raisins, plug the processor back in, and pulse again to incorporate.
2. The tapenade may be refrigerated in an airtight container for up to 1 day.

Stuffed Mushrooms

MAKES 2 DOZEN MUSHROOMS, SERVING 4 TO 6
PREP TIME: 30 MINUTES
COOK TIME: 25 MINUTES

As anybody who watches *Cake Boss,* or read my first book, knows, my father died much too young, when I was just seventeen years old. After his death, it was all hands on deck at Carlo's. Even my mother had to pitch in. One of the hardest things about this for her was that she couldn't keep her house in her usual proud way, or cook dinner for me every night. It was just the two of us living there, because my sisters had all moved out to live on their own or had married. When Mom finally accepted that she couldn't do it all herself, she hired Olga, a sweet Ukrainian woman, to be her housekeeper. Olga was a great, natural cook, but she didn't have the same Italian-American palate as Mama, so my mom sent her to my Aunt Nina's house for a crash course in Italian-American cooking. One of the things she wanted Olga to learn was the family recipe for stuffed mushrooms, and I'll tell you something: Aunt Nina was as good a teacher as she is a cook, because Olga's stuffed mushrooms could pass for the real thing any day of the week.

*2 dozen large white button mushrooms (about 1 pound),
    stems removed and reserved*
1 tablespoon plus 1 teaspoon olive oil
1 medium shallot, minced
2 large garlic cloves, pressed
3 tablespoons unsalted butter
Kosher salt
Freshly ground black pepper
¼ cup dry white wine, such as Sauvignon Blanc
½ cup Homemade Breadcrumbs (page 295)
*½ cup plus 2 tablespoons (2½ ounces) finely grated
    Parmigiano-Reggiano*
2 tablespoons chopped flat-leaf parsley leaves

1. Position a rack in the center of the oven. Preheat to 400°F.
2. Finely chop the mushroom stems. This is most easily done by putting the stems in a food processor fitted with the steel blade and pulsing a few times, but you can also do it on a cutting board with a good, sharp chef's knife.

3. Heat a wide, deep, heavy sauté pan over medium heat. Add 2 teaspoons oil and heat it until it is shimmering, almost smoking. Add the shallot and garlic and cook, stirring with a wooden spoon, until the garlic is fragrant but not browned, about 3 minutes.

4. Add 2 tablespoons butter to the pan and let it melt, then add the chopped mushroom stems and cook, stirring, until the mushrooms release their liquid, 7 to 10 minutes. Continue to cook until the liquid has evaporated, about another 2 minutes. Season with salt and pepper, stir, then add the wine to the pan, bring to a boil, and boil for 1 minute; do not reduce completely (some moisture in the pan will help incorporate the breadcrumbs). Remove the pan from the heat and transfer the mixture to a large bowl. Stir in the breadcrumbs, ½ cup Parmigiano-Reggiano, and the parsley.

5. Grease a 9-inch x 13-inch x 2-inch Pyrex or ceramic baking dish with the remaining tablespoon butter.

6. Working with 1 mushroom cap at a time, use a teaspoon or demitasse spoon to fill the cavity with the mushroom mixture, stuffing enough in so that it's rounded on top, then place the mushroom in the baking dish, stuffed side up, without crowding.

7. Sprinkle the remaining 2 tablespoons Parmigiano-Reggiano over the mushrooms and drizzle each with a little of the remaining 2 teaspoons olive oil. The mushrooms can be prepared to this stage, covered with plastic wrap, and refrigerated for up to 4 hours; let the baking dish and mushrooms come to room temperature. Be sure to remove the plastic wrap before baking.

8. Bake the mushrooms until cooked through and the tops are golden brown, 20 to 25 minutes. (To test for doneness, slide a sharp, thin-bladed knife, such as a paring knife, into the center of a mushroom, and remove it. If the side of the blade is warm to the touch, the inside is warm.)

9. Use tongs or a spatula to carefully transfer the mushrooms to a serving platter and serve.

Gloria's Fried Artichokes

SERVES 4
PREP TIME: 15 MINUTES
COOK TIME: 10 MINUTES

It wouldn't be Christmas without my mother-in-law Gloria's fried artichokes. Although she doesn't only make them in December, they are something I look extra-forward to every holiday season. The combination of earthy, mineral flavor, the snap and heat provided by frying, and the salt that brings it all to life, is truly one of a kind. Whenever or wherever I eat fried artichokes, one bite takes me right back to the basement of her house, where we all gather when we visit.

I know what you might be thinking: Turning artichokes can be a real pain, and it is. But these are worth the trouble.

Juice of 2 lemons
5 large eggs
½ cup (2 ounces) finely grated pecorino Romano
2 tablespoons coarsely chopped flat-leaf parsley, stems included
Kosher salt
Freshly ground black pepper
8 baby artichokes, about 3 ounces each, trimmed
1 cup all-purpose flour
Olive oil, for frying

1. Half fill a large, wide bowl with cold water; add the lemon juice.
2. Put the eggs, cheese, and parsley in a bowl, season with salt and pepper, and whisk together.
3. Trim the artichoke stems, then use a paring knife to "turn," or trim, the artichokes down to their tender hearts. (See photographs, page 37.) Cut the artichokes in half lengthwise through the stem, then cut each half in half lengthwise so that you have 4 pieces from each artichoke. As each quarter is prepared, drop it into the acidulated water.
4. Once all the artichokes have been quartered, drain them.
5. Put the flour into a large freezer or zipper bag and place the drained artichokes in the bag. Work the bag with your fingers to coat the artichoke quarters in the flour. Remove the artichokes from the bag 1 at a time and roll them in the egg mixture

until coated. As they are coated, set them on a wire rack set over a baking sheet while you prepare the oil for frying.

6. Line a large plate or platter with paper towels.

7. Pour oil into large, heavy Dutch oven or cast iron skillet to a depth of ½ inch. Heat over medium heat until hot, but not smoking.

8. Gently lower half of the artichoke quarters into the hot oil and fry, turning with tongs or a slotted spoon, until golden brown all over, 1 to 2 minutes per side. (Lower one quarter in at a time; if the first one doesn't cause the oil to bubble around it, remove and try again a minute later, repeating until it does.) Use the tongs or spoon to transfer the fried artichokes to the paper-towel–lined plate and season with a pinch of salt as they come out of the oil. Give the oil a chance to heat up, then repeat with the remaining artichoke quarters.

9. When all artichokes are done, transfer them to a serving platter and serve family style, or divide among 4 salad plates and serve individually.

Stuffed Artichokes

SERVES 4
PREP TIME: 15 MINUTES
COOK TIME: 40 MINUTES

This recipe is based on my father's stuffed artichokes, which remain the best I've ever had: Dad didn't just stuff the center of the artichoke with a decadent breading of prosciutto, two cheeses, garlic, and, for a kick, pepper flakes. He also stuffed some of that breading behind each leaf to really put the flavor over the top. Over the years, I've changed the recipe a little. Dad cooked his in the oven, but I make mine on the stovetop in a covered pot to seal in the heat and speed up the cooking process. The artichokes turn out even more moist and delicious than in the original recipe.

1 large lemon
4 globe artichokes, about 12 ounces each
3 cups Homemade Breadcrumbs (page 295)
½ cup (2 ounces) finely grated pecorino Romano
⅓ cup (2 ounces) minced prosciutto
3 large garlic cloves, coarsely chopped
2 tablespoons chopped flat-leaf parsley, stems included
½ teaspoon crushed red-pepper flakes
½ teaspoon freshly ground black pepper
½ cup olive oil
About 1 quart low-sodium chicken stock
12 Parmigiano-Reggiano shards (about 1 ounce),
    shaved from a chunk of cheese with a vegetable peeler

1. Half fill a large, wide bowl with ice water. Zest the lemon, ideally with a microplane grater, taking care not to remove any of the bitter white pith. Set the zest aside. Cut the lemon in half and squeeze the juice into the water, catching the seeds in your hand and discarding them.
2. Prepare the artichokes: Working with 1 artichoke at a time, cut the stem from the bottom so that the artichoke can stand upright. Set the artichoke on a cutting board on its side and use a sharp, heavy chef's knife to cut off the top inch or so, removing the thorny top. Use a pair of kitchen shears or very clean, sharp household scissors to snip the thorns from the remaining leaves. Spread the artichoke open and use a spoon to scoop out the hairy choke from the center. Discard.

Transfer the artichoke to the acidulated ice water to keep it from discoloring, and repeat with the remaining artichokes.

3. Put the breadcrumbs, pecorino, prosciutto, garlic, parsley, red-pepper flakes, pepper, lemon zest, and olive oil in a bowl and stir. Taste and add salt, if necessary.

4. Working with 1 artichoke at a time, remove the artichokes from the water, let them drain briefly, then pat them dry with paper towels. Working over the bowl, spread the artichoke leaves open like a flower and spoon a generous amount of breading into the center, working it behind the individual leaves with your fingers and letting any excess breading fall back into the bowl.

5. Set the artichokes upright in a wide, heavy pot that holds them snugly and for which you have a tight-fitting lid. Pour stock into the pot, until it reaches about one-third up the sides of the artichokes.

6. Bring the stock to a boil over high heat, cover the pot, and lower the heat so the liquid is just barely simmering. Cook until a center leaf pulls out of an artichoke with ease and the flesh is fork-tender, 30 to 35 minutes.

7. Use tongs or a slotted spoon to transfer the artichokes to a serving plate or platter. Serve warm or let cool to room temperature. Garnish each artichoke with 3 shards of Parmigiano-Reggiano.

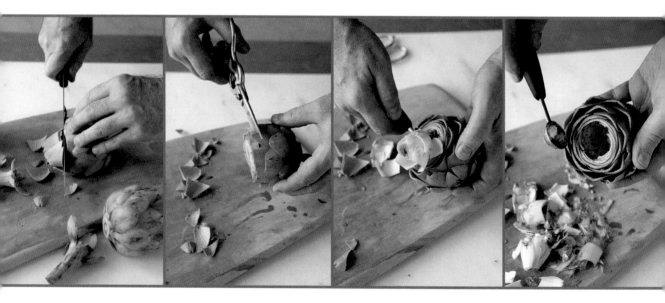

Mozzarella en Carozza

SERVES 4 TO 6
PREP TIME: 10 MINUTES
COOK TIME: 20 TO 25 MINUTES

Italian comfort food at its finest.

If you think *mozzarella en carozza* ("mozzarella in a carriage") is simply a breaded, fried log of cheese, which is how it's served in a lot of American restaurants, think again. The way it's classically prepared is by enveloping the mozzarella in actual pieces of bread like a sandwich, then frying it. In other words, it's even more decadent than the newfangled version; how often does that happen?

The first place I ever saw this dish was at Puccini's restaurant in Jersey City, one of my family's favorite spots to host a gathering when I was growing up. It's another one of those things that I was a little slow to warm up to, finicky eater that I was. My sister Lisa always loved it, and still does to this day: When it comes out of the kitchen, she positively lights up.

This is a very flexible recipe. My mother used to add ham, or whatever she had on hand. If you keep anchovy paste in the house, a little dab in the center of each sandwich really takes this to another level.

1 pound fresh mozzarella
20 slices thinly sliced white bread, such as Pepperidge Farm
  Very Thin Sliced White Bread
3 tablespoons plus 1 teaspoon sun-dried tomato pesto
½ cup all-purpose flour
5 large eggs
1½ cups Homemade Breadcrumbs (page 295)
Canola oil, or other neutral oil, for frying
Kosher salt

1. Trim the rounded ends of the mozzarella ball and save for another use (or snack on them). Slice ten ¼-inch-thick rounds from the mozzarella and set aside. If you have any extra mozzarella, wrap it in plastic wrap and save it for another use.
2. With a 3-inch round cookie cutter, or the rim of a glass or cup with a 3-inch diameter, cut rounds from the center of the bread slices. (You can use the remaining bread to make croutons or breadcrumbs.) Spread 1 teaspoon of tomato pesto on the center of 10 bread rounds, about ¼ inch from the edge.

3. Set up a dredging station in 3 wide, shallow bowls: the flour in one, the beaten eggs in another, the breadcrumbs in the third. Lay the slice of mozzarella in the center of 1 pesto-spread bread round. Repeat with the remaining mozzarella and pesto-spread slices.
4. Top each slice of mozzarella-topped bread with one of the plain bread rounds; the bread should extend slightly beyond the cheese. You should have 10 sandwiches.
5. Line a platter or baking sheet with paper towels.
6. Heat a wide, deep, heavy skillet over medium heat. Pour in oil to a depth of ¼ inch. Heat the oil until it is shimmering, almost smoking.
7. Dip each sandwich in the flour to coat it all over, gently shaking the excess back into the bowl. Dip into the beaten egg, allowing the excess to drip back into the bowl. Then, coat each sandwich in the crumbs, pressing down gently to be sure the crumbs adhere, making sure the sides are covered as well as the top and bottom.
8. Add the sandwiches to the pan in batches without crowding, 3 or 4 sandwiches per batch. Fry until the bottom is golden brown, about 3 minutes, then use tongs or a spatula to turn them over, and fry until the other side is golden brown and cheese is oozing out the sides, about 3 more minutes.
9. As they are finished, transfer the sandwiches to the paper-towel–lined platter and season immediately with salt. (If desired, you can keep finished sandwiches warm in a single layer on a baking sheet in a 200° oven.)
10. Transfer the *mozzarella en carozza* to a platter as soon as they are all done, or—if people are gathered in your kitchen—serve each batch as soon as it's been drained.

Fried Calamari

SERVES 4

PREP TIME: 10 MINUTES (NOT INCLUDING DIPPING SAUCE)

COOK TIME: 5 MINUTES

Fried calamari—the wonderfully crunchy, chewy hors d'oeuvres made with sliced, breaded squid—is a staple in most Italian households, but I first had it in a restaurant, the legendary Park Casino, in Union City, New Jersey, a catering hall where my family attended countless weddings, first communions, and other celebrations. When I was a little boy, my mother really took care of me at those parties, getting me some calamari from the buffet and cutting it up for me, the same way my wife, Lisa, does for our kids today. As a little boy, I was grossed out by the tentacles, but they were my father's favorite part, and—always wanting to be more like him—I developed a taste for them and, wouldn't you know it, today they're my favorite as well because of how crunchy they get when fried.

Personally, I like these with just a squirt of lemon, but the Dipping Sauce and Marinara are popular condiments for calamari and, if that's more to your liking, I say go for it.

1 cup buttermilk
1 teaspoon cayenne pepper sauce, such as Tabasco or Frank's Red Hot
½ teaspoon fine sea salt
1 pound calamari, cleaned by your fishmonger, bodies cut into rings,
*   tentacle clusters left intact*
1⅓ cups Wondra flour
⅔ cup semolina flour or all-purpose flour
¼ cup cornstarch
3 to 4 cups canola or other neutral oil, for deep frying
Kosher salt
1 large lemon, cut into 4 wedges
Calamari Dipping Sauce, optional (recipe follows)
Marinara Sauce, optional (page 141)

1. Put the buttermilk, pepper sauce, and sea salt in a medium bowl and whisk. Add the calamari pieces to the bowl and stir gently to coat. Cover with plastic wrap and refrigerate for at least 1 hour or overnight, to give the flavors a chance to develop.
2. When ready to proceed, line a plate with paper towels.

3. Put the Wondra flour, semolina flour, and cornstarch into a sifter and sift into a medium mixing bowl.
4. Pour oil into a large, wide, heavy pot or deep fryer to a depth of 3 inches. Heat over high heat until the temperature reaches 375°F on a deep-fat thermometer. (see Note)
5. Remove a handful of calamari from the buttermilk mixture, shake gently to allow any excess liquid to run off into the bowl, and place in the flour mixture. Toss gently to coat the pieces evenly, then lift from the mixture and place them in a fine-mesh strainer, shaking any excess flour back into the bowl. Carefully turn the calamari out into the hot oil, not allowing the oil to splash, and fry until a pale golden brown, about 1 minute. Remove with a slotted spoon or Chinese handled strainer and transfer to the paper-towel–lined plate to drain. Season immediately with kosher salt. Repeat with the remaining batches, then transfer to a bowl and serve with lemon wedges and, if desired, Dipping Sauce and Marinara Sauce.

Checking Frying Oil Without a Thermometer

If you don't own a deep-fat thermometer, here's an old trick for testing hot oil to see if it's ready for frying: Get a drop of water (and no more than a drop) on your fingertips and gently flick it into the oil. If it hisses and spits on contact, you're good to go. With a recipe such as this one, you can also test the oil by dropping a few crumbs of extra breading into the oil; if it bubbles and browns on contact, the oil is hot enough for frying.

Wondra Flour

Wondra flour is a granular mix of wheat and barley flour; it crisps very well when fried, so is good to use on its own, or in combination with all-purpose flour and/or cornstarch when frying fish and shellfish.

Calamari Dipping Sauce

MAKES ABOUT 1½ CUPS
PREP TIME: 5 MINUTES

This creamy, spicy sauce is a family favorite for dipping fried calamari, which has enough texture and crunch to stand up to strong flavors. This is also delicious as a sandwich spread, especially on sandwiches or heroes made with fried oysters, fried fish, or leftover roasted pork.

1 cup mayonnaise
2 tablespoons B&G Hot Chopped Pepper Sandwich Topper,
*   or other red-pepper relish, plus more to taste*
2 scallions, white and light green parts only, ends trimmed,
*   very finely chopped*
1 tablespoon freshly squeezed lemon juice
2 tablespoons minced flat-leaf parsley, stems included
Pinch kosher salt

Put all ingredients in a mixing bowl and stir until blended. Taste and add more red pepper relish, if desired, to add more crunch and heat. The sauce can be used right away or refrigerated in an airtight container for 2 to 3 days. Stir before serving.

King Crab Legs with Garlic Butter

SERVES 4 AS AN APPETIZER
PREP TIME: 10 MINUTES
COOK TIME: 10 MINUTES

This is another father-son dish from my repertoire, a recipe that my father made up, and, years later, I made my own. Dad made these crab legs by oven-roasting them, but I slow-cook them in a lemony, garlicky sauce right on the stovetop, letting the flavor seep into the legs. I know that lobster has a reputation as the most luxurious of ingredients, but for my money, succulent, sweet King crab legs are even more delicious and special. I'm not alone: Lisa loves them, too, and we serve them for special occasions.

*3 pounds frozen King crab legs (number of legs will vary), thawed completely in
    the refrigerator*
1 cup (2 sticks) unsalted butter, softened at room temperature
4 large garlic cloves
Finely grated zest of 1 large lemon, plus 1 large lemon cut into 4 wedges
2 tablespoons chopped flat-leaf parsley leaves
Large loaf crusty Italian bread, cut crosswise into slices

1. Break the crab legs into pieces that will fit into a serving dish or bowl. Use kitchen shears to cut the shells along the length of the pieces, leaving them intact.
2. Put the butter and garlic in a heavy saucepan and bring to a simmer over medium heat. Add the lemon zest and parsley and stir to combine. Add the crab pieces to the pot, stir gently to coat the pieces with the seasoned butter, cover with foil, and cook over low heat until warmed through, 10 to 12 minutes.
3. Use a slotted spoon to transfer the crab to a serving bowl. Pour the sauce over and serve with lemon wedges and bread.

Nina's Mussels

SERVES 4 TO 6

PREP TIME: 30 MINUTES

COOK TIME: 3 TO 5 MINUTES

Here's one of my Aunt Nina's classic recipes: mussels on the half shell, breaded and cooked upside-down in a sauté pan. As the juices are released, they are soaked up by the breading; then the mussels are carefully inverted onto a plate for serving. Shucking the mussels is a little hard to do, but it's worth the trouble.

1 pound mussels, washed under cold running water and
debearded, if necessary (Prince Edward Island is a good,
dependable variety.)
1 cup Homemade Breadcrumbs (page 295)
2 large garlic cloves, minced
1 tablespoon chopped flat-leaf parsley
¼ cup plus 2 tablespoons olive oil
1 large lemon, cut into 4 to 6 wedges

1. Shuck the mussels: Start with an immaculately clean kitchen towel or other small towel and a very sharp, thin-bladed paring knife. Between the thumb and fingers of your nondominant hand (which is also holding a towel so you don't stab yourself), press the top of the mussel shell slightly aside so you can slide the tip of your knife into the opening. Slide the blade of the knife down and through to the bottom of the mussel, wiggling the sides apart. Scrape the mussel loose from one half of the shell, guiding it down into the other shell. You will have a mussel on the half shell. Repeat with the other mussels.

2. Put the breadcrumbs, garlic, parsley, and oil in a small mixing bowl and whisk. Spread the breading mixture in an even layer on the bottom of a 12-inch nonstick sauté pan. Arrange the mussels in concentric circles over the mixture and press down very gently to help the breading adhere to the mussels.

3. Set the pan over a burner and turn the heat on high. When the crumbs begin to sizzle, lower the heat to medium. Cook for a few minutes, shaking the pan occasionally to prevent scorching and sticking, until the crumbs brown (turn a few mussels with tongs to check) and smell toasty and the mussels are cooked through, 3 to 5 minutes.

4. Place a large plate over the mussels and very carefully invert the pan. (If you are not comfortable doing this, you can use a kitchen spoon or spatula to lift and carefully turn over a few mussels at a time.) You will have a beautifully crusted plate of mussels.

5. Serve the mussels family style, with lemon wedges.

Clams Posillipo

This clam dish, in which the clams are steamed open in a quick and piquant stew of garlic, tomatoes, and chili, was put on the map by the same guy who put Hoboken on the map: Frances Albert Sinatra, a.k.a. Frank Sinatra, the most famous hometown boy Hoboken has ever or will ever see. Local legend has it that Sinatra loved these clams, and anything that Frank loved was instantly a classic all over town. You might have never heard of Clams Posillipo, but in my neck of the woods, they are iconic.

This dish has an extra-special meaning for me, because whenever my father and I visited my Aunt Franny's house on Long Island, he and I would go clamming in Long Island Sound. We weren't very sophisticated with our technique, wading into the water and feeling around for clams with our toes. (Dad went barefoot but I found the muddy ocean floor frightening, so I wore my socks.) Neither of us was very tall, so when the tide began to roll in, he'd mark the clams with his foot and I'd swim down along the length of his leg and get them.

After the clamming was done, Dad cooked them every which way: in chowder, baked on the half shell, and in this dish, bringing a little bit of New Jersey to Long Island.

¼ cup olive oil
4 large garlic cloves, thinly sliced
1 small fresh green chili, such as serrano or jalapeño,
*   seeded and thinly sliced into rings (wear latex gloves*
*   to protect your hands and wash your hands well after handling)*
¼ cup crisp, light-bodied white wine, such as Pinot Grigio
1 cup canned diced tomatoes with their juice
¼ cup thinly sliced basil leaves (see box)
2 tablespoons coarsely chopped flat-leaf parsley leaves
1 teaspoon sugar
3 dozen middleneck clams, or another small variety,
*   such as cherrystone, well-rinsed and scrubbed of grit*
3 tablespoons cold, unsalted butter, cut into 3 pieces
1 loaf country bread or baguette (optional)

1. Heat a large, heavy skillet, for which you have a tight-fitting lid, and which is wide enough to hold the clams in a single layer, over medium-high heat. Add the oil and heat it until it shimmers, and is almost smoking. Add the garlic and chili and sauté until the garlic is fragrant but not at all browned, about 2 minutes. Immediately pour in the wine, stir, bring to a boil, and let boil until reduced by half, 2 to 3 minutes. Stir in the tomatoes, basil, parsley, and sugar. Bring the liquid to a simmer and let simmer for 30 seconds. Raise the heat to high and add the clams in a single layer.
2. Cover the pan tightly and cook for 3 minutes, shaking the pan periodically to help the clams open, but not hard enough to shatter their shells. Lift the lid and stir the clams gently, taking care not to break their shells; they should be starting to open and exuding their juices. Cover the pan again and cook for about 3 more minutes. Lift the lid and use a slotted spoon to transfer all opened clams to a large serving bowl. Discard any clams that have not opened.
3. Bring the liquid in the skillet to a boil over high heat and reduce it slightly until it thickens enough to coat the back of a spoon, 2 to 3 minutes. Remove the pan from the heat and whisk in the butter, 1 piece at a time.
4. Pour the sauce over the clams in the bowl and serve family style from the center of the table, with the bread alongside for dunking, if desired. Pass another bowl or two for empty shells.

Slicing Basil Leaves

The best, quickest way to slice basil leaves without bruising them is a technique called *chiffonade,* which comes from the French word for "ribbons," because that's what you end up with: ribbons of basil. Stack 5 or 6 basil leaves and roll them up into a small cigar shape. With the seam side down to hold the cigar together, slice it crosswise and the basil will fall in ribbons. This is much prettier than chopping basil; it's also quicker and gives you uniform pieces.

Why Is the Butter Cold?

Having your butter cold before whisking it into the sauce here helps the sauce to emulsify. Rather than melt right in, the cold butter is held in suspension for a richer, creamier effect. Remember to do this whenever whisking butter into a hot sauce.

Baked Chicken Fingers

SERVES 4
PREP TIME: 5 MINUTES
COOK TIME: 14 MINUTES

I came up with this recipe, which bakes rather than fries the chicken, for my kids. It's not that I'd never fry a chicken cutlet or chicken fingers, but the more I learn about nutrition, the more I seek out opportunities for moderating the calories we take in, and these chicken fingers are a perfect example: There's so much flavor in the chicken and breading that you really don't need to fry it to make it delicious. Having said all that, if you or your kids are craving a little greasy goodness, you can by all means pan-fry these.

Chicken fingers can be served with just about anything. You can dip them in marinara sauce, as we do here, or in ranch dressing or sour cream (for a more healthful option, use low-fat or nonfat sour cream, stirring in a little salsa for flavor and texture, if you'd like), or simply squeeze some lemon juice over them.

Nonstick vegetable cooking spray
2 chicken breasts, about 8 ounces each
2 tablespoons olive oil
1 cup unseasoned dried breadcrumbs or Japanese panko
2 tablespoons finely grated Parmigiano-Reggiano
½ teaspoon crumbled dried oregano
½ teaspoon kosher salt
¼ teaspoon freshly ground black pepper
1½ cups Marinara Sauce (page 141), optional

1. Position a rack in the center of the oven. Preheat to 400°F.
2. Spray a baking sheet with nonstick vegetable cooking spray.
3. Cut each chicken breast lengthwise into 1-inch wide strips; you should have 4 or 5 strips per breast. Place in a medium glass or stainless steel bowl. Drizzle with the olive oil and gently stir with a wooden spoon to coat the strips evenly with the oil.
4. Put the breadcrumbs, cheese, oregano, salt, and pepper in a wide, shallow bowl and whisk. One piece at a time, dredge the chicken in the breadcrumb mixture to coat all over, pressing down gently to be sure the coating adheres to the pieces. As they are coated, arrange the pieces on the prepared baking sheet, leaving at least 1 inch between pieces.
5. Bake the chicken pieces for 7 minutes, then carefully turn them over with tongs

and continue to bake until golden brown and cooked through, another 5 to 7 minutes. (To test for doneness, cut one open at the center with a small, thin-bladed knife, such as a paring knife, to be sure there's no trace of pink remaining.)

6. Arrange the chicken fingers on a large plate or platter and serve hot or at room temperature with warmed marinara sauce alongside, for dipping, if you'd like.

Arancini alla Buddy

MAKES ABOUT 36 RICE BALLS, ENOUGH TO SERVE 10 TO 12
PREP TIME: 30 TO 40 MINUTES
COOK TIME: 2 HOURS OR MORE

I've always loved rice balls, but it wasn't until my father took me to Italy when I was fifteen years old that I discovered what they should really taste like. On a visit to our ancestral home, Sicily, staying on the matchbox-sized island of Lipari, I discovered a hole-in-the-wall shop that didn't even qualify as a restaurant: There was a counter where they sold pizza and rice balls, and another counter where you could stand and eat. But the rice balls were to die for: big as softballs and lighter than the often-leaden ones back home. I went back so often that the guys got to know me by name and would scream greetings at me in Italian when I showed up at their door every morning.

In this recipe, I tried to reproduce the texture and flavor of the rice balls made in that little shop: moist yet fluffy rice tossed with an addictively delicious red meat sauce, and a crispy exterior that I always used to think of as gift wrapping. (I should note that these rice balls are smaller, to make them easier to cook through on your home equipment.)

For some notes about making risotto, see page 139.

¼ cup plus 2 tablespoons olive oil
5 tablespoons unsalted butter
1 large Spanish onion, halved, 1 half diced, 1 half minced
2 large garlic cloves, coarsely chopped
1 medium carrot, peeled and finely chopped
2 celery stalks, trimmed and finely diced
¼ pound ground veal
¼ pound ground pork
½ pound ground 80–20 (80% lean, 20% fat) beef
½ cup tomato paste
1 cup robust red wine, such as Nero d'Avola
1 can (28 ounces) crushed plum tomatoes, with their juice
Kosher salt
Freshly ground black pepper
2 cups Arborio rice
6 to 8 cups low-sodium chicken stock
½ cup dry white wine

½ cup (2 ounces) finely grated Parmigiano-Reggiano
¼ cup frozen green peas
6 large eggs
½ cup (3½ ounces) very finely diced mozzarella
About 1½ cups all-purpose flour
½ cup milk
4 cups Homemade Breadcrumbs (page 295)
About 2 quarts canola oil, or other neutral oil, for deep frying

1. To make the meat sauce, heat a wide, deep, heavy saucepan over medium heat. Add 3 tablespoons olive oil and 3 tablespoons butter and cook until the butter melts and the oil is hot, about 2 minutes. Add the diced onion, garlic, carrot, and celery, and cook, stirring with a wooden spoon, until the onion is translucent and the vegetables are soft, about 5 minutes. Add the veal, pork, and beef, and cook, stirring, until browned all over, 15 to 18 minutes. Carefully tip the saucepan over the sink, using a wooden spoon to keep the meat and vegetables from falling out of the pan, and drain the excess liquid.

2. Return the saucepan to the stove and add the tomato paste. Stir to coat the other ingredients with the paste and cook for 2 to 3 minutes, to allow flavors to blend. Pour in the wine, stir, raise the heat to high, bring the wine to a boil, and reduce until almost dry, 10 to 12 minutes. Pour in the crushed tomatoes, bring the liquid in the saucepan to a simmer, and continue to simmer over medium heat until still moist but not soupy, 1 hour and 15 minutes to 1½ hours. (This is a perfect time to make and cool the risotto.) Season with salt and pepper, remove the saucepan from the heat, and let cool completely. You should have about 2 cups of sauce. The sauce can be refrigerated in an airtight container for up to 3 days.

3. To make the risotto: Heat a large, wide, heavy pot over medium heat. Add the remaining 3 tablespoons olive oil and heat it until it is shimmering, almost smoking. Add the minced onions and cook, stirring often with a wooden spoon, until golden but not browned, about 5 minutes. Add the rice and stir to coat with the oil. Continue cooking and stirring the rice until it is opaque at the center, 1 to 2 minutes. Bring the stock to a simmer. Pour in the wine, which should hiss on contact, and cook, stirring, until it evaporates, about 2 minutes.

4. Ladle in ½ cup of the simmering stock and add ½ teaspoon salt. Cook, stirring constantly, until the stock is absorbed. Continue to add stock in approximately half-cup increments, just enough to completely moisten the rice, and cook, stirring vigorously, until the rice has absorbed the liquid. Continue to add stock in the same manner, cooking and stirring and adding the next addition only after the prior one has been completely absorbed. After about 16 minutes, begin adding the

stock more judiciously, a little at a time, until the rice is creamy but still pleasantly al dente. (The best way to check is to taste a few grains.) Remove the pot from the heat and stir in the remaining 2 tablespoons of butter and the grated cheese. Pour the risotto into a shallow baking pan, using the spoon to scrape out as much as possible and spread it out. You should have about 6 cups. Let the risotto cool.

5. While the risotto is cooling, bring a small pot of salted water to a boil over high heat and fill a medium bowl halfway with ice water. Add the peas to the boiling water and cook for 1 minute. Drain in a strainer and dip the strainer in the ice water to shock the peas, stopping the cooking and preserving their color. Drain the peas and set aside.

6. Transfer the risotto to a large, wide bowl. Add 2 of the eggs. Use a spoon or immaculately clean hands to mix the eggs and cheese into the rice.

7. Put the meat sauce in another bowl. Add the peas and mozzarella. Stir, taking care not to mash the peas, and set aside.

8. Set up a dredging line on your kitchen counter: Put the flour in a wide, shallow bowl; the remaining eggs in another wide, shallow bowl with the milk, whisking the two together; and the breadcrumbs in a third.

9. Roll the risotto mixture into balls the size of a small egg; you should have about 36 balls. Use your thumb to make an indentation in the center and fill each one with a teaspoon of meat mixture. (You may not use all the meat.) Close the indentation and roll until smooth. Dredge each rice ball in flour, dip in the egg wash, letting any excess wash run back into the bowl, and roll in the breadcrumbs. As they are prepared, gather them on a large baking tray. (You can freeze the prepared rice balls for up to 2 months. Freeze them on the baking pan, then transfer to freezer bags. Let thaw in the refrigerator before frying.)

10. Heat a large pot of oil to 375°F as measured with a deep-fat thermometer. (See Tip, page 46.) Line a large plate with paper towels.

11. Carefully lower the rice balls into the oil without crowding, about 10 per batch. (Small batches are necessary to keep the oil's temperature from dropping too much when the balls are added.) Fry the rice balls, turning them with a slotted spoon, until golden brown all over, 3 to 4 minutes. Use the slotted spoon to transfer to a paper-towel–lined plate and season with salt if desired.

12. Let the oil return to 375°F and repeat with the remaining batches until all rice balls have been fried and seasoned. Transfer to a platter and serve at once.

Salads

Salads are something that I think should be a part of just about any meal: packed with vegetables and dressed with a vinaigrette, high-quality olive oil, or just lemon juice, they are a way to incorporate something relatively healthful into your everyday eating.

I have a special fondness for salads that are passed family style from the center of the table. There's something about sharing in that way that highlights the values of a meal. "Please pass the *whatever*" is one of my favorite sentences in the world; I just love watching platters and bowls passed around and that anticipation when it comes your way and you get to take as much, or as little, as you want.

As a kid I didn't like salads, mostly because I didn't like raw lettuce, but in time, just as I learned to love other foods, I came to love not only lettuce but also the simplicity of salads: if you put your hands on high-quality ingredients, there are few more simple, elegant ways to show them off.

Here are some salad-making tips.

- Don't sweat the ingredients: With the exception of something that's defined by what's in it, like the Caprese salad, don't get hung up on using the same ingredients that I do: Substitute one kind of lettuce for another, leave out ingredients you don't like, or add others that you do. Who knows? You might end up creating your own house salad. If you do, be sure to name it for yourself or somebody who loves it!

- Unless you buy washed greens, they should be washed, then spun dry to remove as much water as possible, which will maintain their crunch and keep them from wilting. (Too much water will also dilute your dressing.) I suggest you purchase a salad spinner, but if you don't have one, here's an old trick that works: Put the greens in a very clean towel. Gather the towel around the greens so they can't fall out, go outside, make sure nobody is close enough to you to get hit, and swing the towel around and around. Believe it or not, this actually works great.

- When tasting your salad dressing, don't use a spoon or your finger. Since it's going to dress your salad, taste it on a lettuce leaf, or on one of the other ingredients that will go in the salad. That's the best way to see if you've got it where it needs to be.

- I don't make it a step in all these recipes, but if you have time, chill the greens for your salad after they've been washed or dried; this will help them stay nice and crunchy. (Don't try to speed things up by putting your greens in the freezer; that will destroy them almost immediately.) On the other hand, tomatoes should never be refrigerated, and cheeses taste best at room temperature.

- Salads generally don't keep very well, but if you think you may have leftover salad, don't dress the whole thing: Refrigerate your leftover salad and dressing in separate airtight containers and dress the leftovers when ready to serve. By the same token, to keep your salads from becoming soggy, don't dress them until just before serving.

Green Salad
with Italian-American Vinaigrette

SERVES 4 TO 6
PREP TIME: 5 MINUTES

Every Sunday, when my family sits down to our pasta and sauce, or Sunday Gravy, there's always a salad. It's a relatively new addition to the weekly tradition that my wife decided to do. When I was a kid, salad wasn't a part of the meal, but it's the perfect complement to the pasta, meat, and sauce. The crispy lettuce and boldly flavored dressing, zesty with familiar Italian-American flavors such as garlic, oregano, and vinegar, really cut the heaviness of the meal and help the digestion.

More often than not, our salad is a simple one like this, just dressed mesclun greens, but you can build yours out with thinly sliced red onion, green pepper slivers, or halved cherry tomatoes.

12 ounces mesclun or other salad greens, well washed,
*   spun dry, and chilled*
Italian-American Vinaigrette (recipe follows)
¼ cup (1 ounce) finely grated Parmigiano-Reggiano,
*   or a few shavings cut with a vegetable peeler*

1. Put the greens in a large salad or serving bowl, drizzle the dressing over the top, and toss to combine with salad tongs or two wooden spoons. Sprinkle with the grated cheese and toss again. (Alternatively, you may divide the salad among individual salad plates and place a few shards of cheese decoratively over each serving.)
2. Serve immediately.

Italian-American Vinaigrette

MAKES ABOUT 1¼ CUPS
PREP TIME: 10 MINUTES

The ingredients list for this salad reads like a greatest hits of Italian-American flavors: oil, vinegar, garlic, basil, and oregano. Those flavors run through my life, present in just about everything I grew up eating and still eat today. So, this simple dressing tastes like home to me, and will to just about any Italian-American. Normally, oregano is the only herb I used in dried form, but I also use dried basil here, because you need its intensity to make an impact. This dressing can be used on just about any salad greens you like.

The use of two oils, olive and canola, is sometimes called a *blended oil*; I use it to get some of that luscious olive oil flavor without it overwhelming the other ingredients. If you like your dressing especially tangy, you can increase the ratio of vinegar.

2 large garlic cloves, minced
1 teaspoon sugar
1 teaspoon mustard powder, such as Colman's
1 teaspoon dried oregano
1 teaspoon dried basil
3 tablespoons red wine vinegar
Kosher salt
Freshly ground black pepper
½ cup extra-virgin olive oil
½ cup canola oil, or other neutral oil

Put the garlic, sugar, mustard, oregano, and basil in a mixing bowl. Add the vinegar, season with salt and pepper, and whisk together, then whisk in the olive and canola oils. Taste and adjust the seasoning with salt and/or pepper, if necessary. The dressing may be used right away, or stored in an airtight container in the refrigerator for up to 3 days. Whisk again before using to reintegrate the ingredients.

Wake Up Your Herbs

When you're using dried herbs, I suggest rubbing the leaves between your fingers to activate their flavor and wake them up after all the time they spent locked in an airtight container.

Fennel and Apple Salad

SERVES 4 TO 6

PREP TIME: 10 TO 15 MINUTES

Fennel isn't the most popular vegetable in the United States, but if you go to a grocery store in your town's Little Italy, you'll find that it's right up there with onions and carrots, celery and garlic, piled just as high in its bin as those other, better known ingredients. Fennel has a gentle anise flavor, just a hint of licorice in the most unlikely place you'd expect to find it: a crunchy green vegetable. You can sauté fennel, braise it, or grill it, but it's also terrific raw. And it has beautiful fronds that look like fresh dill that you can chop up and scatter over finished dishes the way you would top food with chopped parsley.

If you have some terrific extra-virgin olive oil, you can simply shave some fennel and dress it with oil, salt, and pepper. There's also a popular salad that pairs it with green apple. This salad, based on one they used to serve at Macaluso's—a popular catering hall in New Jersey that was a huge Carlo's Bake Shop account for many years—makes that combination the basis of a full-blown salad with mesclun greens, orange sections, and toasted pine nuts. This is a real crowd pleaser, and will turn everybody who eats it into a bona fide fennel lover.

¼ cup freshly squeezed lemon juice, from 2 large lemons
1 large fennel bulb, halved and cored
1 large Granny Smith apple, halved through the stem end and cored
3 small to medium navel oranges, peeled, separated into segments,
  skin and membrane removed, cut into further segments,
  juice squeezed from membranes and reserved
2 tablespoons champagne vinegar or white wine vinegar
Kosher salt
Freshly ground black pepper
1½ cups extra-virgin olive oil
6 large basil leaves, cut into chiffonade (see box, page 53)
1 medium shallot, minced
5 ounces mesclun greens, well washed and spun dry
3 tablespoons pine nuts, toasted (see box)

1. Half fill a large bowl with cold water and stir in 2 tablespoons lemon juice.
2. Shave the fennel across the grain as thin as possible, ideally on a mandoline or with

a very sharp, heavy chef's knife and a steady hand. Add the slices to the acidulated water to keep them from browning. Slice the apple in the same manner, and add the slices to the water.

3. Add the orange juice, remaining 2 tablespoons lemon juice, and vinegar to a bowl. Add a pinch of salt and pepper. Whisk in the oil. Taste the dressing, and adjust if necessary. Stir in the basil.

4. Drain the apple and fennel slices in a colander, pat dry gently with paper towels, and transfer to a large, wide salad bowl or serving bowl. Add ¾ of the orange segments, the shallot, and the greens. Season with salt and pepper and toss with salad tongs or 2 wooden spoons. Drizzle the vinaigrette over the salad and toss. Taste and adjust the seasoning, if necessary, and toss one last time.

5. Divide the salad among 4 to 6 plates, garnish with the pine nuts and reserved orange segments, and serve.

Toasting Nuts

Toasting nuts is a surefire way to bring out their best flavor, because it activates their essential oils. There are two ways to toast nuts and each works well: One way is to put the nuts in a pan and toast over medium heat, shaking the pan frequently until the nuts are fragrant but not browned, 3 to 5 minutes. Transfer to a plate to allow them to cool as quickly as possible. Alternatively, you can preheat the oven to 350°F, spread the nuts out on a rimmed baking sheet, and toast them in the oven, periodically shaking the pan gently to ensure even toasting and to prevent scorching. Again, as soon as the nuts are fragrant but not browned, transfer to a plate and let cool.

Caprese Salad

SERVES 4

PREP TIME: ABOUT 10 MINUTES

Caprese salads are my wife's favorite way to begin a meal in the late summer. Made with slices of tomato and mozzarella, and topped with olive oil and basil, they never fail to take me back to the town of Gravina, where my entire family and I had dinner at a restaurant perched high atop a cliff. It was there that I had the best version of this salad I ever had: perfect, peak-of-freshness tomatoes, herbaceous basil, its summery aroma wafting from the plate, soft, slightly salty, fresh mozzarella, and a superior extra-virgin olive oil.

That version, and the way it haunts me, points out the essential lesson of this salad: When a dish is this simple, there's nowhere to hide. All of the ingredients must be top notch. In other words, make this only in the late summer when tomatoes and basil are at the height of their season and you can buy them at a farmers' market, farm stand, or maybe even pull them from your own garden.

*2 beautiful large, ripe beefsteak tomatoes, cut across
   the equator into ¼-inch-thick slices*
Kosher salt
*1 pound best-quality fresh mozzarella, sliced into
   ¼-inch rounds (see box)*
15 to 20 fresh basil leaves, assorted sizes
High quality extra-virgin olive oil, for drizzling
Coarsely ground black pepper

1. Arrange the tomato slices on a serving platter and sprinkle them with salt. Let rest 5 to 10 minutes to give the salt a chance to coax out the flavorful juices.
2. Lay the mozzarella slices over the tomato slices in overlapping fashion; you may or may not have the same number of slices of tomato as you do of mozzarella, so adjust accordingly to create a uniform, decorative platter. Season with salt and a few grinds of pepper. Drizzle a little olive oil over and around the salad and scatter basil leaves decoratively over the top.
3. Serve.

Coarsely Grinding Black Pepper

To coarsely grind black pepper, adjust your pepper mill, loosening the dial at the top, which controls how finely the inner blade cuts the pepper. If you don't own a pepper mill, many supermarkets now sell black pepper in disposable mills with an adjustable setting around the neck of the bottle.

Buddy's Chopped Pantry Salad

SERVES 6

PREP TIME: 10 TO 15 MINUTES

A self-taught cook like me always loves a challenge, and the ultimate challenge might just be cooking with foods that you didn't choose for yourself, what they call a *mystery box exercise* in cooking schools. I first devised a version of this salad when I was hungry one night and there was nothing in the house, or so it seemed: I raided the meat and cheese drawer of our fridge and the long-shelf-life jars and cans in our pantry, and came up with this. Not only did it give me a chance to freshen the inventory, but it also used up a few odds and ends from all those holiday gift baskets.

The best thing about this salad is how flexible it is: You can replace the meats and cheese with canned or preserved tuna, or replace the roasted red peppers with pepperoncini or hot cherry peppers if you like some heat, or leave out anything you don't like. It's a great, fun way to improvise in the kitchen and save a little money at the same time.

4 ounces provolone, cut into ½-inch dice (about ⅔ cup dice)

4 ounces Genoa, or other variety, salami, cut into ½-inch dice
   or julienne strips (about ⅔ cup dice)

1 cup (about one 7½-ounce jar) store-bought artichoke hearts,
   drained and quartered

4 pieces store-bought roasted red pepper, cut into 2-inch x ½-inch slices

½ cup Cerignola olives, or other green olives, pitted and thickly sliced

2 celery stalks, thinly sliced crosswise

1 medium red onion, thinly sliced

2 Roma or plum tomatoes, cut into ½-inch dice

1 head romaine lettuce, coarsely chopped (iceberg or Bibb lettuce
   can be substituted)

3 tablespoons red wine vinegar

¼ cup extra-virgin olive oil

½ teaspoon dried oregano

½ teaspoon dried thyme

1 teaspoon sugar

Kosher salt

Coarsely ground black pepper (see box, page 71)

8 sprigs fresh parsley, stems and all, coarsely chopped

1. Put the provolone, salami, artichoke hearts, red peppers, olives, celery, onion, tomatoes, and lettuce in a large, wide salad or serving bowl. Toss well with salad tongs or two wooden spoons.

2. Put the vinegar and oil in a separate, medium mixing bowl. Whisk together, then whisk in the oregano, thyme, and sugar. Season with salt and pepper and whisk again.

3. Drizzle the salad with two thirds of the dressing, toss, and taste a leaf or vegetable. If the salad does not seem adequately dressed, drizzle with the remaining dressing and toss again. (Serve any extra dressing on the side for those who might want more.) Garnish with a scattering of parsley and serve family style.

Caesar Salad with Homemade Croutons

SERVES 4 TO 6

PREP TIME: 10 MINUTES (NOT INCLUDING CROUTONS)

I don't know when I first had a Caesar salad. To me, it's almost like an older relative because, for as long as I can remember, it's just always been there. The most familiar Caesar salad is made with a raw egg, but you can use a coddled egg if you have any concerns about that the safety of raw eggs (see Safety Note). My Caesar salad is topped with my homemade version of store-bought seasoned croutons: dressed with olive oil, salt, pepper, and oregano, and baked. If you've never made your own croutons, you'll never go back to store-bought after trying these.

1 large egg yolk (see note)
¼ cup fresh lemon juice (from about 2 large lemons)
2 large cloves garlic, smashed with the side of a chef's knife
*   and mashed to a paste with 1 teaspoon salt*
½ teaspoon Worcestershire sauce
1 tablespoon Dijon mustard
2 teaspoons anchovy paste or minced, tinned anchovy fillet
*   (from about 1 fillet)*
1⅓ cups olive oil
Freshly ground black pepper
1 large head romaine lettuce, leaves separated, washed,
*   and spun dry or patted dry with paper towels*
½ cup (2 ounces) finely grated Parmigiano-Reggiano
2 cups Homemade Croutons (recipe follows)

1. In a medium bowl, whisk together the egg yolk, lemon juice, garlic paste, Worcestershire, mustard, and anchovy paste. Continuing to whisk, add the oil, first a drop at a time and then in a thin, steady stream, until the mixture comes together as an emulsified vinaigrette. Season to taste with salt and pepper, bearing in mind that anchovy is salty.

2. Arrange the lettuce leaves on 4 to 6 salad plates or a large serving platter. Drizzle with dressing and scatter the cheese over the top. Garnish with croutons and serve.

Safety Note: Raw eggs carry the risk of salmonella, and recipes containing them should not be served to the very young, the very old, pregnant women, or anyone with a compromised immune system. An alternative is to use a coddled, or partially cooked, egg. To coddle an egg, bring a very fresh egg to room temperature by immersing it in warm water, otherwise it might crack when coddled. Drain the egg and set it in a heatproof vessel. Bring a small pot of water to a boil and pour boiling water around the egg until it is covered. Let stand for exactly 1 minute, then immediately run cold water into the bowl until the egg can be easily handled, at which point you can peel and use it.

If you'd rather not use coddled or raw egg in this dressing, replace the egg with ½ cup store-bought mayonnaise and use about ½ cup olive oil.

Note: The easiest way to separate an egg is to work next to your sink, or over a bowl, and carefully crack it around its equator, letting some of the whites run out, and catching the yolk and remaining white in one half. Carefully pour the yolk back and forth between the two halves, letting some of the white run out with each transfer until you are left with the yolk. Gently transfer the yolk to a bowl, taking care to keep it intact and not let it collapse.

Homemade Croutons

MAKES ENOUGH CROUTONS TO GARNISH 4 TO 6 SALADS
PREP TIME: 5 TO 10 MINUTES
COOK TIME: ABOUT 20 MINUTES

Use these croutons to add crunch and flavor.

⅓ to ½ loaf day-old hearty bread, such as Tuscan,
  Italian, or country bread
¼ cup olive oil
½ teaspoon dried oregano
Kosher salt
Freshly ground black pepper

1. Position a rack in the center of the oven. Preheat to 375°F.
2. Trim and discard the crust from the bread and dice the bread into ¾-inch cubes, placing them in a wide, medium mixing bowl. You should have about 2 cups of cubed bread.
3. Drizzle the oil over the cubes and scatter the oregano, salt, and pepper over them. Toss to coat bread with the oil and seasoning, then spread the cubes out on a rimmed baking sheet.
4. Bake until just golden brown and crisped through, 12 to 15 minutes, shaking the pan halfway through the cooking time to prevent scorching and ensure even toasting.
5. Remove the baking sheet from the oven and let the croutons cool completely. Use at once or transfer to an airtight container and store at room temperature for up to 2 days.

Panzanella

SERVES 4

PREP TIME: 25 MINUTES (INCLUDING 15 MINUTES RESTING TIME)

Like bruschetta, panzanella underscores the resourcefulness and parsimony of Italian home cooks: It's another way of using day-old bread. For panzanella you toss the bread with water, then the salad ingredients, including oil and vinegar. After it rests for a time, the bread softens and soaks up the flavors of the dressing and vegetable juices, making for a dish in which bread isn't an accompaniment, but an integral part of the salad itself. In addition to serving as a starter, panzanella is a wonderful picnic dish, and a side dish, especially with grilled meats.

One 12-inch loaf rustic Italian bread, such as Pugliese or
    ciabatta (preferably one-day old), crust removed and
    discarded, cut into 1-inch dice
¼ cup water
2 medium vine-ripened or similar round tomatoes, cut into
    ½-inch dice
1 medium cucumber, peeled, cut in half lengthwise, seeded,
    and cut into ¼-inch slices
1 small red onion, thinly sliced and rinsed under cold water
¼ cup pitted black olives (such as Alfonso or Gaeta),
    coarsely chopped
1 tablespoon capers, soaked for 10 minutes in warm water,
    drained, and rinsed
¼ cup loosely packed fresh basil leaves
¼ cup extra-virgin olive oil
3 tablespoons red wine vinegar
Pinch dried oregano
Kosher salt
Freshly ground black pepper

1. Put the bread and water in a large mixing bowl and gently stir. Add the tomatoes, cucumbers, onion, olives, capers, basil, oil, vinegar, and oregano. Toss and season to taste with salt and pepper. Let stand for 15 minutes before serving. The salad may also be covered with plastic wrap and refrigerated for up to 4 hours; let come to room temperature before serving.

Seafood Salad

SERVES 6 TO 8

PREP TIME: 15 MINUTES

COOK TIME: ABOUT 1 HOUR

This chilled seafood salad really shows off the shellfish itself, a mix of calamari (squid), clams, scallops, shrimp, mussels, and octopus. It's dressed and chilled, at which point you can leave it in the refrigerator for several hours. But I suggest serving it as soon as it reaches the desired temperature, so that the individual flavors of the different shellfish remain distinct.

You don't have to use the same shellfish mix that I do: As long as you have about the same total amount (by weight) that the recipe calls for, you'll be fine. My favorites are octopus, squid, and shrimp; those are the ones I would always include, but let your own taste be your guide.

1 celery stalk, cut crosswise into thirds
1 medium carrot, peeled and cut crosswise in half or thirds
1 small onion, peeled and halved through the root end
1 bay leaf
1 tablespoon plus ½ teaspoon kosher salt
1 pound calamari bodies, cleaned by your fishmonger and
    cut into 1-inch-thick rings
½ pound sea or bay scallops, muscle removed
1 pound medium or large shrimp, peeled and deveined
1 pound littleneck clams, or other small clams, such as cherrystone
    or middleneck
1 pound mussels (Prince Edward Island is a good, dependable variety)
1 pound octopus
2 tablespoons chopped fresh flat-leaf parsley leaves
2 large garlic cloves, finely chopped
Juice of 2 large lemons (about ¼ cup)
½ cup extra-virgin olive oil
Freshly ground black pepper

1. Put the celery, carrot, onion, bay leaf, and 1 tablespoon of the salt in the bottom of a large, heavy pot or saucepan for which you have a colander or straining insert.

Fill the pan a little more than halfway with cold water. Set over high heat and bring the water to a boil, then lower the heat so the water is simmering.

2. Have a large, dry bowl at the ready for the poached seafood.

3. Begin poaching the seafood: Put the calamari in the colander, lower into the simmering water, and cook until just firm and white, 2 minutes. Lift the colander out of the water, letting any excess water run back into the pot, and transfer the calamari to the bowl.

4. Put the scallops in the colander, lower into the simmering water, and cook until white, about 1 minute for small bay scallops, 3 to 4 minutes for the larger sea scallops. Lift the colander out of the water, letting any excess water run back into the pot, and transfer the scallops to the bowl with the calamari. (If your bowl is large enough, keep each type of seafood apart from the others, so that they can each cool completely.)

5. Place the shrimp in the colander, lower into the simmering water, and poach until firm and pink, about 3 minutes. Lift the colander out of the water, letting any excess water run back into the pot, and transfer the shrimp to the bowl with the calamari and scallops.

6. Put the clams and mussels in the colander, suspend the colander over the simmering water, and steam them open, about 5 minutes. (This is best done in a steaming basket or pasta pot that fits in the larger pot.) Discard any clams or mussels that have not opened and add the open ones, in their shells, to the bowl.

7. (Once it is cool enough to handle, cut the shrimp in half lengthwise. If using sea scallops, once cool enough to handle, cut them in half vertically; leave bay scallops whole.) Cover the bowl with plastic wrap and refrigerate while you cook and cool the octopus.

8. Set the colander aside and carefully lower the octopus into the simmering water, adding more water if necessary to completely cover it. Raise the heat to high and bring the water to a boil, then lower the heat so the water is simmering, and continue to simmer until the tentacles begin to pull away from the body and are fork tender, 40 to 50 minutes. Transfer the octopus to a large bowl and rinse under cold running water until it is completely cooled, about 5 minutes.

9. Use your fingers and a small paring knife to remove the outer skin. Discard the hard mouth (beak) and head sac. Cut the tentacles diagonally into 1-inch pieces and add to the bowl with the other seafood.

10. To make the salad, scatter parsley and garlic over the seafood, then drizzle with the lemon juice and olive oil. Toss well with salad tongs or 2 wooden spoons. Season with ½ teaspoon of salt and generous grindings of pepper. Cover with plastic wrap and chill in the refrigerator for at least 1 hour, and up to 4 hours. Serve cold on individual plates, or family style, passing an empty bowl or two for collecting mussel and clam shells.

Iceberg Wedges with Pancetta and Chunky Gorgonzola Dressing

SERVES 6

PREP TIME: 15 MINUTES

COOK TIME: 15 MINUTES

The iceberg wedge with bacon and blue cheese dressing is nothing new: It's one of the great American salads. But, a few years ago, I went to a steakhouse where there must have been an Italian in the kitchen: They served me a version of the salad made with pancetta, or Italian bacon, instead of slab bacon, and the dressing was especially delicious because it was made with one of the world's great blues, Gorgonzola, also from Italy. The complex flavor of the pancetta against the cool, creamy dressing really took the whole thing to another level.

The radishes and cherry tomatoes are much more than a garnish here: They provide crucial sweetness, acidity, and crunch that balance the richness of the other ingredients. That's why this salad isn't tossed: It's good to be able to alternate bites of dressed greens with those lighter elements.

1 tablespoon olive oil
½ pound pancetta, or thick-cut bacon, cut into 1-inch pieces
1 large head of iceberg lettuce, cut into 6 wedges, each with
    some core attached
Gorgonzola Dressing (recipe follows)
4 radishes, ends trimmed, thinly sliced
10 cherry tomatoes, halved

1. Line a plate with paper towels.
2. Heat a wide, heavy sauté pan over medium heat. Add the oil and heat until warm but not too hot. Add the pancetta to the pan and cook, stirring with a wooden spoon to ensure even cooking, until it has rendered most of its fat and is golden brown and crispy, 5 to 7 minutes. Use the spoon to transfer the pancetta to the paper-towel–lined plate to drain and let cool to room temperature.
3. Arrange 1 iceberg wedge on each of 6 salad plates. Spoon two-thirds of the dressing over the wedges and garnish with pancetta, radishes, and cherry tomato halves. Serve, with the extra dressing alongside.

Gorgonzola Dressing

SERVES 6 (ABOUT 2 CUPS, TOTAL)

You can use other blue cheeses in this dressing. They don't even have to be Italian; Roquefort or Maytag would be delicious. Only serve it with, or on, sturdy greens that won't be overwhelmed by its big flavor, or squashed by its weight.

1 tablespoon Dijon mustard
3 tablespoons apple cider vinegar or white balsamic vinegar
1 tablespoon freshly squeezed lemon juice
Kosher salt
Freshly ground black pepper
⅓ cup olive oil
1 cup (6 ounces) crumbled Gorgonzola
⅓ cup sour cream
About 2 tablespoons milk

1. Put the mustard, vinegar, and lemon juice in a bowl and season with salt and pepper. Slowly whisk in the olive oil. Add ½ cup of the Gorgonzola to the bowl and mash with a fork. Whisk in the sour cream and 2 tablespoons of milk to make a thick but pourable dressing; you may need to add a little more milk to achieve the desired pourable consistency. Season with salt and pepper and crumble in the remaining ½ cup Gorgonzola.
2. Use the dressing right away or refrigerate in an airtight container for up to 2 days.

Breads, Pizzas, and Sandwiches

That old expression "breaking bread," a shorthand way of referring to the act of coming together to share a meal, has real meaning for the Valastros. Although we don't bake bread at Carlo's, bread is a part of just about every family dinner. From the first meal I can remember to the one I had last night, there has always been a loaf of bread on the table.

To me, bread is part of an extended family that also includes pizza and sandwiches. Just as I ate a lot of bread as a kid, I ate a lot of pizza. On many Friday nights, when my parents went out for dinner, they'd order in pizza for us kids and, as I got older, I became a pizza connoisseur, trying pies from various places around northern New Jersey. My wife Lisa's family owned a pizzeria for years, and they are wonderful pizza makers. When she and I were dating, I'd sometimes go to her family's shop in Union, New Jersey, and give her father, Mauro, a hand on Friday nights, which was their busiest day of the week. I learned a lot about pizza making there, and making pizza always reminds me of that wonderful time in my life when our families were starting to come together.

I encourage you to try making pizza at home: It's really not that hard, and pizza parties, where you make and serve a variety of pizzas straight from the oven, are a lot of fun, especially for kids.

As for sandwiches, when you're as busy as I am, they are the ultimate quick fix, a perfect food that allows you to work while you eat without the need for a knife and fork: There's probably nothing that the guys and gals who work at Carlo's order in for lunch more than sandwiches. Away from the bakery, they're also a fun way to improvise in the kitchen.

Something all of these bready foods have in common is that everybody seems to love them, so no matter whom you're feeding, whether your own family or a larger group of friends and relatives, I honestly feel like you can't go wrong with these dishes.

The recipes in this chapter are pretty simple and straightforward, but here are a few tips and suggestions:

- For dishes that call for store-bought bread, the options available today are incredible. From artisanal bakeries to markets such as Whole Foods, you can get great bread no matter where you live. Take the time to seek out the best bread you can find and use it, whether on its own, or for Garlic Bread (page 91), Pizza Bread (page 93), or sandwiches.

- When making sandwiches, it's fine to add and subtract ingredients, so long as you pay attention to one of the few rules: The ratio of bread to filling must be respected. It's different for every sandwich, but the idea is to taste both without either one dominating. Basically, sturdier, thicker breads can take on a greater volume of filling and bigger flavors than thinner or more delicate breads.

- When building sandwiches, put wet ingredients, such as roasted peppers, pickles, marinated vegetables, and so on in the center, so the meats and cheeses can act as a buffer, keeping the liquids from soaking through the bread. This is especially important with sandwiches that will be pressed or cooked in some fashion.

- A pizza stone is really the best way to bake pizza. There are a variety of pizza stones available in all different price ranges. My two favorites are square or rectangular stones that take up the better part of a rack, turning it into a shelf like you'd find in the oven of a pizzeria, and stones with handles built right onto them. Both of those formats make it easy to get pizza in and out of the oven. Less appealing are pizza stones that rest in a wire rack because the rack doesn't sit very well on an oven rack.

- If you don't have a pizza stone, you can use an inverted baking tray, although you'll have to make a rectangular pizza and be very careful not to let the cornmeal roll off the tray and onto the floor of the oven.

Garlic Bread

SERVES 4 TO 6
PREP TIME: 5 MINUTES (NOT INCLUDING COMPOUND BUTTER)
COOK TIME: ABOUT 10 MINUTES

We ate a lot of garlic bread in the Valastro home when I was a kid: It's another one of those things that always seemed to be around, and which never fails to bring me right back to that table. My dad used to make it, and as my sisters got older, Mary took over garlic bread duty, and still makes a mean one today.

A lot of people make garlic bread by simply smearing bread with butter and some pressed or minced garlic. There's nothing wrong with that, but with just a little more work, you can turn a taken-for-granted item into something really special. The trick is to make a compound (flavored) butter with garlic, parsley, and lemon zest, spread it onto the bread, and bake it. When the butter melts, those flavors are absorbed and baked right into the bread itself, filling it with awesome flavor.

1 loaf Italian bread
½ cup Compound Butter (recipe follows)

1. Position a rack in the center of the oven. Preheat to 375°F.
2. Cut the bread lengthwise into two equal halves. Spread the cut side of each half with a generous amount of butter. Place the bread on a baking tray, cut side up, and bake until the butter is melted and the bread is golden brown, 7 to 10 minutes.
3. Remove the bread from the oven, transfer to a serving plate, and slice crosswise with a serrated knife into 6 to 8 slices per half, to make it easy for everybody to take a piece. Serve.

Scarpetta

If there's one thing that Italian-Americans do when we eat, it's dip. We dip bread in salad dressings and pasta sauces and the leftover drippings from everything from fish to steak. The hunk of bread that we use to do this is called *scarpetta*, which actually means "little shoe." The only thing better than dipping is dipping with this garlic bread.

Compound Butter

MAKES ½ POUND (1 CUP) COMPOUND BUTTER
PREP TIME: 5 TO 10 MINUTES

A compound butter is a flavored butter made by letting butter soften enough to work in flavoring agents. When the butter is baked or broiled along with other foods, or spread on hot foods, it melts right in, transmitting those flavors wherever the butter goes.

½ pound (2 sticks) unsalted butter
3 large garlic cloves, peeled and pressed
¼ cup (loosely packed) flat-leaf parsley, including stems
Finely grated zest of 1 lemon
Pinch kosher salt

Let the butter soften to room temperature. Put all ingredients in the bowl of a food processor fitted with the steel blade and pulse to combine. Being extremely careful of the steel blade, transfer the butter to another container. Use at once on garlic bread or wrap tightly in plastic wrap and keep in the refrigerator for up to 6 weeks, or freeze for up to 6 months.

Compound Butters

Compound butters are also wonderful finishing agents: Melt a slice on top of a just-grilled steak and its flavors will penetrate the meat, mash some into mashed potatoes, or toss a little with some hot pasta, along with a little of the pasta's cooking liquid to emulsify it, for an instant sauce. You can also play with compound butters to create your own: popular additions are minced shallots, other herbs such as thyme and oregano, and—for an especially terrific steak-appropriate compound butter—red wine.

Pizza Bread

SERVES 4 TO 6

PREP TIME: ABOUT 10 MINUTES

COOK TIME: ABOUT 15 MINUTES

Back in my family's first bakery on Adams Street, the sweet smell of sugar always hung in the air, because we were either mixing it into dough, or dusting finished pastries with powdered sugar. Even to this day, in our massive facility in Jersey City, that sweet, yeasty scent in the air never fails to take me back to Adams Street, where I first learned the nuts and bolts of the family business.

But there was one hour each day when things changed: lunchtime, when my dad would cook for the crew. The aroma of Dad's food was unmistakable. He was a larger-than-life guy and his food reflected that, so when he made lunch, the telltale smells of the bakery were replaced by the punch of garlic, the pungency of oregano, the delightful funkiness of melting cheese.

Danny Dragone was with the bakery way back in those days, and his favorite lunch was this pizza bread. He loved it so much that Dad had to bake two of them: one for Danny and one for the rest of us to split. One bite of this treat never fails to bring me right back to those lunches: It's hard to believe, given how enormous our operation is now, but there were only five of us back then—me, my dad, Danny, Sal, and (on the weekend) Uncle Frankie. When lunchtime came around, we'd all pull flour bins up to the bench and use them as chairs. When we dug in, it was dead silent, everybody communing with his food, taking it in, savoring it.

1 can (14 ounces) whole peeled plum tomatoes or
    3 vine-ripened tomatoes, cored, seeded (see page 30),
    and coarsely chopped
¼ cup extra-virgin olive oil
2 large garlic cloves, minced
¼ cup torn basil leaves
Pinch crushed red-pepper flakes
1 tablespoon finely grated Parmigiano-Reggiano
Kosher salt
1 day-old bottom half of a Pugliese loaf
6 deli slices provolone cheese (about 4 ounces)
1 tablespoon finely grated pecorino Romano

1. Position a rack in the center of the oven. Preheat to 400°F.
2. Put the tomatoes in a bowl. Add the olive oil, garlic, basil, red-pepper flakes, Parmigiano-Reggiano, and a generous pinch of salt. Mash the ingredients together with a potato masher or the back of a fork and let rest for 5 minutes.
3. Put the bread, cut side up, on a baking sheet. Top with the tomato mixture and any juices from the bowl. Top with the provolone slices and the pecorino. Bake until the cheese has melted and the bread is nice and crispy, about 10 minutes.
4. Remove the pizza bread from the oven, transfer to a cutting board, and let cool for 2 to 3 minutes. Use a serrated knife to slice into 4 to 6 pieces, dividing among individual plates or arranging on a platter, and serve.

Pizza Dough

Pizza dough is one of those things that a lot of home cooks seem to fear, but I've never understood why. Maybe it's because once you're seen professional pizza makers twirling the dough in the air, you assume that every pie requires incredible finesse. But you don't need to be able to perform those kinds of tricks to make pizza dough. The only real trick is to develop a sense of when the dough has the right level of moisture and elasticity: You should be able to pull pizza dough like taffy, but it should separate into strands more quickly than taffy. There's a little trial and error involved, but not much. Once you've made two or three pizzas, you will find that your dough is as good as, if not better than, what you get at most pizzerias.

All that said, if you don't want to make your own pizza dough, many supermarkets now sell it in the dairy section. I'll let you in on a little secret: Most pizzerias will be more than happy to sell you some.

Note that, because of changes in humidity, your dough might take different amounts of time to expand in different seasons: less in the summer, more in winter.

¾ teaspoon active dry yeast
About 15 ounces unbleached all-purpose flour (about 3¼ cups)
About 1 cup plus 2 tablespoons lukewarm water
1½ teaspoons kosher salt
3 tablespoons olive oil

1. Put the yeast in a small, heatproof bowl. Warm ¼ cup water in a small pot over medium heat and pour it over the yeast. Stir with a fork and let proof for 10 minutes.

2. Put the flour, water, salt, and 2 tablespoons olive oil in the bowl of a stand mixer fitted with the paddle attachment. Add the yeast and paddle on low speed until the mixture comes together. Switch to the dough hook attachment and continue mixing, on medium-low speed, until the dough comes together in a ball, another 3 to 4 minutes. Check the dough: If it's too dry, mix in a bit more water. If too sticky, add a bit more flour.

3. Lightly flour a clean work surface. Turn the dough onto the surface and knead until smooth and elastic, 5 to 7 minutes. Form the dough into a ball. Grease a medium mixing bowl with the remaining tablespoon of olive oil and set the ball

of dough in the bottom of the bowl and rotate to coat with the oil. Top the bowl loosely with plastic wrap or a slightly damp kitchen towel. Let rest in a cool, dark place until the dough increases by about half its size, 30 to 45 minutes.

4. Clean and reflour your work surface and transfer the dough to the surface. Press down on it to deflate it. Cut the dough into thirds (or desired portions), and form into tight balls to press out the excess air.

5. At this point, you may place the balls of dough on a floured baking sheet covered with oiled plastic or a damp towel, and let rise for 1 hour if you plan to use the dough on the same day. Alternatively, you may place the dough on a lightly floured sheet, cover with a piece of plastic wrap moistened on the underside with oil, and refrigerate overnight. Allow the dough to rest at room temperature for 10 to 15 minutes before shaping/baking.

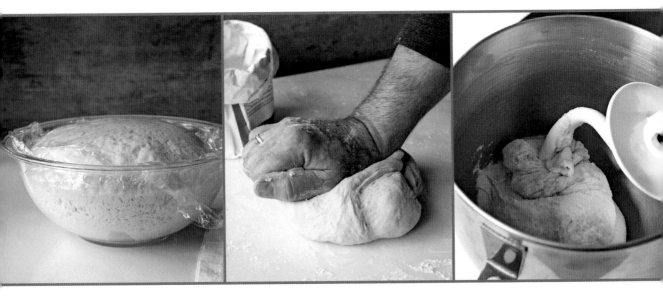

Pizza Sauce

MAKES ABOUT 2½ CUPS, ENOUGH FOR 4 TO 6 PIZZAS
PREP TIME: ABOUT 10 MINUTES

If you're used to American pizzeria sauces, defined by the flavors of tomato paste, garlic powder, and oregano, then you might be surprised by the clean, fresh flavor in this sauce that isn't cooked until it's ladled onto the pizza and baked. This is pizza sauce the way I love it, and I hope you do, too.

1 can (28 ounces) whole peeled tomatoes, mostly drained,
*   left just a little wet*
2 tablespoons extra-virgin olive oil
2 large garlic cloves, minced
2 tablespoons (½ ounce) finely grated Parmigiano-
*   Reggiano cheese*
1 tablespoon sugar
Kosher salt

Pass the tomatoes through a food mill set over a large bowl. Add the oil, garlic, Parmigiano-Reggiano, and sugar to the bowl, season with salt, and let rest at room temperature for 1 hour to give the flavors a chance to develop. The sauce can be refrigerated in an airtight container for up to 2 days.

Pizza Margherita

MAKES ONE 9- TO 10-INCH PIZZA, ENOUGH TO SERVE 1 TO 2
PREP TIME: ABOUT 10 MINUTES (NOT INCLUDING DOUGH AND SAUCE)
COOK TIME: ABOUT 15 MINUTES

My first taste of pizza Margherita was at a little joint called Café Capri in East Rutherford, New Jersey, where my parents took me to eat when I was a little kid. But it wasn't until my dad took me to Italy when I was fifteen years old that I learned the story behind the name of pizza Margherita: the colors of this classic pie—the white of the mozzarella, the green of the basil, and the red of the tomato sauce—are the colors of the Italian flag, and the pizza was named for Queen Margherita.

Cornmeal, for dusting your work surface and pizza peel
⅓ Pizza Dough recipe (page 95)
¼ cup Pizza Sauce (page 97)
4 ounces fresh mozzarella, sliced into ¼-inch-thick rounds
    and drained on paper towels
6 leaves fresh basil
Kosher salt
Extra-virgin olive oil, for serving

1. Position a rack in the bottom of the oven and set the pizza stone on the rack. Preheat to the highest setting, 450° to 500°.
2. Lightly dust your work surface and a pizza peel with cornmeal. Pat and stretch or roll out the dough to a 9- to 10-inch round. In one swift movement, lift the dough by one edge and drag it onto the peel.
3. Use a ladle to spoon the sauce into the center of the dough, then use the back of the ladle to spread it around, leaving a ½-inch border. Scatter the mozzarella decoratively over the pizza.
4. Open the oven and very carefully slide the prepared pizza onto the stone. Bake until the crust is golden brown and the cheese bubbles, 10 to 12 minutes. Remove the pizza with the peel. Scatter the basil over the pizza, season with a pinch of salt, and drizzle with extra-virgin olive oil.
5. Transfer the pizza to a serving platter. Slice or cut it into 6 slices, and serve.

Pizza with Prosciutto, Arugula, Tomatoes, and Shaved Parmesan

MAKES ONE 9-TO-10 INCH PIZZA, ENOUGH TO SERVE 1 TO 2
PREP TIME: ABOUT 25 MINUTES (NOT INCLUDING PIZZA DOUGH)
COOK TIME: ABOUT 15 MINUTES

This pizza is like an entire meal coming together in one dish: a white sauceless pizza topped with a salad of arugula and tomatoes. There's even some extra protein in the prosciutto. Make sure to add the prosciutto just before serving, so that it doesn't curl and shrink from the heat of the pizza.

2 tablespoons extra-virgin olive oil
1 large garlic clove, smashed with the side of a chef's knife
½ teaspoon crushed red-pepper flakes
Cornmeal for dusting your work surface and pizza peel
⅓ Pizza Dough recipe (page 95)
8 ounces fresh mozzarella, torn by hand into pieces and
*   drained on paper towels*
2 cups loosely packed baby arugula, tough stems trimmed
½ cup (5 ounces) sweet grape tomatoes, halved lengthwise
Kosher salt
Freshly ground black pepper
4 large slices prosciutto (about 4 ounces), torn by hand
*   into small pieces*
12 shavings Parmigiano-Reggiano, cut with a vegetable
*   peeler (from about 1 ounce cheese)*

1. Position a rack at the bottom of the oven and set a pizza stone on the rack. Preheat to the highest setting, 450°F to 500°F.
2. Put the oil, garlic, and pepper flakes in a small bowl and stir together.
3. Dust your work surface and a pizza peel with cornmeal.
4. Pat, stretch, and roll the dough out to a 9- to 10-inch circle and, in one swift movement, lift and drag it onto the peel. Use a pastry brush to brush the dough with seasoned oil, leaving a ½-inch border (you will not use all the oil). Scatter the mozzarella evenly over the dough.
5. Slide the dough onto the stone and bake until golden and crisp, 10 to 12 minutes.

6. While the pizza is baking, put the arugula and tomatoes in the bowl, and toss with the remaining seasoned oil, a pinch of salt, and a few grinds of black pepper.
7. When the pizza is done, carefully slide it onto the peel and transfer it to a serving plate or platter.
8. Pile the salad over the hot pizza, arrange the prosciutto pieces on top, and finish with shavings of Parmigiano-Reggiano. Cut or slice into 6 slices, and serve.

Four-Cheese Pizza

MAKES ONE 9-TO 10-INCH PIZZA, ENOUGH TO SERVE 1 TO 2
PREP TIME: ABOUT 25 MINUTES (NOT INCLUDING PIZZA DOUGH)
COOK TIME: ABOUT 15 MINUTES

This is my version of the classic Roman four-cheese pizza, which often includes a blue cheese, but I prefer to use an assortment of mild and funky white cheeses—mozzarella, ricotta, caciocavallo, and Fontina—that harmonize beautifully when they melt together. You can play around with different ratios of cheeses or substitute your own favorite cheeses; just be sure to use good melting cheeses. Taleggio, for example, would get along very well here. You can also dress up the ricotta by stirring olive oil and/or herbs into it to enrich it and add even more flavor.

Cornmeal, for dusting your work surface and pizza peel
1 ball Pizza Dough (one-third of recipe, page 95)
2 ounces fresh mozzarella, torn into 1-inch pieces
2 ounces Fontina, shredded on the large holes of a box grater
   (about ¼ cup grated)
2 ounces caciocavallo (or sharp provolone), shredded on the large
   holes of a box grater (about ¼ cup grated)
2 ounces (about ¼ cup) fresh ricotta
Pinch coarsely ground black pepper
1 tablespoon grated pecorino Romano

1. Position a rack in the bottom of the oven and set the pizza stone on the rack. Preheat the oven to the highest setting, 450°F to 500°F.
2. Lightly dust your work surface and a pizza peel with cornstarch. Pat and stretch or roll out the dough to a 9- to 10-inch round. In one swift movement, lift the dough by one edge and drag it onto the peel.
3. Scatter the mozzarella, Fontina, and caciocavallo evenly over the surface of the pizza, leaving a ½-inch border, then use a small spoon to drop dollops of ricotta over the pizza, avoiding the border. Season with the black pepper and sprinkle the pecorino over the other cheeses.
4. Open the oven and very carefully slide the prepared pizza onto the stone. Bake until the crust is golden brown and the cheese bubbles, 10 to 12 minutes. Remove the pizza with the peel.
5. Transfer the pizza to a serving platter. Slice or cut it into 6 slices, and serve.

Pizza with Anchovies, Olives, and Capers

MAKES ONE 9-TO 10-INCH PIZZA, ENOUGH TO SERVE 1 TO 2
PREP TIME: ABOUT 25 MINUTES (NOT INCLUDING PIZZA DOUGH)
COOK TIME: ABOUT 15 MINUTES

With its salty toppings of anchovy, olives, and capers, this pizza pays tribute to the traditional ingredients of Sicily.

Cornmeal, for dusting your work surface and pizza peel
⅓ Pizza Dough recipe (page 95)
¼ cup Pizza Sauce (page 97)
1 small clove garlic, very thinly sliced
3 anchovy fillets, coarsely chopped
4 ounces fresh mozzarella, cut into ¼-inch-thick slices,
*   then torn into smaller pieces*
1 tablespoon capers, rinsed under cold water and patted dry
¼ cup coarsely chopped pitted black olives, such as Gaeta or Alonso
Pinch crushed red-pepper flakes
½ teaspoon dried oregano
1 tablespoon extra-virgin olive oil

1. Position a rack in the bottom of the oven and set the pizza stone on the rack. Preheat the oven to the highest setting, 450°F to 500°F.
2. Lightly dust your work surface and a pizza peel with cornmeal. Pat and stretch or roll out the dough to a 9- to 10-inch round. In one swift movement, lift the dough by one edge and drag it onto the peel.
3. Use a ladle to spoon the sauce into the center of the dough, then use the back of the ladle to spread it around, leaving a ½-inch border. Scatter the garlic and anchovies over the sauce, then evenly distribute the mozzarella, capers, and olives over the other ingredients and season with the pepper flakes and oregano.
4. Open the oven and very carefully slide the prepared pizza onto the stone. Bake until the crust is golden brown and the cheese bubbles, 10 to 12 minutes. Remove the pizza with the peel.
5. Transfer the pizza to a serving platter and drizzle the oil over it. Slice or cut it into 6 slices, and serve.

Calzone

MAKES 6 CALZONES
PREP TIME: ABOUT 20 MINUTES (NOT INCLUDING PIZZA DOUGH)
COOK TIME: ABOUT 45 MINUTES

Calzones intensify the pizza experience by encasing the toppings with dough, rather than placing them on top of the dough. When the calzone bakes, the ingredients come together the same way they would in a burrito or a crock pot. My calzone touchstone is the one they used to make at Delfino, a pizzeria around the corner from our old bakery on Adams Street. It was a great calzone, the chewy crust giving way to an ooze of ricotta, mozzarella, and sausage. I make my calzones with sausage, mozzarella, and ricotta to this day, but you can vary the cheeses and other fillings.

My mother in-law, Gloria, used to make a similar treat called *frittelle*, and she always changed it up to use whatever she had on hand at home; she even made a version with tuna. You can do the same with calzones; some of my favorite variations are made with ham, prosciutto, and scallions.

It's very important to cut slits in the calzone to vent it, so that the heat doesn't build up inside, which could cause the calzone to explode.

¼ cup olive oil
3 small sweet Italian sausage links (2 ounces each)
1 small Spanish onion, thinly sliced
1 small green bell pepper, seeds and ribs removed,
    sliced into ¼-inch strips
Cornmeal, for dusting a work surface and pizza peel
Pizza Dough (page 95), divided and shaped into six balls
8 ounces smoked mozzarella, cut into ¼-inch dice
8 ounces fresh mozzarella, cut into thin slices
1 cup (8 ounces) fresh ricotta
¼ cup plus 2 tablespoons (1½ ounces) finely grated
    Parmigiano-Reggiano, plus 2 additional tablespoons
    for scattering over baked calzones (additional 2
    tablespoons optional)

1. Preheat a grill pan or sauté pan over medium high heat. Add 2 tablespoons of the oil and heat until shimmering, almost smoking. Cook the sausages, turning with tongs or a wooden spoon, until nicely browned on all sides, 10 to 12 minutes

total cooking time. Transfer to a cutting board and let cool. When cool enough to handle, coarsely chop the sausage.

2. Heat a wide, heavy sauté pan over medium heat. Add the remaining 2 tablespoons of oil and heat until it's shimmering, almost smoking. Add the onion and pepper and cook, stirring with a wooden spoon, until tender, 8 to 10 minutes. Set aside and let cool in the pan.

3. Position a rack in the bottom of the oven and position a pizza stone in the center of the rack. Preheat the oven to 475°F.

4. Dust your work surface and pizza peel with cornmeal.

5. Working with one ball of dough at a time, pat and stretch, or roll, the dough into an 8-inch circle on your work surface, then lift onto the peel in one swift movement. Working quickly, arrange one-sixth of the sausage, onion, pepper, fresh and smoked mozzarella, parmesan, and ricotta in the center of the calzone. Gently fold the top of the dough over, stretching as needed to meet the edges of the other half. Pinch the edges to seal with your fingers, or with the tines of a fork. Use a sharp, thin-bladed knife to slash 2 small vents in the top.

6. Carefully transfer the calzone to the pizza stone. Bake until nicely golden brown cheese is bubbling through the vents, 8 to 10 minutes.

7. As the calzone bakes, make the next one and add it to the pizza stone. Work as quickly as you can and remove calzones as they are finished by sliding them onto the pizza peel and transferring them to individual serving dishes. Scatter more parmesan over the top of the baked calzones, if desired, let rest for 5 minutes, then serve hot. If you work quickly and efficiently, the last calzone should be finished just a few minutes after the first one and you will be able to serve them all at once because they retain a lot of heat.

Pesto Chicken Panini

MAKES 4 SANDWICHES
PREP TIME: 20 MINUTES
COOK TIME: 3 TO 5 MINUTES

When the panini, or pressed sandwich, craze hit America in the early 2000s, I got swept up in the fervor right along with everybody else. I love the way the flavors in a panini get fused under the weight and heat of the press. I'm not an especially adventurous panini maker: the combination of basil pesto, sun-dried tomato pesto, and chicken here is nothing new, but it's delicious and satisfying.

1 pound chicken cutlets
Kosher salt
1 clove garlic, smashed with the side of a chef's knife
2 tablespoons olive oil
Eight ½-inch-thick slices artisanal sourdough bread
¼ cup basil pesto
¼ cup sun-dried tomato pesto
8 thin slices provolone

1. Put the chicken cutlets in a baking dish or other shallow vessel. Salt the chicken and rub with the smashed garlic clove. Drizzle with the olive oil and turn to coat. Let rest at room temperature for 15 minutes.
2. Preheat a grill pan or cast iron pan over medium-high heat. Grill the chicken cutlets until done, about 5 minutes per side. Transfer to a plate and let rest while preparing the sandwiches.
3. Preheat a panini grill according to the manufacturer's instructions.
4. Spread 1 tablespoon of the basil pesto over each of 4 slices of bread. Top the pesto with 2 slices of provolone. Slice each chicken breast diagonally, and put the pieces of 1 breast over the cheese on each sandwich. Spread one tablespoon of sun-dried tomato pesto over the remaining 4 slices of bread and top the sandwiches with these slices, pesto side down. Brush the tops of the sandwiches with oil. Place on the panini pan, oiled side down, brush the tops with oil, and press until nicely browned and crisp and the cheese is oozing, 4 to 5 minutes.
5. Transfer the sandwiches to a cutting board, cut in half, and serve warm.

Prosciutto, Mozzarella, and Roasted Red Pepper Panini

MAKES 4 SANDWICHES
PREP TIME: 25 MINUTES
COOK TIME: ABOUT 5 MINUTES

This sandwich is a combination of the old and the new in my life: The old is the prosciutto, mozzarella, and peppers combination—a version of a classic Italian combo hero, like the one I used to get from Fiore's Deli on Adams Street. The new is taking that combo and pressing it into a panini to create a turbo-charged version of the traditional.

1 large garlic clove, minced
1 teaspoon minced rosemary
¼ cup olive oil plus more for brushing sandwiches
Eight ½-inch slices artisanal sourdough bread
8 thin slices prosciutto (about 6 ounces)
Eight 1-inch-wide strips jarred roasted red pepper
Eight ¼-inch-thick slices (about 12 ounces) fresh mozzarella

1. About 20 minutes before you plan to assemble the sandwiches, put the garlic, rosemary, and olive oil in a small bowl and stir together.
2. Preheat the panini maker according to the manufacturer's instructions.
3. Brush the upward-facing side of all eight slices of bread with the garlic-rosemary oil. Top 4 of the slices with two slices of prosciutto each, folding and overlapping it to fit onto the bread. Top the prosciutto on each bread slice with 2 pieces of roasted pepper, then two slices of mozzarella.
4. Cover each open-faced sandwich with an oiled slice of bread, oiled side down. Brush the tops of the sandwiches with some olive oil and place oiled side down on the griddle. Brush oil on the tops. Grill the panini until browned and crisp, and the cheese is melted and oozing, 4 to 5 minutes.
5. Remove the sandwiches from the press, cut in half, and serve warm.

Sausage and Pepper Sandwich

MAKES 4 SANDWICHES
PREP TIME: 10 MINUTES
COOK TIME: 30 MINUTES

Nothing says street fair like a sausage and pepper sandwich. If you grew up like I did, in a community that throws a lot of festivals and block parties, one of the first things you look for in that setting is the line of grills on which sausages and peppers are cooked, one batch after another, all day long, being worked over until they're crisped and blackened along the edges, and then scooped up by a spatula and slipped between the halves of a seeded Italian roll. As a kid, I went to a lot of street fairs, usually with my cousin Frankie Amato.

I remember the sausage and pepper sandwiches of my youth the way you remember old friends: there was the one they served at the Madonna Dei Martiri Feast in Hoboken (now the Italian Festival in Hoboken Park), where the grills were set up right outside the family bakery; there was the Lions Club carnival in the parking lot of Valley Fare supermarket (today a Shop Rite) when our family moved there. There's a carnival in the town where my family and I live today and the first thing I look for when we hit the scene is that smoke from the grill, calling out to me, telling me that my next sausage and pepper sandwich is just moments away.

I have two tricks for making these sandwiches: I pull a little of the bread out to make room for as much sausage and pepper as possible, and I parboil the sausages in boiling water ahead of time to be sure they're cooked through and shorten the time they need on the grill to just a few minutes to mark and reheat them.

This is another of those recipes that I don't think it's worth firing up the grill for. If you happen to have your grill lit and ready to go, by all means grill the sausages on it, but you can get a perfectly delicious result on a grill pan or even a sauté pan.

8 sweet Italian link sausages, 2 ounces each
2 tablespoons olive oil
1 medium Spanish onion, peeled and thinly sliced lengthwise
1 medium red pepper, cored, seeded, and sliced into ¼-inch-thick slices
1 medium green pepper, cored, seeded, and sliced into ¼-inch-thick slices
1 Cubanelle pepper, cored, seeded, and sliced into ¼-inch-thick slices
Kosher salt
1 large garlic clove, minced
½ teaspoon dried oregano
4 seeded Italian rolls, halved lengthwise but still attached at the edge

1. Bring a large pot of salted water to a boil. Line a large plate with paper towels.
2. Prick the sausage with a fork and boil until cooked through, about 10 minutes. Drain on a paper-towel–lined plate and set aside.
3. Heat a large griddle, grill, or sauté pan over medium-high heat and brush with 1 tablespoon of the olive oil. When the oil is shimmering, almost smoking, add the onions, peppers, and a pinch of salt. Stir well with tongs or a wooden spoon, then spread the vegetables out on the grill and lower the heat to medium-low. Cook, stirring occasionally, until the vegetables begin to soften, 5 to 7 minutes. Add the garlic, oregano, and another pinch of salt; continue cooking until all is softened, juicy, and delicious, another 1 to 2 minutes. (It's fine, even desirable, if the vegetables brown a little and crisp up around the edges.)
4. Transfer the vegetables to a bowl and cover with aluminum foil to keep them warm. Add the remaining olive oil to the grill pan and spread it out with a brush or your spoon. Add the sausages and cook, turning, until browned and crispy and reheated, about 5 minutes. If using a grill pan, make sure you have nice grill marks on the sausages.
5. Pull out and discard (or snack on) some bread from the top and bottom interiors of each roll, leaving enough that the sausage and peppers won't soak through. Nestle 2 sausages in each roll, top with some of the pepper mixture, and serve.

Frying Peppers

If you come from an Italian family, then you might know Cubanelle peppers by another name: *frying peppers*. That's what my mom used to call them and what many of us still call them to this day.

Soups

Italian-American soups aren't fancy affairs. Often they were created, or adapted on a daily basis, to use up whatever ingredients might be on hand or left over, whether that was pasta, vegetables, fish, or meats.

That's certainly the case with the soups I've selected for this chapter, which were either nightly dinners in our home, called on to use up the bounty of a fishing expedition, or cooked up to satisfy a longing for something special from our family's ancestral home.

Personally, I will always see soups as belonging to winter; the only soup we ever ate in the summer was fish soup. (I think I also associate soup with winter because both my mother and my wife turn to soup as a remedy for colds, and I really believe that nothing makes a sore throat feel better than chicken broth.) But you can, of course, make these soups at any time of year.

As for making soup, here is some general advice.

- I love adding pasta to soups, but this is one place where you need to be a little careful with the substitutions: generally speaking, you want to confine yourself to small, tubular pasta such as ditalini, small macaroni, tubetti or tubettini, or mini farfalle. (If you have kids, little star-shaped pastina are also fine.) Larger pasta shapes will cloud your soup with their starch and soak up too much of the liquid.
- Keep the season in mind when making soups. To me they are among the dishes that should be most in synch with the season because soups almost seem to infuse *you* when you eat them: They go right to the soul. Save the hearty soups with bacon in the base and thicker, reduced broths for the colder months and the lighter ones for the warmer months.
- When making a fish or chicken soup, bones are very important to the flavor. For a vegetable-based soup, it's fine to use store-bought stock, but it's best to use a real, homemade stock or to use the bones themselves in preparation of the soup, to get the deepest possible flavor.
- Italian tradition dictates that you don't combine fish and cheese, but we Valastros grate cheese, usually Parmigiano-Reggiano, over all our soups, even fish soups.

Minestrone Soup

SERVES 6 TO 8
PREP TIME: 10 MINUTES
COOK TIME: 30 MINUTES

Minestrone isn't really a specific soup: it's just a catch-all use of the Italian word for soup, *minestra*, adapted to mean vegetable soup among Italian-Americans in the United States. My grandmother Madeline made a minestrone, and so did my mother. I decided to cram mine full of all my favorite veggies and herbs: potatoes, Swiss chard, rosemary, and white beans. It's a hearty soup, made all the more so by the inclusion of pancetta, or Italian bacon, in the base.

This is another one of those recipes that I love because it's so flexible: You can leave out things you don't like, or change what's here to suit your own taste; use whatever small pasta shape you like, replace the Swiss chard with spinach or kale, and/or use different beans.

Leftover soup can be refrigerated in an airtight container for up to two days.

2 tablespoons olive oil
1 small onion, coarsely chopped
2 medium carrots, peeled and coarsely chopped
2 medium celery stalks, coarsely chopped
4 ounces thinly sliced pancetta, coarsely chopped (about ½ cup)
2 large garlic cloves, crushed with the side of a chef's knife
Kosher salt
1 pound Swiss chard, stems trimmed, leaves coarsely chopped
1 Idaho potato, peeled and cubed
1 can (28 ounces) crushed tomatoes with their juice
1 tablespoon finely chopped rosemary
8 cups low-sodium chicken broth
1 cup dried tubetti pasta, or other small pasta shape such as
   ditalini or small macaroni
1 can (15 ounces) cannellini beans, drained and rinsed
Freshly ground black pepper
½ cup (2 ounces) finely grated Parmigiano-Reggiano
2 tablespoons coarsely chopped fresh basil leaves
Extra-virgin olive oil, for serving

1. Heat a large, wide, heavy pot or Dutch oven over medium-high heat. Add the oil and heat until shimmering, almost smoking.
2. Add the onion, carrots, celery, pancetta, garlic, and a pinch of salt. Cook, stirring frequently, until the vegetables are softened but not browned and some fat has rendered from the pancetta, 6 to 7 minutes. Add the Swiss chard, potato, tomatoes, rosemary, and chicken broth. Raise the heat to high, bring the liquids to a boil, then reduce the heat so the liquid is simmering, and let simmer for 10 minutes.
3. Meanwhile, bring a small pot of salted water to a boil. Add the pasta and cook until al dente, about 8 minutes. Drain in a colander and set aside.
4. Stir the cannellini beans into the soup and cook until the beans and other vegetables are tender, about 10 more minutes. Stir in the pasta and cook 1 additional minute to rewarm it. Season the soup to taste with salt and pepper.
5. To serve, ladle the minestrone into 6 to 8 bowls and top with the grated cheese and basil. Drizzle with extra-virgin olive oil and serve.

Using Dried Beans

If you prefer to use dried beans in this or other recipes, put the beans in a bowl, cover with cold water, and soak overnight. There's a quick-soak method that involves soaking the beans for a shorter time in boiling hot water, but I find that the results aren't as dependable.

Mom's Chicken Soup

SERVES 8

PREP TIME: 15 MINUTES

COOK TIME: ABOUT 3 HOURS

This soup was sometimes featured in my mother's weekly dinner menus, but I remember eating it when I or one of my sisters was under the weather. We didn't know it in those days, but it's since been proven that chicken soup really does help get you better, especially when you do what Mama did and make it with homemade chicken stock. If you want to make a more hearty soup, add cooked mini farfalle (bowtie pasta) to the finished soup and/or finish each serving with a generous grating of pecorino Romano cheese.

3 pounds mixed chicken bones, such as necks, backs,
  and wings (see note)
2 tablespoons olive oil
1 large Spanish onion, cut into ¼-inch dice
1½ pounds boneless, skinless chicken breasts, cut into
  bite-sized pieces
2 medium carrots, peeled, and thinly sliced crosswise
3 medium stalks celery, thinly sliced crosswise
1 large russet potato, peeled and cut into ½-inch dice
1 cup fresh or frozen corn kernels
Herb sachet (1 sprig parsley, 1 sprig sage, and 1 sprig
  fresh oregano, tied in a cheesecloth bundle)
Kosher salt
Freshly ground black pepper

1. Put the chicken bones in a stock pot or other wide, deep, heavy pot. Pour in 6 quarts of cold water. Bring to a simmer over medium heat, then lower the heat and simmer gently for 2 hours, skimming any impurities from the surface of the soup with a straining wand or the edge of a wooden spoon. Strain the broth through a fine-mesh strainer set over a large bowl. Discard the bones and reserve the broth.

2. Carefully wipe out the pot and return it to the stovetop over medium heat. Add the olive oil and heat until shimmering, almost smoking. Add the onions and chicken, and cook, stirring, until the onions are softened and the chicken starts to brown, 5 to 7 minutes.

3. Pour in the reserved broth and add the carrots, celery, potato, corn, and herb sachet. Season with salt and pepper. Bring to a simmer over medium heat, lower the heat to low, and simmer until the chicken is cooked through and the soup tastes of chicken, about 90 minutes.
4. Ladle the soup into bowls, making sure you get a good mix of chicken and vegetables in each serving. Serve at once.

Note: Most butchers will be happy to sell you bones for making stock, whether chicken, other poultry, beef, or other meats.

Pasta e Fagioli

(Pasta and Bean Soup)

SERVES 6

PREP TIME: 10 TO 15 MINUTES (NOT INCLUDING OVERNIGHT SOAKING OF BEANS)

COOK TIME: ABOUT 2 HOURS

Every region of Italy makes its own version of *pasta e fagioli,* or pasta and bean soup, but most people associate it with Venice. It's also one of those recipes that no two cooks make exactly the same way. The essentials are some kind of white bean, small tubular pasta, such as tubettini or tiny macaroni, and rosemary. After that, it's open to interpretation: A lot of versions begin with bacon or another pork product in the base, some puree the beans into the broth, others leave it soupy, and so on. My mother's version, which was part of the weekly repertoire of dinners in our house during the winter months, incorporates some tomato paste for thickness and sweetness, and kale for color and texture, turning it into a hearty dish perfect for the season. You can even adjust the soup throughout the year, making a lighter, soupier version in the warmer months.

Note that the beans must be soaked overnight.

2 cups dried borlotti beans
2 tablespoons olive oil
1 small Spanish onion, cut into ¼-inch dice
1 medium celery stalk, cut into ¼-inch dice
1 large carrot, peeled and cut into ¼-inch dice
Kosher salt
3 large garlic cloves, minced
Pinch crushed red-pepper flakes
2 tablespoons tomato paste
1 small sprig rosemary
2 cups small macaroni (elbows, tubetti, or ditalini)
1 cup (loosely packed) coarsely chopped kale leaves
    (spinach or Swiss chard may be substituted)
Extra-virgin olive oil
Coarsely ground black pepper
12 Parmigiano-Reggiano shards (about 1 ounce),
    shaved from a chunk of cheese with a vegetable peeler

1. Soak the beans overnight in enough cold water to cover. Drain.
2. Heat a large, wide, heavy soup pot over medium heat. Add the olive oil and heat until shimmering, almost smoking. Add the onion, celery, carrot, and a pinch of salt. Sauté over low heat until the vegetables are softened, about 10 minutes. Add the garlic and red-pepper flakes, and sauté until the garlic is fragrant, 2 to 3 minutes. Add the tomato paste and stir to coat the other ingredients with the paste. Pour in 6 cups of water and add the rosemary and beans. Bring the liquid to a boil over high heat, then lower the heat and simmer until the beans are tender, about 2 hours, adding more water as necessary to make sure the solids are covered, but not so much that the soup becomes excessively brothy.
3. About 90 minutes into the soup's cooking time, bring a pot of salted water to a boil and add the pasta. Cook until al dente, about 8 minutes, and drain in a colander. Set aside.
4 When the beans are almost tender, add the drained pasta to the pot, along with the kale. Cook just enough to wilt the kale and warm the pasta through, 2 to 3 minutes.
5. Ladle the soup into bowls and top with a drizzle of extra-virgin olive oil, black pepper, and Parmigiano-Reggiano shards.

Fish Soup, Sicilian Style

SERVES 4 TO 6
PREP TIME: 10 MINUTES
COOK TIME: 20 MINUTES

Once in a while, my late Grandma Grace would get a craving for a taste of the old country, and—generous soul that she was—want to share it with the rest of the family. At moments like those, she'd come to the bakery, a shopping bag of ingredients in tow, and cook something up for us, More often than not, this Sicilian fish soup, a simple pot of fish stock, tomatoes, and fennel served with grilled bread spread with saffron aioli, was the outlet for this impulse; and it was always a treat for the rest of us.

¼ cup extra-virgin olive oil
1 small Spanish onion, cut into ½-inch dice
1 medium fennel bulb, cut into ½-inch dice
Kosher salt
Freshly ground black pepper
2 large garlic cloves, thinly sliced
1 cup dry white wine, such as Sauvignon Blanc
1 can (14½ ounces) peeled plum tomatoes, crushed by hand,
*   with their juices*
2 quarts homemade Fish Stock (page 302) or store-bought
*   seafood stock*
2 pounds filet of white-fleshed fish, such as halibut, snapper,
*   sea bass, or cod, skin removed, cut into 1-inch cubes*
2 tablespoons coarsely chopped flat-leaf parsley
Ciabatta bread cut into 4- to 6-inch slices, toasted
Saffron Aioli (recipe follows)

1. Heat a wide, deep, heavy pot over medium heat. Add the olive oil and heat until it is shimmering, almost smoking. Add the onion, fennel, and a pinch of salt and pepper. Lower the heat and sauté until the vegetables are softened and translucent but not browned, about 5 minutes. Add the garlic and sauté another minute. Pour in the wine, raise the heat to medium, bring the wine to a boil, and reduce by about half, 4 to 5 minutes Add the tomatoes and stock, bring to a simmer, and continue to simmer for 5 minutes. Season with salt and pepper.

2. Add the fish to the pot, pushing down gently with a wooden spoon, if necessary, to be sure it is fully submerged in the hot liquid.
3. Cover the pot and cook at a low simmer, until the fish is firm, white, and cooked through, 5 to 7 minutes. Add the parsley and give the contents a gentle stir. Taste and adjust the seasoning with salt and pepper, if necessary.
4. Ladle the soup into 4 to 6 wide, shallow bowls and serve with the toast and aioli alongside.

Saffron Aioli

MAKES ABOUT 1 CUP
PREP TIME: ABOUT 5 MINUTES

This golden saffron mayonnaise is spread on grilled toast as the classic accompaniment to fish soup. It's also delicious served alongside grilled fish, especially white fish, such as cod and halibut.

1 pinch saffron
2 tablespoons boiling water
1 large egg yolk (see Safety Note, page 75)
1 large lemon, zested and juiced
½ cup olive oil
½ cup canola oil
Kosher salt
Freshly ground black pepper

1. In a small bowl, steep the saffron in the boiling water for 5 minutes, then drain and set aside.
2. Put the egg yolk, lemon zest, lemon juice, and saffron in the bowl of a food processor fit with the steel blade. With the motor running, slowly pour in the oils until the mixture is emulsified. Carefully transfer to a small bowl and season the mixture with salt and pepper. Set aside or refrigerate for up to 1 day.

Sea Robin Soup

SERVES 6
PREP TIME: 10 MINUTES
COOK TIME: 2½ HOURS

My father had a fishing buddy, Larry, who owned a condo next to our weekend place in Sandy Hook, New Jersey. Larry was Italian but much more Americanized than my father, so the only fish he caught and ate was fluke. But my father, hailing as he did from the waste-not-want-not culture of Italy, had his own slogan, and I still use it to this day: "If we catch it, we eat it!" (He also used to say, "If you hook 'em, you cook 'em.") So, my father was constantly stopping Larry from throwing fish back into the ocean.

One of the fish we caught a lot of was sea robin, which gets its name from its big pectoral fins, which look like a bird's wings when it swims. Because of its bone structure, sea robin is a real pain to eat or clean, but makes the most incredibly delicious broth. We caught what seemed like thousands of these fish. What we didn't use, my father would give away to my Uncle Frankie, who came from Molfetta, Bari, a little coastal town. "The Muffies will eat them," he'd say, and Frankie, proud of his heritage, would take the fish home and do just that.

¼ cup olive oil, plus 1 to 2 teaspoons for brushing the bread
1 medium onion, coarsely chopped
1 medium fennel bulb, coarsely chopped
1 large carrot, peeled and coarsely chopped
1 stalk celery, coarsely chopped
2 large garlic cloves, 1 finely chopped, 1 cut in half crosswise
4 medium sea robins, about 1 pound each, gutted, filleted, and roughly chopped
    (similar-sized fish ,such as sea bass or grouper, can be substituted)
Kosher salt
Freshly ground black pepper
1 cup dry white wine, such as Sauvignon Blanc
1 tablespoon tomato paste
1 can (28 ounces) whole peeled tomatoes, crushed by hand, with their juice
¼ cup flat-leaf parsley leaves, plus 2 tablespoons coarsely chopped leaves for serving
1 bay leaf
1 cup orzo, cooked and drained
Six ½-inch-thick slices country bread
Freshly grated parmesan

1. Heat a large, wide, deep, heavy pot over medium-high heat. Add the olive oil and heat over medium-high heat until shimmering, almost smoking. Add the onions, fennel, carrot, celery, chopped garlic, and sea robins. Season with salt and pepper. Cook, stirring occasionally, until the vegetables have softened, about 8 minutes.
2. Pour in the wine, raise the heat to high, bring it to a boil, and let reduce for 2 minutes. Add the tomato paste, lower the heat to medium, and stir to coat the other ingredients with the paste. Add the tomatoes and about 8 cups of cold water, or enough to completely cover the other ingredients. Stir in the parsley and bay leaf. Bring to a low simmer and cook at a gentle simmer until the broth is nicely thickened, about 1½ hours.
3. Meanwhile, bring a pot of salted water to a boil. Add the orzo and cook until al dente, about 8 minutes. Drain in a colander and set aside.
4. When the soup is almost done cooking, heat a grill pan over medium-high heat, or preheat the oven to 350°F. Drizzle the bread lightly with olive oil on both sides. Grill the bread, turning once, until toasted, or bake directly on the rack of the oven until nicely golden brown, 2 to 3 minutes. Remove from grill or oven and rub one side of the bread with the cut side of the cut garlic clove. (See page 27 for tip on rubbing bread with garlic.)
5. When the soup is done, strain it through a fine-mesh strainer set over a large bowl, pressing down on the solids with a wooden spoon or the bottom of a ladle to extract as much flavorful liquid as possible. Discard the solids.
6. Carefully wipe out the soup pot and pour the strained soup back into the pot. Add the orzo. Cook over medium heat, stirring occasionally, just until the orzo is heated through, 1 to 2 minutes.
7. Ladle the soup into bowls and garnish with the grated cheese and chopped parsley. Serve immediately with the garlic toasts alongside.

Tortellini Soup

SERVES 6
PREP TIME: 15 MINUTES
COOK TIME: 2 HOURS

I didn't think I could love this soup more than I loved my mother's version, which she made when I was kid, especially as a home remedy when I was sick. (It's a popular soup in the family; my father's sister, Auntie Anna, makes it for her husband, my Uncle Cosmo, as well.) But my wife, Lisa, makes it even better. There's something about the way it all comes together in her hands that's really special. Hers is the best tortellini soup I've ever had, even better than any restaurant version.

2 pounds cross-cut flanken short ribs, cut into
single-rib portions
2 beef bouillon cubes
1 small onion, finely diced
1½ cups peeled, thickly sliced carrots (from about
1 large carrot)
3 stalks celery, finely diced
3 large garlic cloves, finely chopped
1 medium Idaho potato, peeled and cut into ½-inch pieces
2 vine-ripe tomatoes, diced
Freshly ground black pepper
9 ounce package (about 2 cups) fresh or frozen prepared
cheese tortellini
2 tablespoons coarsely chopped flat-leaf parsley,
including stems
About 1 tablespoon finely grated pecorino Romano,
for serving

1. Put the meat in a wide, deep, heavy pot and cover by 1 inch with cold water; you will need about 2 quarts of water. Bring to a boil over high heat, then lower the heat and simmer until the meat is fork tender, about 45 minutes, skimming any impurities from the surface with a skimming wand or the edge of a wooden spoon as needed. When the meat is tender, use tongs to remove the meat from the pot and set aside on a plate until cool enough to handle.
2. While the meat cools, add 4 cups of water to the beef broth and bring to a sim-

mer over medium heat. Add the bouillon cubes and stir to dissolve them. Add the onion, carrots, celery, garlic, potato, tomatoes, and a few grinds of pepper. (You don't need to add any salt because the bouillon is salty.) Simmer over low heat until the ingredients are tender, about 45 minutes.

3. Meanwhile, bring a pot of salted water to a boil and add the tortellini. Cook until they float to the surface, about 1 minute for fresh and 2 to 3 minutes for frozen. Drain the tortellini in a colander and set aside.

4. When the meat is cool enough to handle, remove the meat from the bones and cut or pull it into bite-sized pieces. Set aside on a plate or in a bowl.

5. Add the meat and tortellini to the soup about 5 minutes before the soup is done, to warm them through. Stir in the parsley, ladle the soup into individual bowls, top with grated cheese, and serve.

Pasta and Risotto

After his family, there's nothing more near and dear to the heart of an Italian-American than pasta.

I could go on all day about all the reasons I love pasta: It's filling and it gets along with just about everything; it can stand up to a hearty meat sauce or a rich cream sauce or turn the spotlight over to more gentle flavors like shrimp or eggplant.

More generally, if you grew up in a family like mine, pasta is the thing that's always there: if you're a little kid, and you get sick, your mom makes you pasta *en bianca,* or white pasta, with just butter and grated parmesan cheese; on Sunday nights, pasta is a ritual, families and extended families gathering for the same combination of pasta and meat sauce that they enjoy together every week, with the leftovers a day or two later. (The Valastro family's own Sunday Gravy traditions are described on page 179.) Pasta is what our mothers put into soup to beef it up, toss with leftovers to keep from wasting anything, and have in their cupboards at all times.

I'm not sure, but I don't believe anybody in my family has ever tried to go on a no-carb diet, and it's not because most of us work at Carlo's Bake Shop. It's because of the pasta!

Before we dive into the Valastros' favorite pasta recipes, here are some tips for making the best pasta possible:

- When cooking pasta, you want the water to be boiling aggressively, like there's a hurricane blowing through the pot, and to add the pasta a little at a time, but in quick succession. (The times you don't want the pasta boiling too hard are when cooking ravioli and other filled pasta, or gnocchi, all of which can fall apart.) Both of these tips will help keep the pasta from sticking together.
- Don't add olive oil to the water; somewhere along the line people starting believing that doing that would keep pasta from sticking or clumping, but it's not true.
- You want to taste the pasta itself, so you need to season it, the same way you need to season anything else. To pull this off, add salt to the pasta's cooking water; a good rule of thumb is 1 tablespoon of kosher salt to 2 quarts of water.

- Don't get hung up on the pasta shapes in my recipes or any recipes. It's good to try to stay in the same ballpark, but you don't need to use exactly what I call for: Replace short tubular shapes like penne with similar shapes such as rigatoni; longer strands like spaghetti with linguine, fettuccine, and so on. But there are almost no recipes I know of—except maybe lasagna—where it's essential to use the exact shape that's called for in a recipe. If you have different pasta in your pantry, or another one was on sale at the supermarket that day, or another one just makes you or your kids happy, then it's fine to substitute.

- As far as I'm concerned, there's only one way to eat pasta, and that's *al dente,* which means "to the tooth." Al dente pasta has a bite to it, just a little resistance that makes it more pleasing to eat and makes it feel more substantial. You can certainly cook pasta longer than I do, but I really encourage you to try to develop a taste for al dente pasta; it's really the only way to go. For this reason, with the exception of gnocchi, cavatelli, and ravioli, where there's not really a choice, I only use dried pasta in my recipes. Fresh pasta can be delicious, but I love that toothsome effect of perfectly cooked dried pasta. A great tip for getting your pasta to come out al dente is to shave one minute off the cooking time on the pasta's package.

- If pasta is going to be tossed into a hot sauce, don't cook the pasta all the way in the water when you boil it. Instead, let it finish cooking in the sauce; it'll soak up some of the sauce, helping the two components meld. When the outer edge of your pasta begins to turn a chalky white, indicating the beginning of doneness, that's a good time to drain the pasta and add it to the sauce.

- If you find tomatoes too acidic for your taste, when making a red sauce, add 1 teaspoon of sugar along with the tomatoes to help offset their acidity.

- Make sure you have a good colander, or *sculapasta,* as my mother called it. It's the only way to properly drain a pound of pasta and makes it easy to transfer the strained pasta into a pan or serving bowl.

- The best way to get pasta and a sauce to come together is to toss them with each other in a sauté pan. If you don't have the skills to do that (and you should be a careful if you don't), you can also use salad tongs to toss the pasta a different way.

- Most of the recipes in this chapter serve 4 to 6 people, although some serve more. The exact number of people depends on how you'll serve the pasta: Whether it's a starter as it would be in Italy, or a main course, as it often is here in America, not to mention how big each person's appetite is.

- When checking for seasoning, taste pasta sauce on a piece of bread, which simulates the carby feel of pasta.

As for risotto, I usually group it with pasta because the two are very similar: a starchy primary component cooked in a liquid (risotto is usually made with stock rather than water), to which you add just about anything you want.

Pasta and risotto are also interchangeable in a meal: You'd never serve risotto and pasta in the same meal, although probably nobody would mind if you did!

Here are a few of my secrets for making great risotto.

First of all, it's always important to use a heavy-bottomed pot when cooking, but it's especially crucial when making risotto, because the rice flirts with dryness so often that it's easy for it to scorch. You should also be sure to buy an appropriate risotto rice: the most common type is Arborio, but Vialone Nano and Carnaroli are also fine. Because risotto is infused with stock, you should buy a good, gourmet brand, or make your own; I've included recipes for chicken and fish stock in the basics chapter of this book mainly because of how important they are in making risotto.

It's also very important, when making risotto, that the stock is simmering before you ladle it into the risotto pot; having the risotto and stock at a similar temperature helps keep the risotto cooking at a constant pace and prevents it from seizing up on itself.

Finally, generations of home cooks have struggled with how to make risotto for a dinner party, because it requires you to be away from the table for 20 minutes. Well, let me share with you a trick that restaurants use to make risotto *à la minute,* or at the last second, to order: Prepare risotto according to the recipe, but stop before adding the last addition or two of stock. Spread the risotto out on a cookie or baking sheet in an even layer (use a rubber spatula to do this) so that it cools as quickly as possible, then transfer the risotto to an airtight container for up to 2 hours. When you're ready to serve the risotto, bring your remaining stock to a simmer, heat the risotto in a clean pot, and proceed with the recipe, finishing the risotto and folding in any other ingredients, such as sautéed mushrooms.

Spaghetti Marinara

SERVES 4 TO 6

PREP TIME: 5 MINUTES

COOK TIME: 10 MINUTES (NOT INCLUDING MARINARA)

Spaghetti Marinara isn't a complicated dish to make, but I had to include it in the book because it's such a touchstone for me. In every house I've ever lived in, both the one my mother kept and today the one that Lisa keeps for me and our kids, there's always marinara sauce in the freezer, ready to become the source of a quick but wonderful meal. Its simplicity is its brilliance, and the addition of basil and cheese is all it takes to make this something special every time.

Kosher salt
3 cups Marinara Sauce (recipe follows)
¼ cup (loosely packed) torn basil leaves
1 pound dried spaghetti
Chunk of Parmigiano-Reggiano, at least 3 ounces,
    for serving

1. Bring a large pot of salted water to a rolling boil over high heat. Meanwhile, warm the sauce in a wide, deep sauté pan set over medium heat.
2. Cook the spaghetti in the boiling water until al dente, about 8 minutes.
3. Drain the pasta in a colander, add it to the sauté pan, and toss. Scatter the basil over the pasta, give one more toss, then use tongs to divide the pasta among 4 to 6 plates or wide, shallow bowls. Grate some cheese over each portion and pass the Parmigiano-Reggiano and grater alongside, inviting everybody to add more to their plate.

Marinara Sauce

MAKES ABOUT 2 QUARTS
PREP TIME: 10 MINUTES
COOK TIME: ABOUT 25 MINUTES

This is my recipe for a basic marinara sauce. My trick is adding basil twice: Once during the cooking and again at the end, so you a depth of flavor in the sauce and a fresh, herbaceous kick when you serve it.

¼ cup extra-virgin olive oil
2 large cloves garlic, thinly sliced
2 cans (28 ounces) crushed tomatoes with their juice
2 cans (14½ ounces) diced tomatoes with their juice
1 teaspoon kosher salt
1 sprig fresh basil plus ½ cup (loosely packed) basil leaves,
    torn into small pieces

1. Heat a large, heavy pot over medium-high heat. Add the oil and heat until shimmering, almost smoking. Add the garlic and cook, stirring, until it becomes golden and fragrant, about 30 seconds. Stir in the tomatoes, salt, and basil sprig. Keep cooking and stirring until the sauce comes to a boil, then lower the heat and simmer, stirring occasionally, until the sauce is thickened and richly flavored, 15 to 20 minutes. Adjust the seasoning with additional salt, if necessary, and stir in the basil leaves.

2. Use the sauce in other dishes, toss with the pasta of your choice, or use as a dip for fried foods. Extra sauce may be refrigerated in an airtight container for up to 2 days or frozen for up to 1 month.

Note: To make this recipe with fresh tomatoes, peel and seed (see pages 233 and 30 for instructions) 5 pounds (18 to 20 tomatoes) plum or Roma tomatoes. Proceed with the recipe, stirring in 2 tablespoons of tomato paste after softening the garlic. Simmering time will vary based on the water content of the tomatoes, but should take 1 hour to 1 hour 15 minutes to achieve the desired effect.

Pasta e Lenticchie
(Pasta and Lentil Soup)

SERVES 4 TO 6
PREP TIME: 10 MINUTES
COOK TIME: ABOUT 1 HOUR

My brother-in-law Mauro and I didn't grow up in the same house, but we have a common fondness for this soupy pasta dish because our mothers made it for us. He remembers his mom making this soup for, among other things, its affordability: "For a buck, you could feed the family," he says. In our house, this dish was in my mother's weekly dinner rotation during the cold months: When I think of it, I remember coming home late in the afternoon on a winter Tuesday or Wednesday and smelling the hearty aromas: smoky bacon, sweet garlic, and rich parmesan. You took all of that in, and you knew what was coming, and how one bite would warm you up.

Italian tradition says that you eat lentils for New Year's Eve, to bring luck in the coming year, and that's one of, but far from the only, times we always ate this pasta. I don't know if it brought us luck, but it warmed the soul, that's for sure.

1 teaspoon olive oil
2 slices extra-thick cut bacon, cut into ¼-inch dice (see Note)
1 small Spanish onion, finely chopped
1 stalk celery, trimmed and finely chopped
1 medium carrot, peeled and finely chopped
Kosher salt
2 large garlic cloves, peeled and minced
1 cup dried brown lentils, picked free of any impurities or
*   pebbles, rinsed, and drained*
1 can (14½ ounces) plum tomatoes with their juice,
*   broken up by hand into large pieces*
5 cups water
Piece of parmesan rind, optional
1 cup ditalini or other small pasta shape
2 tablespoons extra-virgin olive oil, plus more for serving
Chunk of Parmigiano-Reggiano, at least 2 ounces, for serving
Coarsely grated black pepper

1. Heat a large, heavy soup pot over medium heat. Add the oil and let it warm up, then add the bacon and stir to coat. Cook, stirring with a wooden spoon, until the bacon has softened and some fat has rendered, about 8 minutes. Add the onion, celery, and carrot, and stir to coat. Season with a pinch of salt, stir, and continue to cook, stirring, until the vegetables are softened but not browned, about 10 minutes. Stir in the garlic and cook, stirring periodically, until fragrant but not browned, about another 2 minutes. Stir in the lentils, then stir in the tomatoes with their juices, 5 cups water, a pinch of salt, and the parmesan rind, if using. Raise the heat to high and bring to a boil, then lower the heat and simmer, stirring occasionally, until the lentils are tender but still al dente, 20 to 30 minutes.
2. Meanwhile, bring a small pot of salted water to a rolling boil. Add the ditalini and cook until al dente, about 2 minutes. Drain in a colander and set aside.
3. When the lentils have reached the desired consistency, stir in the ditalini and cook until the pasta is fully cooked, about 10 more minutes. Taste and add more salt, if necessary.
4. Ladle the soup into 4 to 6 bowls and finish with a drizzle of extra-virgin olive oil, some grated cheese, and black pepper. Serve at once with the cheese, with a grater alongside for grating over each serving.

Note: Bacon can be a little greasy and slippery. If you need to dice it in a recipe, a cool trick is putting it on a piece of plastic wrap in the freezer for 10 minutes to firm it up and make it easier to slice. By the time you get it in the pan, it'll be back to room temperature and ready to go.

Potato Gnocchi

MAKES A GENEROUS POUND OF GNOCCHI, ENOUGH TO SERVE 4 TO 6 PEOPLE
PREP TIME: ABOUT 1 HOUR 15 MINUTES
COOK TIME: ABOUT 5 MINUTES

This is another dish that my father used to make, and it also happens to be a favorite of my sister Lisa. I love it, too. What's not to love? A pasta made out of potato: Starch heaven, baby.

Contrary to popular belief, gnocchi are not that difficult to make: once you've done it, and seen how they come out so you can adjust, you'll be a pro in no time at all. The main thing is not to overwork the dough, which will cause the gnocchi to become leaden and gummy.

I offer my Dad's mushroom sauce to go with gnocchi, but you don't have to go to the trouble of making a sauce; gnocchi are so soft and delicious themselves that you can simply toss them with a simple tomato sauce, or with melted butter and minced herbs.

3 large Idaho potatoes (about 2½ pounds total)
2 large egg yolks, beaten
1 to 2 cups all-purpose flour (you may not need it all),
*   plus more for dusting your work surface*
½ teaspoon fine sea salt
Pinch freshly grated nutmeg, optional

1. Position a rack in the center of the oven. Preheat to 400°F.
2. Prick the potatoes all over with a fork, arrange on a rimmed baking tray, and bake, turning every 15 minutes or so to ensure even cooking, until a sharp, thin-bladed knife, such as a paring knife, slides easily into the center of a potato, 45 to 60 minutes.
3. Remove the potatoes from the oven, use tongs to transfer them to the cutting board, and use the knife to make slashes lengthwise across the potatoes. As soon as they are cool enough to handle, press on the ends of the potatoes with your hands to force out the steam. (In order to make less gummy gnocchi, the potatoes need to be as dry as possible.)
4. While the potatoes are still quite warm, scoop out the potato flesh and rice them in a ricer or transfer to a bowl and mash with a potato masher. Measure out 3 (loosely packed) cups.
5. Lightly flour a work surface and transfer the 3 cups of potato to the surface. Add ½

cup flour, gently knead, and form into a mound. Make a well in the center and add about ¾ of the egg to the well. Use a fork to work the egg into the mixture. When almost incorporated (the mixture will begin crumbling), sprinkle another ¼ cup flour over the mixture and work it in with the fork , then gently knead together. If the mixture seems too dry, add more of the yolk. Continue just until the mixture comes together in a slightly shiny and fragile dough—adding more flour and egg yolk, as necessary.

6. Lightly press the dough together into a ball and set it aside. Scrape any stuck-on dough from your work surface, then dust lightly with flour.

7. Working on the freshly floured surface, fold and knead the dough just enough for it to hold together. If the dough is sticky, add a little more flour, but as little as possible; the less flour you add and the less you work the dough, the lighter and more tender the gnocchi will be.

8. Lightly flour a rimmed baking sheet. Cut the dough into four equal pieces. Working with 1 portion of dough, roll it into a long rope, about ½ inch in diameter. With the bench scraper, cut 1-inch pieces of dough from the rope and place on the floured sheet. These are your gnocchi. The gnocchi may be frozen on the baking sheet, then transferred to a freezer bag and frozen for up to 1 month. There is no need to defrost the gnocchi before cooking them.

9. To cook gnocchi, bring a pot of salted water to a gentle boil over high heat. Add the gnocchi. They are done after they bob to the surface then cook for 1 additional minute, about 2 minutes total for fresh gnocchi, 3 to 4 for frozen. Use a slotted spoon to transfer the gnocchi either to mixing bowls to gently toss with other ingredients (see headnote), to pans full of sauce (as in Mushroom Sauce for Gnocchi, page 148), or directly to serving dishes.

Mushroom Sauce for Gnocchi

MAKES ENOUGH SAUCE FOR A POUND OF GNOCCHI
PREP TIME: ABOUT 20 MINUTES
COOK TIME: ABOUT 40 MINUTES (INCLUDING SOAKING)

This sauce, which my father used to make, pulls off a neat trick: There's no meat in it, but the texture of the cremini mushrooms and the intensity of the reconstituted dried porcini create a meatlike effect. The real magic is in the porcini's soaking liquid, which is like liquid gold: I use it to intensify the sauce. You can use it for the same purpose in mushroom soups and risottos.

This sauce is also wonderful with broad pasta shapes, especially pappardelle.

2 cups homemade Chicken Stock (page 303), or low-sodium
    chicken broth
1-ounce package dried porcini mushrooms
3 tablespoons olive oil
1¼ pounds cremini mushrooms, wiped clean, ends trimmed,
    and thinly sliced (see Box)
Kosher salt
2 large cloves garlic, minced
½ teaspoon crushed red-pepper flakes
¼ cup dry white wine, such as Sauvignon Blanc
⅓ cup coarsely chopped flat-leaf parsley
Gnocchi (page 145)
2 to 3 tablespoons unsalted butter
1 tablespoon white truffle oil
¼ cup (about 1 ounce) finely grated Parmigiano-Reggiano,
    for garnish
Freshly ground black pepper

1. Heat the chicken stock in a small pot set over high heat. Put the dried porcini mushrooms in a small, heatproof bowl and pour the stock over them. Let soak at least 20 minutes to hydrate, then use a slotted spoon to transfer to a cutting board. Coarsely chop the mushrooms, then set aside. Line a fine-mesh strainer with cheesecloth and strain the mushroom's soaking liquid through the cheesecloth into a cup and set aside. (If you don't have cheesecloth, a paper towel or coffee filter may be used.)

2. Heat a wide, deep, heavy sauté pan large enough to hold the gnocchi and sauce over medium-high heat. Add the olive oil and heat until it is shimmering, almost smoking. Add the cremini mushrooms and a pinch of salt. Cook, stirring, until the mushrooms release their juice, it comes to a boil, and nearly evaporates, about 7 minutes. Stir in the porcini, garlic, and red-pepper flakes and continue to cook until the mixture is nicely fragrant and almost dry, 1 to 2 minutes.

3. Pour in the wine, bring it to a boil, and let it reduce, about 1 minute. Pour in ½ cup of the mushroom-soaking liquid, bring it to a boil, and reduce until almost dry, about 2 minutes. Pour in another ½ cup of the liquid, and boil and reduce until almost dry, about 1 more minute. Stir in the parsley. Taste and add salt, if necessary.

4. Transfer the cooked gnocchi to the mushroom sauce, using a slotted spoon. Raise the heat to medium-high and add another ½ cup mushroom cooking liquid, stirring the gnocchi to coat it with the sauce. If the gnocchi looks as though it can absorb more stock, add a little more, but take care to not let it become too soft. Fold in the butter and truffle oil.

5. Spoon the gnocchi and sauce into 4 to 6 wide, shallow bowls or plates and garnish with grated cheese and pepper.

Note: Mushrooms soak up liquid, so don't clean them in water. Simply take a slightly damp paper towel and gently wipe off any dirt or grit. Some people also use a mushroom brush, but I don't think they're necessary; in fact, I think they tend to break up mushrooms.

Pasta alla Norma

SERVES 4 TO 6
PREP TIME: ABOUT 1 HOUR (INCLUDING SALTING THE EGGPLANT)
COOK TIME: ABOUT 25 MINUTES

I first had Pasta alla Norma when visiting Taormina in Sicily as a child. It's a classic Sicilian pasta, named for Vincenzo Bellini's opera *Norma*. I put my own spin on it, topping the pasta with slices of one of my favorite treats, fried eggplant, rather than simply including diced eggplant in the sauce, although I also do that.

2 medium eggplants, about 1 pound each
Kosher salt
½ cup plus 2 tablespoons olive oil
1 small Spanish onion, peeled and cut into small dice
3 large garlic cloves, minced
1 can (28 ounces) crushed tomatoes with their juice
1 tablespoon unsalted butter
1 bunch fresh basil, stems discarded, roughly chopped
Freshly ground black pepper
1 cup all-purpose flour
2 large eggs, beaten
2 cups Homemade Breadcrumbs (page 295)
1 pound short pasta, such as gemelli, penne, or rigatoni
¾ cup (4 ounces) crumbled ricotta salata

1. Cut the ends off the eggplants and peel them. With a sharp, heavy chef's knife, slice 1 eggplant crosswise into ⅛-inch rounds. Cut the other eggplant into ½-inch dice. Put the eggplant rounds in a colander, sprinkle with about 1½ teaspoons salt, toss, and set in the sink, pushing the rounds to one side of the colander; the salt will coax the moisture and bitterness out of the eggplant. Put the diced eggplant on the other side of the colander, salt with about 1½ teaspoons of salt, mixing it with your fingers to distribute the salt, and allow it to drain for 1 hour. If you have 2 colanders, you can of course drain the two eggplants in separate colanders.

2. Rinse the eggplant under gently running cold water and let drain briefly. Remove the sliced eggplant from the colander, pat dry with paper towels, and set aside. Dry the diced eggplant and set aside separately.

3. Heat a medium, heavy saucepan over medium high. Add 2 tablespoons of the olive

oil and heat it until it is shimmering, almost smoking. Add the onion and a pinch of salt and cook, stirring with a wooden spoon, until the onion is soft and translucent, about 5 minutes. Add the garlic and cook until fragrant but not browned, a few more minutes. Add the diced eggplant and cook, stirring, until soft but not mushy, about 5 minutes longer. Stir in the tomatoes and bring the sauce to a simmer, then lower the heat and let simmer until the juices begin to evaporate and the sauce thickens slightly, about 5 minutes. Stir in the butter and basil. Taste and adjust the seasoning with salt and/or pepper, if necessary.

4. Bring a large pot of salted water to a boil and cook the pasta until al dente, about 8 minutes.

5. Set a wire rack over a baking sheet.

6. Spread the flour out in a wide, shallow bowl. Beat the eggs in another bowl, and spread the breadcrumbs out in a third. Working with 1 eggplant slice at a time, dip in the flour, shaking any excess off into the bowl, dip it in the egg, letting any excess drip into the bowl, then dip it in the breadcrumbs, pressing down gently to be sure the breadcrumbs adhere to the slices. As the slices are prepared, place them on a wire rack.

7. Line a large plate with paper towels.

8. Heat the remaining ½ cup olive oil in a wide, heavy sauté pan until it is shimmering, almost smoking.

9. Carefully add the eggplant rounds to the pan in batches without crowding, and cook until golden brown, 1 to 2 minutes per side, turning the slices with tongs or a spatula. When they are done, transfer them to the paper-towel–lined plate to drain. Add additional oil to the pan as needed.

10. Drain the pasta in a colander, add it to the pan with the eggplant sauce, and toss well. Transfer to a serving platter. When cool enough to handle, slice each fried eggplant round into 3 strips and place atop the pasta. Garnish with the crumbled ricotta and serve immediately.

Nina's Famous Meatless Meatballs

MAKES 1 DOZEN
PREP TIME: 10 MINUTES
COOK TIME: 30 MINUTES

My parents' best friends were a couple named Nina and Mario. They had a lot in common: Each couple had five kids, and vacationed in Acapulco together every January. Every few months, they'd get the two families together. If they came to our house, my father would cook; when we went to their house, Nina hit the stove. This was one of her specialties, another Italian-American dish that evolved because of limited financial resources in Italy, where many families couldn't afford meat for sauce, and thus became expert at faking it. (My mother-in-law, Gloria, makes a wonderful version of these with, of all things, matzo mix.)

Now here's the thing about these meatless meatballs, known in some circles as *egg balls*: You would never know that you were missing out on something. One bite and you'd think you'd died and gone to heaven. I actually know some people who like them better than the real thing. If you have any vegetarians in your life, make this for them.

1 cup Homemade Breadcrumbs (page 295)
5 large eggs, beaten
¾ cup whole milk
¾ cup to 1 cup (3 to 4 ounces) finely grated pecorino
*   Romano*
1 large garlic clove, pressed
1 cup coarsely chopped flat-leaf parsley leaves
Kosher salt
Freshly ground black pepper
About 2½ cups canola or other neutral oil
1 medium Spanish onion, finely diced
1 can (28 ounces) whole peeled tomatoes, with their juice,
*   crushed by hand*
1 teaspoon sugar
¼ cup water, if needed
¼ cup torn basil leaves

1. Put the breadcrumbs, eggs, milk, cheese, garlic, parsley, a pinch of salt, and a pinch of pepper in a large bowl. By hand or using a wooden spoon, mix or knead into a uniform mixture. Let rest at room temperature for 15 minutes.

2. Line a large plate or platter with paper towels.

3. Pour oil into a wide, deep, heavy cast iron pan or sauté pan to a depth of ¾ inch. Heat over medium heat. The oil is ready for frying when a breadcrumb carefully dropped into the oil bubbles and browns.

4. Use 2 tablespoons to form balls from the meatball mixture, Drop spoonfuls of the meatball mixture into the hot oil and pan-fry, rolling them with a slotted spoon as they cook, until golden brown all over, about 6 minutes total cooking time. Work in batches to keep from overcrowding the pan and, thus, lowering the temperature too much.

5. As they are done, use the slotted spoon to transfer the meatballs to the paper-towel–lined plate.

6. Wipe out the same pan, or start with a new sauté pan and heat 2 more tablespoons of oil over medium heat. When the oil is shimmering, almost smoking, add the diced onion to the pan and cook, stirring, over medium heat until soft and translucent, but not browned, about 5 minutes. Stir in the tomatoes and sugar, season with salt and pepper, and bring the liquids to a boil. Lower the heat and cook at a brisk simmer for 10 minutes, adding a little water if the sauce becomes too dry.

7. Add the meatballs to the sauce and cook until warmed through, about 10 minutes. Stir in the torn basil.

8. Serve the meatballs over pasta or as a side dish.

Kids' Cavatelli with Broccoli

SERVES 6 KIDS
PREP TIME: 5 MINUTES
COOK TIME: ABOUT 10 MINUTES

My kids love pasta and broccoli, but it wasn't easy to make that happen: My wife, Lisa, tricked them into it by cooking a version of this recipe in which she boiled the broccoli to death, until it was falling apart. Each time she made it, she cooked the vegetable less and less, until the kids developed a taste for al dente broccoli, which is more nutritious. Before we knew it, they had grown to like not only broccoli, but also cauliflower and other vegetables. The irony is that I came to love the sort-of-green sauce created by overcooking the broccoli: This recipe meets the two recipes in the middle by cooking the pasta in the same pot as the softer-than-al-dente broccoli and tossing it all together with a quick garlic oil.

Kosher salt
4 to 5 cups broccoli florets and tender stems,
    from 1 large bunch of broccoli
1 pound fresh or frozen plain (not ricotta) cavatelli
2 tablespoons olive oil
3 large garlic cloves, minced
½ cup (2 ounces) finely grated Parmigiano-Reggiano

1. Bring a large pot of salted water to a boil. Half fill a large bowl with ice water.
2. Add the broccoli to the boiling water and cook until softer than al dente, but not mushy, 3 to 4 minutes. Use a slotted spoon to transfer the broccoli to the ice water to shock it and preserve the beautiful green color.
3. Let the salted water return to a simmer and add the cavatelli. Cook until they float, about 1 minute for fresh, 2 to 3 minutes for frozen. Reserve about a cup of the pasta cooking liquid in a heatproof measuring cup, then drain the pasta in a colander.
4. Heat a large sauté pan over medium heat. Add the oil and heat until shimmering, almost smoking. Add the garlic and cook over low heat, not allowing the garlic to brown or burn, about 1 minute. Add the broccoli to the pan with the pasta, and toss, adding a little of the pasta's cooking liquid if the mixture seems too dry. Divide among 6 small plates or bowls and serve at once, passing the grated cheese.

Spinach and Ricotta Ravioli

MAKES ABOUT 24, ENOUGH TO SERVE 4 TO 6
PREP TIME: ABOUT 10 MINUTES
COOK TIME: ABOUT 15 MINUTES

Italian-American women in tight-knit communities always have to have something on hand to serve up for last-minute company, often two or three times a week. I call dishes like those *back-pocket recipes,* dishes that you can have in your back pocket, ready to heat and serve on a moment's notice. One of the all-time greatest back-pocket recipes is ravioli, and my favorite is spinach and ricotta. These can be made and frozen in advance and boiled in a matter of minutes; you don't even have to defrost them.

Serve these with Marinara Sauce (page 141) and/or plenty of parmesan, or brown butter with sage and parmesan.

1 pound fresh spinach, tough stems trimmed and discarded
1 tablespoon unsalted butter
¼ cup minced shallot
1 heaping cup fresh ricotta
½ cup (2 ounces) finely grated Parmigiano-Reggiano
2 large egg yolks
Several gratings whole nutmeg
Kosher salt
Homemade Fresh Pasta Sheets (page 304)

1. Pour water into a pot that can accommodate a steamer basket to a depth of 1 inch, and bring to a simmer over high heat. Half fill a large bowl with ice water. Add the spinach to the steamer and steam over the boiling water until cooked through, 3 to 5 minutes. (If you don't have a steamer basket, you can suspend a colander over the water.) Transfer the spinach to the ice water to stop the cooking and preserve the spinach's color. When it's cool enough to handle, drain and squeeze any excess liquid from the spinach and coarsely chop it. You should have about 1 cup chopped spinach.

2. Heat a heavy sauté pan over medium-high heat. Add butter and cook until it melts and is foamy. Add the shallot and cook, stirring, until softened but not browned, about 2 minutes. Remove the pan from the heat and let cool.

3. Place the spinach, shallot, ricotta, Parmigiano-Reggiano cheese, egg yolks, nutmeg, and a pinch of salt in a large bowl and stir until blended.

4. Working with 1 sheet of pasta at a time, trim each length sheet to a 4-inch width. Place heaping teaspoons of filling in a line about 1 inch from the bottom of the pasta sheet, leaving about 1¼ inches between each mound of filling.

5. Lay another sheet of pasta on top of the first one and let it drop and conform to the mounds of filling. If the pasta is not moist enough to adhere to itself, brush streaks of water along the edges and press and seal at the edges. Use a fluted pastry wheel to trim along outer edges and in between mounds to cut ravioli.

6. To freeze ravioli, arrange them in a single layer on a baking sheet and freeze, then transfer them to zipper or freezer bags and freeze for up to 1 month. Do not thaw before cooking.

7. Bring a large pot of salted water to boil. Cook the ravioli, in batches if necessary, until they float, 3 to 4 minutes for fresh, a minute or 2 longer for frozen. Drain gently in a colander and serve.

Auntie Anna's Manicotti

SERVES 4 TO 6

PREP TIME: 1 HOUR 15 MINUTES (INCLUDES 1 HOUR RESTING TIME)

COOK TIME: 50 MINUTES

My father's sister, Auntie Anna, is a naturally gifted home cook whose food never fails to make me happy. As kids, if we weren't eating at home, or at Grandma Madeline's in Hoboken, you could probably find us at Anna's house in Weehawken. Of all her dishes, one that is incredibly popular among my family is her legendary manicotti, which are the most delicious, dreamiest, creamiest manicotti you could imagine. Where many modern cooks take a shortcut and use pasta for their manicotti, Auntie Anna does it the old-fashioned way, with homemade crepes, and that makes all the difference; the way those crepes soak up all the flavors in the baking pan is really special.

If you're wondering why this recipe has potato in it, it's Anna's trick to help neutralize the acidity of the tomatoes.

This recipe makes ten to twelve crepes, but you only need ten for the manicotti. It's one of the great mysteries of cooking that the first crepe never comes out right, so plan to discard that one; you'll still have enough.

½ cup water
½ cup whole milk
4 large eggs
3 tablespoons melted unsalted butter, plus solid butter for greasing a baking dish
1 cup all-purpose flour
Kosher salt
1½ pounds fresh whole-milk ricotta
1 heaping cup (6 ounces) coarsely grated mozzarella
¼ cup (1 ounce) finely grated pecorino Romano
2 large garlic cloves, minced or pressed
2 tablespoons minced flat-leaf parsley leaves
3 tablespoons chopped fresh basil leaves
3 tablespoons olive oil
8 ounces sweet Italian sausage, purchased loose, or squeezed from casings
1 cup peeled, grated russet potato
1 can (28 ounces) pureed tomatoes
Freshly ground black pepper
Pinch sugar, optional
1 cup (4 ounces) finely grated Parmigiano-Reggiano

1. Make the crepe batter: Put the water, milk, and 2 eggs in a standing blender, then add 2 tablespoons butter. (Add the butter last to keep it from cooking the eggs; the cold milk will cool it instantly.) Blend for a few seconds, then stop the motor and add the flour and a pinch of salt. Blend again until smooth and free of lumps, just a few seconds. Pour the batter into a bowl, cover with plastic wrap, and refrigerate for at least 1 hour, or up to 4 hours. (If you like, this is a good time to jump ahead and make the filling and sauce.)

2. Heat an 8-inch, nonstick skillet over medium heat. Using a pastry brush, lightly grease the skillet with the remaining melted butter. When the butter is hot, ladle 2 to 3 tablespoons of batter into the center of the pan and quickly tilt the pan in a rotating motion until the batter forms a thin, round, uniform layer. Let cook until the bottom is set and starting to lightly brown, about 30 seconds.

3. Lift a set edge of the crepe with a fork or small offset spatula and, quickly but carefully, turn the crepe over. Cook until the bottom is set, about 30 seconds more; the crepe will be a bit shiny in places, but that's all right. Transfer the cooked crepe to a plate.

4. Continue to make crepes, stacking them on the plate, and adding more melted butter to the pan as necessary, until all the batter has been used; you should have 10 to 12 crepes. (If not preparing the manicotti immediately, separate the cooked crepes with squares of waxed paper or paper towels.)

5. Make the filling: Put the ricotta, mozzarella, pecorino, 2 eggs, half the garlic, the parsley, and 1 tablespoon basil in a large mixing bowl and stir the ingredients together. The filling may be made up to 4 hours in advance, and refrigerated in an airtight container.

6. Make the sauce: Heat a wide heavy sauté pan over medium heat. Add 1 tablespoon olive oil and heat until shimmering, almost smoking. Add the sausage and cook, turning and crumbling with a wooden spoon or a fork, until beginning to brown, with no trace of pink remaining, 8 to 10 minutes. Remove the pan from the heat.

7. Meanwhile, heat a large saucepan over medium heat. Add the remaining the olive oil and heat until shimmering, almost smoking. Add the remaining garlic and the potato, stirring and cooking until the garlic is fragrant (do not allow the potato to crisp and brown). Add the pureed tomatoes, sausage and its accumulated juices, a pinch of salt, and a few grinds of pepper. Bring to a low boil, then lower the heat and simmer until thick and flavorful, 20 to 30 minutes. Taste and, if desired, stir in the sugar. Taste again and adjust the seasoning with salt, if necessary. Stir in 1 tablespoon of the basil. Remove from the heat and let cool for at least 10 minutes.

8. To assemble and cook the manicotti: Position a rack in the center of the oven and preheat to 375°F. Lightly grease a 13-inch x 9-inch x 2-inch (deep) ovenproof

Pyrex or other nonmetallic baking dish with butter. Ladle just enough sauce onto the bottom of the dish to coat.

9. Select your 10 most beautiful crepes. Working on a cutting board or clean work surface, arrange the crepes with the shinier side (the second side cooked) up. Scoop about 2 tablespoons of filling along the center of each crepe, all the way to the ends, and work it into a cigar shape. Working with one crepe at a time, roll the crepe around the filling and arrange the manicotti snugly in the prepared baking dish, seam-side down so they do not unravel. Snuggle them together; 10 will fill the dish perfectly. Pour the remaining sauce over the manicotti and sprinkle with the Parmigiano-Reggiano.

10. Bake the manicotti, uncovered, until hot and bubbling, 35 to 40 minutes. If you'd like to brown the cheese, broil for a few minutes. Remove from the oven and let rest for 10 minutes before serving.

11. To serve, scatter the remaining basil over the manicotti, divide the manicotti among 4 to 6 plates, and serve.

Rigatoni "alla Vodka"

SERVES 4 TO 6
PREP TIME: 10 MINUTES
COOK TIME: 20 MINUTES

If you look at the ingredients list for this recipe, you might think something's missing: the vodka!

Here's the story: I developed this recipe in my teens, after I ate rigatoni alla vodka in a restaurant and fell in love with the strong flavors and the cool undercurrent of flavor provided by the vodka. My mother wouldn't let me cook with vodka in those days, so I came up with this recipe that pumps up the flavor with lots of garlic and basil to create a similar effect.

Kosher salt
2 tablespoons olive oil
½ small Spanish onion, coarsely chopped
6 thin slices (4 ounces) prosciutto or pancetta
3 large garlic cloves, minced
Freshly ground black pepper
1 can (28 ounces) crushed tomatoes with their juice
1 teaspoon sugar
1 pound dried rigatoni pasta
1 cup heavy cream
¼ cup (loosely packed) basil leaves
¼ cup (1 ounce) finely grated Parmigiano-Reggiano

1. Bring a large pot of salted water to a boil.
2. Heat a wide, heavy sauté pan over medium heat. Add the oil and heat until shimmering, almost smoking. Add the onion and cook, stirring with a wooden spoon, until softened but not browned, about 5 minutes. Add the prosciutto and garlic, season with salt and pepper, and cook, stirring, for 1 minute. Stir in the tomatoes and sugar, bring to a simmer, and let simmer until the juices reduce slightly, about 15 minutes.
3. Meanwhile, add the rigatoni to the boiling water and cook until al dente, 10 to 12 minutes.

4. Pour the cream into a mixing bowl and whip with a hand mixer until peaks form. Fold the cream gently into the tomato sauce.

5. Drain the rigatoni in a colander, add it to the sauce, and toss well. Taste and add salt and pepper, if necessary. Transfer to a serving bowl, top with grated cheese and basil, and serve immediately.

Shrimp Scampi

SERVES 4 TO 6
PREP TIME: 15 MINUTES
COOK TIME: ABOUT 10 MINUTES

This super garlicky take on the classic Italian-American pasta and shrimp dish is another Auntie Anna classic. (A lot of people make fun of the name of this dish because it means "shrimp shrimp," but the flavors are no joke.) This recipe goes so far back that nobody is sure where it first came from, but Anna probably learned it from her mother or mother-in-law. All I can tell you is that its balance of garlic, lemon, and herbs is right on the money. It is so good that a number of other family members have been inspired to try their own versions over the years: My father used to make it, and my sister Mary does as well, but nobody can rival Auntie Anna, who has the magic touch with this and manicotti (page 159).

Auntie Anna sometimes serves this over rice.

Kosher salt
1 pound dried linguine
¼ cup olive oil
4 tablespoons unsalted butter
4 large garlic cloves, minced
1 pound large shrimp, peeled and deveined
Freshly ground black pepper
1 teaspoon dried oregano
2 tablespoons chopped fresh flat-leaf parsley leaves
½ cup Homemade Breadcrumbs (page 295)
¼ cup (1 ounce) finely grated pecorino Romano
Juice of three large lemons

1. Bring a large pot of salted water to a boil. Add the linguine and cook until al dente, about 8 minutes.
2. Meanwhile, heat a large, heavy sauté pan over medium heat. Add the oil and butter and heat until the butter melts and the oil is hot. Add the garlic and cook until fragrant but not browned, about 1 minute. Add the shrimp and season with a few pinches of salt and some pepper. Cook, stirring, for 2 to 3 minutes, then stir in the oregano and parsley and cook, stirring, until the shrimp are firm, pink, and cooked

through, about another 3 minutes. Stir in the breadcrumbs and cheese and coat the shrimp with them. Stir in the lemon juice.

3. To serve, drain the pasta in a colander and divide it among 4 to 6 individual plates. Spoon shrimp and sauce over each serving.

Why Oil and Butter?

Putting oil and butter in the pan together lets you get the butter hotter than would be possible on its own, because the oil has a higher smoke point.

Linguine with Shrimp
and Oven-Roasted Tomatoes

SERVES 4 TO 6

PREP TIME: ABOUT 20 MINUTES

COOK TIME: ABOUT 1 HOUR

This killer pasta is my wife Lisa's recipe, which I believe she first learned from her Aunt Gina. It's bursting with flavors and textures created by roasting well-seasoned tomatoes and garlic separately in the oven, then tossing them with shrimp and herbs. The tomatoes themselves are so good that sometimes Lisa serves pasta tossed with them alone. Roasting adds a real depth of flavor that makes seasonality irrelevant; if you're looking for a way to enjoy tomatoes outside the summer months, look no further than this year-round recipe.

1 large head garlic, about ½-inch cut off the top,
*   plus 1 large garlic clove, coarsely chopped*
¼ cup plus 2 tablespoons plus 1 teaspoon extra-virgin olive oil
1 pint cherry or grape tomatoes, red, or a mix of red and orange
Kosher salt
¼ cup Homemade Breadcrumbs (page 295)
1 pound dried linguine fini
2 tablespoons unsalted butter
1 pound large shrimp, peeled and deveined
½ cup dry white wine, such as Sauvignon Blanc
1 large lemon, halved
4 ounces (about 1½ cups loosely packed) baby spinach
½ cup coarsely chopped flat-leaf parsley leaves

1. Position a rack in the center of the oven. Preheat to 375°F.
2. Roast the garlic: Put the garlic head in a small piece of aluminum foil, cut-side up, and drizzle with a teaspoon of the oil. (You can also roast the garlic in a small ovenproof ramekin covered with foil or in a ceramic vessel specially made for roasting garlic.) Wrap the garlic tightly in the foil and place in the oven. Roast until the garlic is fragrant and the cloves are golden and a sharp, thin-bladed knife, such as a paring knife, slides easily to the center of a clove or two, 30 to 40 minutes. When the garlic is done, remove it from the oven, unwrap the foil, and let the garlic cool.

(Do not turn off the oven.) When cool enough to handle, pop the roasted garlic cloves out of the skin.

3. Meanwhile, put the tomatoes in a medium mixing bowl. Add the chopped garlic, ¼ cup oil, ½ teaspoon salt, and stir gently to coat. Spread the tomatoes evenly in a single layer on a rimmed baking sheet.

4. As the garlic cools, roast the tomatoes in the oven, shaking the pan occasionally to prevent scorching, until the tomatoes burst, about 10 minutes. Roast another 5 minutes, shake the pan, and scatter the breadcrumbs evenly over the tomatoes. Roast until the breadcrumbs are toasted, another 5 minutes.

5. While the tomatoes roast, bring a large pot of salted water to a boil over high heat. Add the pasta and cook until al dente, about 8 minutes.

6. Meanwhile, heat a large, heavy sauté pan over medium-high heat. Add 2 tablespoons of oil and 1 tablespoon of butter. When the butter is melted and foamy and the oil is hot, add the shrimp in one layer, and season lightly with salt. When one side is pink and firm, 1 to 2 minutes, turn the shrimp over with tongs or a wooden spoon and season the other side lightly with salt. Continue cooking until the upward-facing side is firm and pink and the shrimp are cooked through, 1 to 2 more minutes. Just before the shrimp are finished cooking, pour in the wine, raise the heat to high, and bring it to a boil. Squeeze some lemon juice into the pan, catching the seeds in your hand. Stir and let cook for 1 minute, then remove the pan from the heat and swirl in the remaining tablespoon of butter.

7. Use a heatproof measuring cup to reserve about a cup of the pasta's cooking liquid, then drain the pasta and add it to the pan, tossing or stirring to finish it in the sauce. If the sauce is too dry, stir in a little of the cooking liquid.

8. Remove the pan from the heat and add the roasted tomatoes and their juices, along with the roasted garlic cloves. Stir in the spinach and parsley. Mix the ingredients together, transfer to a bowl, and serve family style.

Pasta Carbonara

SERVES 4 TO 6
PREP TIME: 10 MINUTES
COOK TIME: 20 MINUTES

For me, this classic pasta dish of barely cooked eggs, cheese, pancetta, and black pepper goes all the way back to my childhood, when my sister Lisa and I had it in a restaurant, and she later asked me to cook it for her. It's a bit of an unusual dish, because the eggs aren't cooked on the stove, but by the heat of the pasta itself, so it took me some experimenting to nail it down, but I stuck with it and mastered it. This is the same recipe I've been using ever since; it captures the silky, peppery quality of any great carbonara. The trick is to cook the eggs just enough that they are safe to eat but not truly scrambled.

You can mix these same ingredients into a risotto, stirring the eggs in at the very end to cook them in the heat of the rice.

1 pound dried spaghetti
3 large very fresh eggs, preferably organic
1 cup (4 ounces) freshly, finely grated Parmigiano-Reggiano
2 tablespoons olive oil
8 ounces pancetta, cut into ½-inch dice (about 1 cup diced)
2 large garlic cloves, minced
1½ teaspoons coarsely ground black pepper

1. Bring a large pot of salted water to boil. Add the spaghetti and cook until al dente, 7 to 8 minutes.
2. Put the eggs in a large mixing bowl and beat them, then stir in the cheese.
3. Meanwhile, heat a large, heavy sauté pan over medium heat. Add the oil and warm slightly. Add the pancetta and cook, stirring, until it renders its fat and starts to brown, 4 to 5 minutes. Add the garlic and cook, stirring, until fragrant but not browned, another 30 seconds. Remove the pan from the heat and set aside.
4. When the pasta is done, reserve 1 cup of the cooking water, then drain the spaghetti in a colander. Immediately transfer the spaghetti to the bowl with the egg-and-cheese mixture. Toss thoroughly to coat, cooking the egg slightly with the heat of the pasta. Add the pancetta and garlic and toss to coat. If the mixture appears dry, add a little of the pasta's cooking liquid and toss again.
5. Season the pasta with the pepper, divide among 4 to 6 plates or large, shallow bowls, and serve.

Pasta with Ham, Peas, and Cream

SERVES 4 TO 6

PREP TIME: 10 MINUTES

COOK TIME: 15 MINUTES

One Sunday evening, when Lisa was pregnant with Marco, she spent the night tossing and turning and unable to get comfortable.

"You hungry?" I asked her. "Let's order something in."

"No," she said. "I want to sleep."

That turned out to be a mission impossible, and a little later, just after all the area restaurants had closed up shop, she was starving.

"Wait here," I said, and headed downstairs to the kitchen, where the cupboards were pretty bare. (Lisa usually shops on Monday, so we were down to the last of our food for the week.) But, after some poking around, I found a few things to work with: ham, Parmigiano-Reggiano, a can of peas, and some heavy cream that was two days from expiring. I knew things were going to turn out all right because ham and cheese are two of the biggest cravings Lisa experiences when she's pregnant.

I used those ingredients to whip up this dish. Although I'd planned on serving her dinner in bed, Lisa smelled it cooking and came downstairs.

"I can't believe you whipped this up from *nothing,*" she said. And, with that, we sat down to a midnight snack and a new house favorite.

Kosher salt
1 pound long ruffled pasta, such as mafalde
6 ounces sliced baked ham (about 6 slices)
3 tablespoons unsalted butter, 1 tablespoon chilled and cut into small pieces
2 large shallots, minced
2 large garlic cloves, pressed
1 cup defrosted frozen peas
1 cup heavy cream
½ cup (2 ounces) finely grated Parmigiano-Reggiano
Freshly ground black pepper

1. Bring a large pot of salted water to a boil. Add the pasta and cook until al dente, about 9 minutes.
2. Meanwhile, stack the slices of ham, roll lengthwise, and cut crosswise into ¼-inch ribbons. Separate the ribbons.

3. Heat a large, heavy sauté pan over medium-high heat. Add 2 tablespoons butter and cook until it melts and becomes foamy. Add the shallot and garlic and cook, stirring, until the shallots are softened but not browned, 2 to 3 minutes. Add the ham, stir with a wooden spoon, and cook until frizzled and cooked through, 2 to 3 minutes. (It's okay if the ham browns a little.) Add the peas and cook, stirring, until heated through, about 2 minutes.

4. When the pasta is done, reserve about a cup of the cooking liquid, then drain the pasta and add it to the pan, along with the remaining butter. Add a tablespoon or 2 of the cooking liquid to help the ingredients melt, and toss until the butter has melted and coated the pasta. Add the cream and cheese, and toss over low heat just until the butter, cream, and cheese come together into a sauce and coat the pasta, adding a little more of the pasta's cooking liquid if necessary, about 3 minutes. Add a few grinds of black pepper, and stir one last time.

5. Divide the pasta among 4 to 6 plates or wide, shallow bowls, and serve immediately.

Grandma Madeline's Sausage Lasagna

SERVES 10 TO 12

PREP TIME: ABOUT 2 HOURS (INCLUDES SAUCE TIME; SAUCE CAN BE MADE IN ADVANCE)

COOK TIME: ABOUT 1 HOUR 20 MINUTES (INCLUDES 20 MINUTES RESTING TIME)

My Grandma Madeline's lasagna really showed off all her impeccable cooking instincts: First of all, there was the combination of meats: beef, pork, and veal are the same combination that makes meatballs and meatloaf work because the beef provides flavor, the veal texture, and pork the essential fat that binds it all together. To that, she added spicy Italian sausage, which was really a stroke of genius because the sausage fat transmits all of its spices and flavors throughout the lasagna. And *then* to provide a wonderful texture, she used a combination of crushed and pureed tomatoes. This is one of the best lasagnas you will ever have, and the best part is that it really doesn't take any more work than making a more traditional recipe.

This recipe uses spicy sausage, but if it's too hot for you, you can use sweet sausage or a combination of the two.

¼ cup olive oil
½ pound ground (80–20) beef
½ pound ground pork
½ pound ground veal
1 pound hot Italian sausage, casings removed
4 large garlic cloves, minced
½ teaspoon dried oregano
2 tablespoons tomato paste
1 can (28 ounces) peeled whole tomatoes with their juices, crushed by hand
1 can (28 ounces) tomato puree
Kosher salt
Freshly ground black pepper
2 pounds fresh ricotta cheese
¼ cup finely chopped flat-leaf parsley, including stems
2 tablespoons finely chopped basil leaves
1½ cups (6 ounces) finely grated Parmigiano-Reggiano, divided
1½ pounds fresh whole mozzarella, grated on the large holes
    of a box grater (about 2 cups), divided
2 large eggs, beaten
1 pound fresh lasagna sheets, or dried lasagna noodles

1. Make the sauce: Heat a large, heavy-bottomed pot over medium-high heat. Add the oil and heat until it is shimmering, almost smoking. Add the beef, pork, veal, and sausage, and cook until nicely browned, 10 to 15 minutes, using a wooden spoon or fork to break up and blend the meats. Stir in the garlic and oregano and cook, stirring, until the garlic is fragrant, 1 to 2 minutes. Stir in the tomato paste and cook, stirring, until the meat is coated with the paste, about 2 minutes. Pour in the tomatoes with their juices and the tomato puree, season with salt and pepper, and bring to a boil. Lower the heat and simmer over medium heat, stirring occasionally, until the sauce is thickened, about 1½ hours. Remove from the heat and let cool. The sauce can be refrigerated in an airtight container for up to 2 days or frozen for up to 1 month. Let come to room temperature before making the lasagna.

2. Put the ricotta, parsley, basil, 1 cup of the Parmigiano-Reggiano, 1 pound of the shredded mozzarella, and the eggs in a large bowl, season with salt and pepper, and blend well.

3. Cook the lasagna noodles, if necessary. (Fresh pasta and no-cook lasagna do not require any precooking. Dry, curly-edged lasagna noodles need only be par-cooked for 3 minutes in boiling, salted water. Drain, rinse in cold water, and pat dry with paper towels.)

4. Position a rack in the center of the oven. Preheat the oven to 375°F.

5. Spread 1 cup of the sauce in the bottom of a 9-inch x 13-inch x 2-inch glass or ceramic baking dish. Line the bottom of the dish with overlapping noodles. Spread ⅓ of the cheese mixture over the noodles, sprinkle with a little Parmigiano-Reggiano and shredded mozzarella, then top with 1½ cups of the sauce and another layer of noodles. Repeat this layering sequence twice, finishing with a layer of pasta and 1½ cups of sauce. (There may be some sauce left over; save it for another use.)

6. Put the remaining ½ cup of mozzarella and ½ cup of Parmigiano-Reggiano in a small bowl, stir together, and scatter evenly over the lasagna.

7. Cover the lasagna with aluminum foil and bake for 40 minutes. Remove the foil and continue to bake until the top is golden and crisp around the edges and the filling is bubbling, about another 20 minutes. Remove the lasagna from the oven and let rest for 20 minutes before slicing and serving.

Note: Put a rimmed cookie or baking sheet into the oven under the lasagna pan to catch any spills and boil-over.

Baked Ziti with Creamy Mortadella Sauce

SERVES 6
PREP TIME: 10 MINUTES
COOK TIME: ABOUT 40 MINUTES

We used to call this pasta, yet another Grandma Madeline special, "baked macaroni," and it's been one of my favorites for as long as I can remember. If you've never had Fontinella cheese, it's similar to provolone and melts beautifully. This is a wonderful dish to serve when entertaining because you can prepare the ziti in advance, freeze it, and bake it for a dinner party. (If frozen, the best way to thaw it is gradually, by transferring it to the refrigerator for two days.)

2 tablespoons unsalted butter, plus extra for greasing baking dish
Kosher salt
1 pound ziti rigati
2 cups heavy cream
¼ cup (2 ounces) fresh ricotta cheese
1 cup grated Fontinella, Italian fontina, or mild provolone
1 can (14½ ounces) diced tomatoes in their juice
6 ounces mortadella, cut in one thick slice, cut into ¼-inch
  dice (about ¾ cup diced)
½ cup Homemade Breadcrumbs (page 295)

1. Position a rack in the center of the oven and preheat to 400°F. Butter a 9-inch x 13-inch x 2-inch Pyrex or ceramic baking dish.
2. Bring a large pot of salted water to a boil. Add the ziti and cook until just barely al dente, about 6 minutes.
3. Meanwhile, put the cream, ricotta, Fontinella, and 1 teaspoon salt in a large bowl and whisk together. Fold in the tomatoes and their juices and the mortadella.
4. When the pasta is done, drain, and add it to the bowl with the other ingredients. Stir, then pour into the prepared baking dish.
5. Bake, uncovered, for 15 minutes, then stir the contents of the baking dish, and spread them evenly. Scatter the breadcrumbs evenly over the top, and dot with butter. Continue baking until bubbling and hot, about 15 more minutes. Remove the tray from the oven and let cool for 10 minutes before serving.

Mortadella

Mortadella is an Italian bologna, a mix of pork and beef with pistachios added for texture. While other kids had Oscar Meyer in their lunchboxes, this is what I had in mine. If you can't find mortadella, you can make this with prosciutto, ham, or—come to think of it—American bologna.

Sunday Gravy

SERVES 8 TO 10 WITH LEFTOVERS
PREP TIME: ABOUT 20 MINUTES (NOT INCLUDING MEATBALL AND BRACIOLE PREPARATION)
COOK TIME: 2½ TO 3½ HOURS

Sunday gravy is the cornerstone of the week in the Valastro family, and has been since I was a kid. It's much more than a meal: It's a time when the world stops and we all get together to wrap up the weekend and fortify ourselves for the week ahead; it's a chance to connect with the most important people in our lives no matter what else is going on; and it's an opportunity to eat a meal so delicious and satisfying that we never tire of it.

I'll put it another way: In these times, it's nice to have something constant in your life and, crazy as it may sound, Sunday gravy is one of those things for us, and has been for my entire life. As a kid, the only question about it every week was at whose house we would eat it; on Saturday night, there'd be a call and the decision would be made. These days, most of the time, we have it at my house, in part because Lisa is such a pro at the sauce-making: She can get the whole thing prepped and simmering in just an hour, then spend the rest of the day with the family. And her sauce is always, *always* perfect. That's impressive!

A lot of families haven't been able to keep up the tradition of Sunday gravy, which I understand: It requires a fair amount of shopping, and time to prepare, which is hard to accomplish on a weekly basis. But we hold onto this tradition with both arms, and always will.

This recipe makes a ton of sauce and meat. Serve it with as much pasta as you like (we go through four pounds of dried pasta on a normal Sunday, two on a light one), and refrigerate the leftover sauce and meats to enjoy a day or two later with a pot of freshly cooked pasta, just as we do.

¼ cup olive oil
1 meaty lamb neck bone (about 1 pound), cut crosswise into
    2-inch pieces with a heavy knife (Ask your butcher to do this.)
Salt
1 pound sweet Italian sausage links (about 8 links)
Braciole (recipe follows)
1 large Spanish onion, diced
5 large garlic cloves, pressed
2 tablespoons coarsely chopped fresh basil leaves
1 tablespoon coarsely chopped fresh oregano leaves
Three 28-ounce cans whole plum tomatoes with their juice

Three 28-ounce cans crushed tomatoes with their juice
1 empty 28-ounce tomato can, filled with cold water
2 tablespoons sugar
Meatballs (recipe follows)
Chunk of Parmigiano-Reggiano, for serving

1. Heat a heavy stockpot or other wide, deep, heavy pot over medium heat and add the oil. Heat it until it is shimmering, almost smoking.
2. Lightly salt the lamb pieces, add them to the pot, and sear them, stirring, until golden brown all over, 5 to 7 minutes. Transfer to a plate and set aside.
3. Add the sausage links to the pan and sear them, turning as they cook, until browned all over, 5 to 7 minutes. Transfer the sausages to the plate with the lamb. Add the braciole to the pot and sear it all over, 5 to 7 minutes. Transfer the braciole to the plate with the other meats.
4. Add the onions to the pot and cook, stirring, until softened but not browned, about 5 minutes. Stir in the garlic, basil, and oregano, and cook, stirring, for 1 minute. Pour in the tomatoes and water, and add the sugar. Stir and cook until the sauce comes to a boil. Lower the heat to bring the sauce to a simmer. Return the meats to the pot, along with the meatballs.
5. Cook the sauce, adjusting the heat to keep it at a low simmer, and stirring occasionally to ensure that nothing scorches, until cooked to your desired thickness—it can range from thin and mildly flavored to thick and richly flavored. When done to your taste, 2 to 3 hours, use tongs to transfer the meats to a platter. Stir the sauce and reduce further, if necessary. Taste and, if necessary, add more salt.
6. Slice the sausage crosswise into individual portions. Remove the string or toothpicks from the braciole and slice it crosswise into portions. Arrange the meats and meatballs on a platter, including the neck bone pieces for those who wish to pick the meat from them.
7. Serve the sauce with cooked pasta and grated cheese, passing the platter of meatballs and sliced meats.

Braciole

MAKES 2 PIECES

PREP TIME: 10 MINUTES

COOK TIME: ABOUT 10 MINUTES (LESS IF COOKING IN THE SUNDAY GRAVY)

Braciole is a traditional Italian recipe that wraps breadcrumbs and cheese in beef. It can be seared and served on its own, or in a Sunday gravy.

2 thin slices beef round cut for braciole,
*   about 8 ounces each*
Kosher salt
3 large garlic cloves, minced
½ cup Homemade Breadcrumbs (page 295)
¼ cup finely grated pecorino Romano
1 tablespoon chopped flat-leaf parsley leaves
Freshly ground black pepper
2 tablespoons olive oil (if not cooking in
*   Sunday Gravy)*

1. Lay the beef between layers of plastic wrap and pound gently with a meat mallet until about ¼-inch thick. Remove the plastic and lightly salt the top. Top each piece of meat with garlic, breadcrumbs, pecorino, parsley, and a few grinds of black pepper. Fold in the short sides of the beef, then the bottom, followed by the top, to enclose and create a long bundle. Secure the meat with toothpicks or butcher's twine.
2. If cooking the braciole in Sunday Gravy, proceed with the instructions on page 179. Otherwise, heat the olive oil in a wide, heavy pan until it is shimmering, almost smoking. Add the braciole without crowding and cook, turning them with tongs or a wooden spoon, until nicely seared on the outside and cooked through, about 10 minutes.

Meatballs

MAKES ABOUT 15 MEATBALLS
PREP TIME: ABOUT 20 MINUTES
COOK TIME: ABOUT 20 MINUTES

If not making these for Sunday Gravy, you can finish them by baking them on a rimmed baking tray in a 350°F oven until cooked through, 15 to 20 minutes.

4 slices fresh white bread
8 ounces ground sirloin
8 ounces ground veal
8 ounces ground pork
5 large garlic cloves, coarsely chopped
2 large eggs, beaten
2 tablespoons minced flat-leaf parsley
½ cup (2 ounces) finely grated pecorino Romano
½ cup Homemade Breadcrumbs (page 295)
2 teaspoons kosher salt
1 teaspoon freshly ground black pepper
1 cup canola oil or other neutral oil

1. Tear the bread into small pieces and put it in a small bowl. Add ½ cup water and soak for 5 minutes.
2. Put the sirloin, veal, and pork in a large bowl. Squeeze the excess water from the bread and add the bread pieces to the bowl with the meats. Add the garlic, eggs, parsley, pecorino Romano, breadcrumbs, salt, and pepper to the bowl and knead the ingredients together. Form the mixture into about 15 meatballs, about 2 inches in diameter.
3. Heat a wide, deep, heavy sauté pan over medium-high heat. Add the meatballs in batches without crowding, and shallow fry them, turning them with a slotted spoon as they cook until golden-brown all over, 6 to 8 minutes total cooking time.
4. Proceed with cooking instructions for Sunday Gravy (page 179).

Bolognese

MAKES 5 TO 6 CUPS, ENOUGH FOR 8 TO 10 SERVINGS OF PASTA
PREP TIME: 15 MINUTES
COOK TIME: 2½ TO 3 HOURS

As much as I love the weekly ritual of Sunday Gravy, I also love a meaty Bolognese, which has more vegetables than Sunday Gravy, with the ground meats mixed in rather than served separately. The key to a great Bolognese is that, when you eat it over pasta, you have a perfect balance of pasta, meat, and sauce in every bite.

Toss this over whatever pasta you like—my favorites are tagliatelle and fettuccine—topped with grated Parmigiano-Reggiano or pecorino Romano.

¼ cup unsalted butter
1 medium Spanish onion, cut into
*   small dice*
2 medium carrots, peeled and cut into
*   small dice*
2 medium celery stalks, trimmed and cut
*   into small dice*
Kosher salt
1 pound ground beef chuck
1 pound ground pork
½ cup dry white wine, such as Sauvignon Blanc
1 can (28 ounces) crushed tomatoes
1 cup water
1 bay leaf
Freshly ground black pepper
Whole nutmeg, for grating

1. Heat a wide, deep, heavy pan over medium heat. Add the butter and cook until it melts. Add the onion, carrots, celery, and a pinch of salt. Lower the heat and cook, stirring, until the vegetables are very tender, about 10 minutes. Add the beef and pork and cook, stirring to break up the meats, over low heat until cooked through but not seared or browned, 10 to 15 minutes. Pour in the wine, raise the heat, bring to a boil, and let boil until reduced by half, 1 to 2 minutes. Add the tomatoes, water and bay leaf.

2. Let the sauce simmer, partially covered, stirring occasionally, until nicely thick-

ened and richly flavored, 2 to 2½ hours. Taste and add more salt and/or pepper, if necessary. Grate some nutmeg into the sauce and stir.

3. Serve the Bolognese with the pasta of your choice. Extra sauce may be refrigerated in an airtight container for up to 3 days or frozen for up to 1 month.

Saffron Risotto

SERVES 6 AS A SIDE DISH
PREP TIME: 10 MINUTES
COOK TIME: 20 TO 25 MINUTES

Saffron risotto was created for one reason and one reason only: to go under the classic braised veal shank, osso buco (page 269). The two go together like bread and butter, with the golden risotto soaking up the braising liquid. Because that's what it's meant for, the portion size of this recipe is smaller than for the other risotto recipes in this chapter.

6 cups homemade Chicken Stock (page 303) or
    low-sodium chicken stock
½ teaspoon saffron threads
5 tablespoons unsalted butter
⅓ cup minced Spanish onion
1½ cups Arborio rice
½ cup dry white wine, such as Sauvignon Blanc
½ cup (2 ounces) finely grated Parmigiano-Reggiano

1. Bring the stock to a simmer in a pot placed over medium heat.
2. Put the saffron in a small, heatproof bowl and ladle ½ cup of stock over it. Let macerate while you begin making the risotto.
3. Heat a wide, deep, heavy pot over medium heat. Add 3 tablespoons butter. When the butter melts, add the onion and cook, stirring, until softened but not browned, about 5 minutes. Add the rice and stir with a wooden spoon to coat the rice. Continue to cook until the rice is opaque in the center, about 1 minute. Pour in the wine—it should hiss on contact—and cook, stirring, until it is absorbed by the rice, about 3 minutes. Add the saffron mixture and stir until almost completely absorbed, about 1 minute.
4. Ladle in ½ cup of the simmering stock. Cook, stirring constantly, until all the stock has been absorbed. Continue to add stock in approximately half-cup increments, just enough to completely moisten the rice, and cook, stirring vigorously until the rice has absorbed the liquid. Continue to add stock in the same manner, cooking and stirring and adding the next half cup only after the prior one has

been completely absorbed. After about 16 minutes, began adding the stock more judiciously, a little at a time, until the rice is creamy but still pleasantly al dente. (The best way to be sure is to try a few grains.) Remove the pot from the heat and stir in the remaining 2 tablespoons of butter and the grated cheese.

5. Serve.

Mushroom Risotto

SERVES 4 TO 6

PREP TIME: 30 TO 40 MINUTES

COOK TIME: 45 MINUTES

Even though I was a finicky eater as a kid, I've always loved mushrooms. As far as I'm concerned, dried porcini mushrooms are the secret to great mushroom risotto, especially the juice from soaking them: Use it here in place of a final addition of chicken stock.

1 ounce dried porcini mushrooms
2 cups boiling water
6 cups homemade Chicken Stock (page 303) or
    low-sodium chicken broth
¼ cup olive oil
1 large clove garlic, minced
1 medium Spanish onion, minced
1 pound white button mushrooms, coarsely chopped
    (about 4 cups)
2 cups Arborio rice
⅓ cup dry white wine, such as Sauvignon Blanc
Kosher salt
½ teaspoon freshly ground black pepper
2 tablespoons unsalted butter
⅔ cup (about 3 ounces) finely grated Parmigiano-Reggiano,
    plus more for serving

1. Put the mushrooms in a bowl and pour the boiling water over them. Let soak for 30 minutes. Use a slotted spoon to transfer the mushrooms to a cutting board. You should have 2 cups of mushroom soaking liquid; if not, add enough water to make 2 cups. Coarsely chop the mushrooms and set aside.
2. Strain the mushroom soaking liquid through a fine-mesh strainer into a small pot. Add the chicken stock and bring to a simmer over medium heat.
3. Add 2 tablespoons of oil and heat until shimmering, almost smoking. Add the garlic and sauté until softened but not browned, about 3 minutes. Add the mushrooms and a pinch of salt, raise the heat slightly, and cook, stirring, until they give

up their liquid and begin to dry, about 5 minutes. Remove the pan from the heat and set aside.

4. Heat a large, wide, heavy pot over medium heat. Add the remaining 2 tablespoons of oil and heat until it is shimmering, almost smoking. Add the onion and cook, stirring, until softened but not browned, about 5 minutes. Add the rice and stir with a wooden spoon to coat the rice and continue cooking until the rice is opaque in the center, about 1 minute. Pour in 1 cup of the wine, which should hiss on contact, and stir until it is absorbed by the rice, about 2 minutes. Pour in the remaining cup of wine and continue to cook, stirring, until it is absorbed by the rice, about 2 more minutes.

5. Ladle in ½ cup of simmering stock. Cook, stirring constantly, until all stock has been absorbed. Continue to add stock in approximately half-cup increments, just enough to completely moisten the rice, and cook, stirring vigorously until the rice has absorbed the liquid. Continue to add stock in the same manner, cooking and stirring and adding the next half cup only after the prior one has been completely absorbed. After about 16 minutes, began adding the stock more judiciously, a little at a time, until the rice is creamy but still pleasantly al dente. (The best way to be sure is to try a few grains.) Remove the pot from the heat and stir in the butter. Taste and adjust the seasoning, if necessary, with salt and/or pepper.

6. Divide the risotto among 4 to 6 plates and serve, passing extra cheese for topping the rice.

Seafood Risotto

SERVES 4 TO 6
PREP TIME: ABOUT 15 MINUTES
COOK TIME: ABOUT 25 MINUTES

Seafood risotto was served at just about every special event I attended at the Park Casino, a catering hall in Union City, which became my dad's first restaurant account after he bought Carlo's Bake Shop. Not only was it an important business relationship for us, but we had a strong personal connection as well, because we used to throw all of our parties there. The owner, Joe, whom we all called Joe Park Casino, got to be a very good friend of my father. Joe was a great chef and, in time, a little of his personal flair wore off on Dad.

This recipe is based on the one Joe served at the Park Casino, loaded with lots of mussels, clams, and shrimp. Feel free to vary the mix of seafood based on your own taste or what looks good at the market.

2 cups homemade Chicken Stock (page 303)
*   or low-sodium chicken broth*
¼ teaspoon saffron threads
¼ cup olive oil
1 small Spanish onion, finely chopped
1 cup Arborio rice
4 large garlic cloves, finely chopped
Kosher salt
Freshly ground black pepper
½ cup dry white wine, such as Sauvignon Blanc
1 cup bottled clam juice
1 pound mussels, rinsed and debearded, about 24 mussels
*   (Prince Edward Island is a good, dependable variety)*
1½ pounds littleneck clams (about 12 clams); middleneck or
*   cherrystone may be substituted*
12 ounces large shrimp (about 12 shrimp), peeled
*   and deveined*
1 medium vine-ripened tomato, seeded (see page 30)
*   and coarsely chopped*
2 tablespoons unsalted butter, softened at room temperature

1. Put the broth in a pot and bring it to a simmer over medium heat. Stir in the saffron threads and keep the liquid at a simmer.

2. Heat a wide, deep, heavy pot over medium heat. Add 2 tablespoons of oil and heat it until it is shimmering, almost smoking. Add the onion and cook, stirring, until softened but not browned, about 5 minutes. Add the rice and 3 of the chopped garlic cloves, season with salt and pepper, stir with a wooden spoon to coat the rice, and continue cooking until the rice is opaque in the center, about 1 minute. Pour in the wine, which should hiss on contact, and stir until it is absorbed by the rice, about 3 minutes. Add the saffron broth and stir until almost completely absorbed, about 1 minute.

3. Ladle in ½ cup of the simmering stock. Cook, stirring constantly, until all the stock has been absorbed. Continue to add stock in approximately half-cup increments, just enough to completely moisten the rice, and cook, stirring vigorously until the rice has absorbed the liquid. Continue to add stock in the same manner, cooking and stirring and adding the next addition only after the prior one has been completely absorbed. After about 14 minutes, begin adding the stock more judiciously, a little at a time, until the rice is creamy but still al dente. (The best way to check is to simply taste a few grains.)

4. In a separate sauté pan with a cover, heat the remaining 2 tablespoons of the oil. Add the remaining garlic and sauté for 1 minute. Add the mussels, clams, and shrimp; stir gently; and cover. Cook until the mussels and clams have opened, about 6 minutes. Discard any clams and mussels that have not opened. Gently fold the mussels and clams into the risotto, along with the tomatoes. Fold in the butter.

5. To serve, divide the risotto among 4 to 6 wide, shallow bowls, making sure to spoon an equal amount of shellfish into each serving. Pass an extra bowl or two alongside for discarding shells.

Red Wine Risotto

SERVES 4 TO 6

PREP TIME: ABOUT 10 MINUTES

COOK TIME: ABOUT 25 MINUTES

Red wine risotto isn't as well known in the United States as it is in Italy, so it's a surprising dish to serve, and goes over especially well with those who, like me, love a good red wine. It wasn't until I grew up and developed an appreciation for wine that I came to love this risotto, but I turn to it often now as a way to enjoy one of my favorite flavors in a fun way that doesn't take any more work than the more familiar, white-wine-based risottos.

8 cups homemade Chicken Stock (page 303)
*   or low-sodium chicken broth*
3 tablespoons unsalted butter
6 ounces pancetta, in ¼-inch-thick slices
*   (about 4 slices), cut into ½-inch dice*
1 small onion, finely chopped
1 teaspoon dried rosemary
1 teaspoon dried oregano
2 cups Arborio rice
2 large garlic cloves, finely chopped
2 cups dry red wine, such as Chianti
2 tablespoons coarsely chopped flat-leaf parsley leaves
½ cup (2 ounces) finely grated Parmigiano-Reggiano
Kosher salt
Freshly ground black pepper

1. Put the broth in a pot and bring it to a simmer over medium heat.
2. Heat a wide, deep, heavy pot over medium heat. Add 1 tablespoon of the butter and the pancetta. When the butter melts and the pancetta has browned and some of its fat has rendered, about 4 minutes, add the onion, rosemary, and oregano, and cook, stirring, until the onion has softened but not browned, about 5 minutes. Add the rice and garlic, stir with a wooden spoon to coat the rice with the fat, and continue cooking until the rice is opaque in the center, about 1 minute. Pour in 1 cup of the wine, which should hiss on contact, and stir until it is absorbed by the rice, about 2 minutes. Pour in the remaining cup of wine and continue to cook, stirring, until it is absorbed by the rice, about 2 more minutes.

3. Ladle in ½ cup of the simmering stock. Cook, stirring constantly, until all the stock has been absorbed. Continue to add stock in approximately half-cup increments, just enough to completely moisten the rice, and cook, stirring vigorously until the rice has absorbed the liquid. Continue to add stock in the same manner, cooking and stirring and adding the next addition only after the prior one has been completely absorbed. After about 16 minutes, began adding the stock more judiciously, a little at a time, until the rice is creamy but still pleasantly al dente. (The best way to be sure is to try a few grains.) Remove the pot from the heat and stir in the parsley, the cheese, and the remaining 2 tablespoons of butter. Taste and adjust the seasoning, if necessary, with salt and/or pepper.
4. Divide the risotto among 4 to 6 plates and serve.

Main Courses

Okay, now it's time for the headliners, the stars of the show, the main events.

Some of the dishes in this chapter reflect the diet I was raised on, like the number of chicken and veal dishes I've included here: Those are meats that I came to love because we ate them so much as children, in part because they were affordable. They may not be the most rarefied of proteins, but they taste like home for me. Many of the recipes here turn them into something special, with ingredients lists and cooking times short enough for nightly family meals, which is how I first discovered most of them myself.

There's a lot of diversity here, from shellfish that can be eaten by hand to roasts that need to be carved. Here's some general advice for when you're deciding which recipes in this chapter to prepare.

- Buy the best fish and meat you can find and afford: These are not very complicated recipes, so each ingredient really makes an impact, and none more so than the protein itself. If you can, use freshly caught fish, and organic and/or free-range poultry and beef. You'll be amazed at how much better a cook you become just by doing some careful shopping.
- Cook within your comfort zone: Use the prep and cook times provided, as well as the times in the recipe instructions, to select main courses that will let you enjoy the act of cooking. Don't try to cram a recipe into your schedule; select ones that can be prepared at a leisurely pace. By the same token, if entertaining, use the prep and cook times to guide your planning so you can spend as much time as possible with your guests. In some cases, you can have a dish cooking in the oven before guests arrive, and let it rest during the pasta course. In others, you may decide *not* to serve a particular dish because it's too labor intensive for a given occasion.
- Sometimes, the number of guests you're planning to serve can narrow your choices as to what to serve: Some of the dishes here are meant for two to four people; others, eight and up.
- Don't try a new dish when you have company coming; instead, if you want to expand your horizons (which I highly recommend), try a new dish out on your immediate family first, to learn what you need to know about it, *then*

make it for a special occasion. Also, serve dishes that are appropriate for different occasions: Although nothing is set in stone, the steak dishes are perfect for a guys' gathering, the roasts for a fancy dinner or holiday party, and the sautéed preparations for more casual or family dinners.

- If planning a menu, try to not repeat primary ingredients from different courses; select your main course, then let other choices flow from there, choosing appetizers, salads, pastas, and sides to complement the centerpiece of the dinner.

- Treat your cooking with the respect it deserves: Take a moment between cooking and serving to be sure you're presenting your food in the most attractive possible way. If you're plating individual dishes in the kitchen, be sure you arrange the protein, sauce, and any sides neatly. If serving family style, select platters and/or bowls that complement the colors of your food. In either case, take a moment to dab away any stray juices or sauce from the rim of the plates or platters with a damp paper towel.

Eggplant Parmesan

SERVES 6

PREP TIME: ABOUT 1 HOUR 15 MINUTES

COOK TIME: ABOUT 45 MINUTES

My wife, Lisa's, eggplant parmesan is one of the things I would eat for my last supper. The first time I ever had a version of this dish was when I was very young and my Grandma Madeline made it for me. Truth be told, this recipe is a combination of our two families' recipes, because when Lisa and I first met, she made eggplant parmesan by flouring the eggplant but not breading it. After one taste of fried eggplant coated in crunchy breadcrumbs, she was sold.

Some people leave the skin on their eggplant, but I've always followed Madeline's example and cut it off to remove its bitterness.

It's always important to fry in hot oil, but it's especially important with eggplant; because it's so soft and porous, it will soak up a ton of oil and become soggy if the oil isn't at the proper temperature.

2 medium-to-large eggplants, about 1½ pounds each, peeled
Kosher salt
2 cups Homemade Breadcrumbs (page 295)
6 large eggs
¾ cup plus 2 tablespoons finely grated Parmigiano-Reggiano
1 cup all-purpose flour
2 to 3 cups olive oil, for frying, plus more for greasing
  baking dish
3 cups Marinara Sauce (page 141)
12 ounces fresh mozzarella cheese, cut into about 12- to
  14¼-inch-thick slices

1. Cut the eggplant crosswise into ¼-inch-thick rounds; you will have about 20 rounds. Put the slices in a colander, salt liberally, toss, and let rest in the sink for 1 hour to draw out the bitterness and excess moisture. Rinse briefly under cold running water, turning to expose all of the eggplant to the water, then drain, remove the slices from the colander, and pat dry with paper towels.
2. Position a rack in the center of the oven. Preheat to 375°F.
3. Arrange a wire rack over a baking sheet. Line a large plate or platter with paper towels.

4. Put the breadcrumbs in a wide shallow bowl. Put the eggs in another bowl with ½ cup of Parmigiano-Reggiano and whisk. Put the flour in a third bowl.

5. Working with 1 eggplant slice at a time, dredge the slices in the flour, then the eggs, then breadcrumbs. As they are prepared, gather them in a single layer on the wire rack.

6. Heat a wide, deep, heavy skillet over medium-high heat. Pour in oil to a depth of ¼ inch, and heat until a few breadcrumbs added to the oil sizzle and brown.

7. Carefully add the eggplant to the oil in batches, without crowding, and fry until golden brown on both sides, 2 to 3 minutes per side, turning the slices with tongs when the first side is browned. As they are done, use the tongs to transfer them to the paper-towel–lined plate and season immediately with salt. Repeat until all the eggplant slices are fried, drained, and seasoned.

8. When the slices are cool enough to handle, lightly oil a shallow glass or ceramic 9-inch x 13-inch x 2-inch baking dish. Ladle a few tablespoons of the marinara sauce onto the dish and use the back of the ladle to spread it and coat the bottom of the dish.

9. Arrange the eggplant slices in overlapping fashion in baking dish. Scatter 2 tablespoons of the Parmigiano-Reggiano over them and ladle more sauce over the cheese. Cover with a layer of mozzarella. Repeat with another layer of eggplant, 2 more tablespoons of Parmigiano-Reggiano, sauce, and mozzarella, and finish with the final 2 tablespoons of Parmigiano-Reggiano.

10. Although best baked right away, the eggplant parmesan may be covered with plastic wrap and refrigerated overnight. Remove the plastic and let come to room temperature before baking.

11. Bake until the cheese is hot and bubbling and the dish is hot throughout, 20 to 30 minutes. Let rest 10 minutes before slicing and serving.

Zucchini and Yellow Squash Casserole

SERVES 4

PREP TIME: 10 MINUTES

COOK TIME: ABOUT 50 MINUTES (INCLUDING RESTING TIME)

My mother used to make this casserole as a side dish for roasted meats, but I include it as a main course to provide a vegetarian entrée. Like a lot of vegetarian dishes, what makes this one work is the richness and texture that fill in for the missing meat: creamy cheese, garlicky pesto, and crunchy breadcrumbs. (If you are making a fresh batch of breadcrumbs for this dish, leave some large for a rustic effect).

This is hearty enough to eat on its own and is also perfect the way we used to eat it, as a side to grilled and roasted meats. It also makes terrific leftovers and can even be enjoyed cold at breakfast or a picnic.

2 medium zucchini, about 8 ounces each
2 medium yellow squash, about 8 ounces each
1 teaspoon kosher salt
¼ cup sun-dried tomato pesto
1 tablespoon chopped fresh oregano
1 tablespoon chopped flat-leaf parsley leaves
½ cup extra virgin olive oil
1 to 2 large shallots, thinly sliced lengthwise
1 cup Homemade Breadcrumbs (page 295)
6 ounces Fontal or Bel Paese cheese, grated on
    the large holes of a box grater (1½ cups)

1. Position a rack in the center of the oven. Preheat to 400°F.
2. Thinly slice the zucchini and yellow squash crosswise into less-than-¼-inch-thick circles. Put the slices in a colander, salt liberally, toss, and let rest in the sink for 15 minutes to draw out the bitterness and excess moisture. Rinse briefly under cold running water, turning to expose all of the squash slices to the water, then drain, remove the slices from the colander, and pat dry with paper towels.
3. Put the pesto, oregano, parsley, oil, and shallots in a bowl and stir with a wooden spoon. Add the squash and toss gently to coat. Transfer the slices to a 12-inch x 7½-inch x 2-inch baking dish, or baking dish with a similar capacity. (Do not wipe out or rinse the bowl.) Spread the slices evenly. Cover the dish with foil and bake for 20 minutes.

4. In the same bowl you used to toss the squash, and without wiping out the oil, toss the breadcrumbs and cheese, until they are well integrated and have absorbed the oil.
5. Remove the foil from the squash and, working quickly, top the squash evenly with the crumb-cheese mixture. Bake an additional 20 minutes, uncovered, until the topping is nicely browned but not scorched, and the side of a sharp thin-bladed knife inserted into the center of the casserole comes out warm to the touch.
6. Remove the baking dish from the oven and let rest 10 minutes before slicing and serving.

Stuffed Jumbo Shrimp

SERVES 4
PREP TIME: 10 MINUTES
COOK TIME: 15 MINUTES

This was one of the fancy dinners my mother used to turn to if we were having company, especially on Fridays during Lent, which, as a Catholic family, was our fish night. The secret to this recipe's success is the vermouth, which infuses the quick sauce with a cool blast of flavor. Mama used to serve the shrimp from a big platter to really show it off, and by the time my sisters and I were done with it, there was never a single one left.

2 pounds large or jumbo shrimp
Kosher salt
Freshly ground black pepper
¼ cup olive oil, plus more for oiling the pie pan
     or baking dish
2 tablespoons unsalted butter
1 large shallot, minced
2 large garlic cloves, minced
Splash dry white vermouth
1½ cups finely chopped Homemade Breadcrumbs
     (page 295)
Pinch cayenne pepper
1½ tablespoons chopped dried oregano
Finely grated zest of 1 lemon, plus 1 large lemon,
     cut into 4 wedges

1. Position a rack in the center of the oven and preheat to 400°F.
2. Peel the shrimp, leaving the last shell segment and tail intact. Butterfly the shrimp along the back and devein them. Open the shrimp so that they lie flat, but take care not to let them come apart. Place them in a large bowl as you work. When all the shrimp are prepared, season them lightly with salt and pepper, drizzle with 2 tablespoons olive oil, and toss to coat the shrimp. Marinate for 15 to 20 minutes.
3. Meanwhile, heat a wide, deep, heavy sauté pan over medium-high heat. Add the butter and 1 tablespoon oil and heat until the butter melts and is foamy. Add the shallot and garlic and cook, stirring, 1 minute. Pour in the vermouth, bring to a boil (this will only take a few seconds), and continue to boil for a few seconds, then

add the breadcrumbs. Stir the ingredients and cook, stirring, until the crumbs begin to smell toasty, 4 to 5 minutes. Quickly remove the pan from the heat and transfer its contents to a heatproof bowl, using a wooden spoon to scrape out as much as possible. Stir in the cayenne, oregano, and lemon zest and let rest for 10 minutes.

4. Oil a 9-inch-diameter, 2-inch-deep pie plate or similar round baking dish. Stuff each shrimp with a tablespoonful or so of the crumbs (the mixture will be loose) and close the sides of the shrimp around the filling. As they are prepared, arrange the shrimp in the pan with the tails toward the center for a pinwheel effect. Scatter any extra breadcrumbs over the top and drizzle with 1 tablespoon of olive oil.

5. Bake until the shrimp are firm, pink, and cooked through, 12 to 15 minutes. Serve family style, with lemon wedges.

Garlic Blue Crabs Park Casino

SERVES 4 TO 6

PREP TIME: 25 MINUTES

COOK TIME: 5 TO 10 MINUTES, DEPENDING ON SIZE OF CRABS

Here's another recipe based on one from my father's pal Joe, owner of the Park Casino. The succulent crabs he served at his catering hall were so good that all the men in the family would be at fancy special events, dressed in our best suits, and sucking every last drop of sauce from the crab shells with little regard for the expensive threads we were wearing. We couldn't resist or let any of this delicious dish go to waste.

You can replace the blue crabs with two pounds of large, shell-on shrimp, peeled and deveined.

6 large garlic cloves, pressed
Juice of 1½ large lemons
½ teaspoon kosher salt
½ cup olive oil
12 blue crabs, 3 to 4 ounces each, freshly killed
*   and cleaned*
¼ cup dry white wine, such as Sauvignon Blanc
2 tablespoons low-sodium soy sauce
½ cup chopped flat-leaf parsley leaves

1. Put the garlic, lemon juice, salt, and oil in a large, wide bowl and stir. Add the crabs, toss gently to coat, and let marinate at room temperature for 20 minutes, tossing occasionally.
2. Heat a wide, deep, heavy sauté pan over high heat until very hot.
3. Working in 2 batches to keep the pan hot throughout the cooking process, add the crabs and some marinade to the pan without crowding, and cook, turning with tongs, until the crabs are cooked through and bright red all over and the marinade is almost completely reduced. Pour in half the wine and half the soy sauce, bring to a boil (this will happen quickly), and cook until reduced to a glaze. Stir in half the parsley, tossing gently to coat the crabs with the sauce and parsley, and transfer the crabs to a platter. Cover loosely with foil while you cook the second batch of crabs with the remaining marinade, wine, soy sauce, and parsley.
4. Serve the crabs family style with plenty of napkins.

Seafood Fra Diavolo

SERVES 4 TO 6
PREP TIME: 15 MINUTES
COOK TIME: 20 MINUTES

The first time I had seafood fra diavolo was at Puccini's restaurant in Jersey City where the chef, Pasquale, is a friend of mine. One night at dinner, I asked him what I should have and he sold me on his fra diavolo, promising me that it wouldn't be too spicy. I ordered it, and loved it. This recipe is based on that dish. As with most mixed seafood dishes, you can change the selection of shellfish in this recipe; an especially luxurious version could be made with cooked lobster meat and nothing else.

The pasta is optional in this dish, but even if you include pasta, it's intense and satisfying.

> ¼ cup olive oil
> 2 shallots, thinly sliced lengthwise
> Kosher salt
> 3 large garlic cloves, sliced as thinly as possible
> 2 small fresh green chilies, such as Serrano or jalapeño,
>   seeded and thinly sliced crosswise (be sure to wear
>   latex gloves to protect your fingers)
> ½ teaspoon crushed red-pepper flakes, plus more to taste
> 12 littleneck, middleneck, or cherrystone clams, scrubbed clean
> 12 mussels (about 5 ounces), scrubbed and debearded
>   (Prince Edward Island is a good, dependable variety.)
> ¾ cup dry white vermouth
> 1 can (28 ounces) crushed tomatoes with their juices
> 8 large shrimp (about 8 ounces), peeled and deveined,
>   tail left on
> 8 ounces calamari, body sliced into thin rings, tentacle
>   portions left whole
> 2 tablespoons torn fresh basil leaves
> 1 tablespoon chopped, fresh flat-leaf parsley leaves
> 1 pound dried linguine, optional

1. Heat a wide, deep, heavy sauté pan that has a tight-fitting lid over medium heat. Add the oil and heat until it is shimmering, almost smoking. Add the shallots and a pinch

of salt and cook, stirring with a wooden spoon, until the shallots begin to soften, about 3 minutes. Add the garlic, chilies, and pepper flakes and cook, stirring, until fragrant but not browned, 1 to 2 minutes. Add the clams and mussels, stir gently, cover, and cook, shaking the pan gently occasionally to prevent scorching and ensure even cooking, until the clams and mussels have opened and released their juices, 3 to 5 minutes. Use a slotted spoon to transfer the clams and mussels to a bowl, discarding any that have not opened.

2. Raise the heat to medium high and pour in the vermouth. Bring to a boil and reduce for 1 to 2 minutes. Stir in the tomatoes and a pinch of salt. Let simmer until slightly reduced, about 5 minutes. Add the shrimp to the sauce, using the spoon to gently make sure they are submerged, and cook for 2 to 3 minutes. When the shrimp begin to firm and turn pink, add the calamari and cook 1 minute longer. Return the clams and mussels to the pan and toss or stir gently to coat in the sauce. Stir in the basil and parsley.

3. Meanwhile, if serving the shellfish with pasta, bring a pot of salted water to a boil over high heat. Add the linguine and cook until al dente, about 8 minutes. Drain.

4. Transfer the seafood fra diavolo to a serving bowl and serve family style. If serving with pasta, put the pasta in the bowl, then pour the seafood and sauce over it.

Whole Fish Roasted in Sea Salt with Warm Lemon Butter Sauce

SERVES 2 TO 4
PREP TIME: 10 MINUTES
COOK TIME: 25 MINUTES

One of my favorite dishes to order in a restaurant is a whole roasted branzino, or sea bass, cooked in a salt crust: I just love the ceremony that often accompanies the presentation of the fish, as the waiter shows it to you before taking it off to be roasted, then returning to the table with the salt-crusted finished product, cracking the crust open, and serving it at the table. But, of course, the most important part is how the fish tastes: The crust, made of salt and egg whites, seals all the moisture into the sea bass, steaming it as it roasts. The result is a decadently moist, silky fish with a clean, pure flavor. While it would be delicious with just a squirt of lemon, I like to finish it with a lemon-butter sauce made with the same herbs that are stuffed into the fish before roasting.

6 or 7 large egg whites
1 box (3 pounds) sea or kosher salt
2 striped sea bass or other white-fleshed fish, 1½ pounds each,
    gutted and scaled
2 bay leaves
4 sprigs fresh oregano, plus 2 tablespoons chopped oregano
4 sprigs flat-leaf parsley, plus 1 tablespoon chopped parsley
4 sprigs fresh thyme
2 large garlic cloves, thinly sliced
4 thin slices lemon
4 tablespoons extra-virgin olive oil
2 tablespoons chopped garlic, from about 3 large cloves
Zest and juice of one large lemon
Kosher salt
Freshly ground black pepper
2 tablespoons unsalted butter

1. Position a rack in the center of the oven. Preheat to 475°F.
2. Line a baking sheet large enough to hold the 2 fish in a single layer with foil.
3. Put 6 of the egg whites and the salt in a large bowl and stir together well until a

grainy consistency, almost like moist sand, is attained. If the mixture seems too dry, stir in the final egg white.

4. Press a ¼-inch-thick layer of the salt mixture onto the baking sheet.

5. Stuff the cavity of each fish with the bay leaves, oregano sprigs, parsley sprigs, thyme, garlic, and lemon slices.

6. Lay the fish on top of salt and pack the remaining salt over the fish to enclose it completely. Set the fish in the oven and lower the temperature to 400°F. Roast until their internal temperature reaches 135°F, 15 to 20 minutes.

7. While the fish is roasting, make the butter sauce: Heat the olive oil in a small, heavy sauté pan set over medium heat. Add the chopped garlic and sauté until softened, 2 to 3 minutes. Stir in the lemon zest, lemon juice, chopped oregano, and chopped parsley. Season to taste with salt and pepper. Remove the pan from the heat and swirl in the butter.

8. When the fish is done, remove from the oven. With the fish still in the baking pan, crack open the sea-salt case, push it to the side, then fillet. Place the fillets onto a plate. Spoon some sauce over the fish on each plate and serve.

Bluefish with Tomato, Garlic, and Onions

SERVES 4
PREP TIME: 10 MINUTES
COOK TIME: 15 MINUTES

This main course fish dish simmers bluefish in a simple stew of tomatoes and onions. Bluefish is oily, so the sauce gets as much flavor from the fish as the fish gets from the sauce. You can leave out the rice, but I really like having another component on the plate to soak up all the delicious sauce.

¼ cup plus 2 tablespoons olive oil
4 bluefish filets, 6 ounces each (trout or mackerel may
*   be substituted)*
1 medium Spanish onion, halved and thinly sliced
2 large garlic cloves, chopped
¼ teaspoon kosher salt
3 fresh tomatoes, coarsely chopped, or 1 can (28 ounces)
*   crushed tomatoes with their juice*
⅛ teaspoon freshly ground black pepper
2 cups cooked rice, for serving

1. Heat a large, heavy sauté pan over medium heat. Add ¼ cup oil and heat it until it is shimmering, almost smoking. Add the fish fillets to the pan and brown lightly on both sides, 2 to 3 minutes per side. Transfer the fillets to a plate.
2. Add the remaining 2 tablespoons of oil to the skillet. Add the onion and garlic, season with a pinch of salt, and cook, stirring, until the onion is translucent, 5 to 7 minutes. Stir in the tomatoes and simmer for about 5 minutes, stirring often.
3. Return the fish to the pan and lower the heat so the tomato mixture is just simmering. Simmer until the fish is cooked through, 3 to 5 minutes. Taste the sauce and add more salt and pepper, if necessary.
4. Spoon some rice onto each of 4 dinner plates. Set a fish fillet alongside and spoon some sauce over the fish and rice.

Perfect Italian Chicken Cutlet

SERVES 4
PREP TIME: ABOUT 15 MINUTES
COOK TIME: ABOUT 15 MINUTES

When we lived in Little Ferry, my mother used to dispatch me to pick up her weekly order from the butcher on Main Street. "I'm here to pick up the meat for Valastro," I'd say after parking my bike outside, and the man behind the counter would hand me a heavy brown paper bag full of chicken cutlets. At home, Mom would bread them and fry them, and I could never resist stealing one as it drained on paper towels. Sometimes, simplicity can be the ultimate sign of perfection, and that's definitely the case with these cutlets, which are so delicious it only takes a squeeze of lemon to finish them.

You can also use this recipe for veal cutlets.

4 boneless, skinless chicken breasts, about 8 ounces each,
*   trimmed of any fat and cartilage*
1½ cups all-purpose flour
3 large eggs, beaten with a fork
¼ cup (1 ounce) finely grated Parmigiano-Reggiano
2¼ cups Homemade Breadcrumbs (page 295)
Kosher salt
Freshly ground black pepper
About ¾ cup olive oil, for frying
1 large lemon, cut into wedges

1. Put a chicken breast half on the cutting board. Put your free hand on top of the breast to steady it. Hold a sharp, chef's knife parallel to the board, and slice through the thickest portion of the breast, separating the breast into two even halves. Repeat with the remaining breasts to create 8 pieces.
2. Working with 1 piece at a time, position the chicken between pieces of plastic wrap and use a meat tenderizer or the bottom of a heavy pan to pound each piece to a uniform thickness of about ¼ inch.
3. Put the flour in a wide, shallow bowl, the eggs whisked with the Parmigiano-Reggiano in another shallow bowl, and the breadcrumbs in a third.
4. Position a wire rack over a baking sheet. Line a large plate or platter with paper towels.
5. Working with 1 piece of chicken at a time, salt and pepper the chicken pieces on

both sides. Coat the pieces on both sides in the flour, tapping off any extra, then the egg, allowing any excess to drip back into the bowl, then the breadcrumbs, also on both sides, pressing gently to help the breadcrumbs adhere to the cutlets. As they are prepared, set the chicken pieces on the rack.

6. Heat a wide, deep, heavy sauté pan over medium heat. Add ½ cup of the oil and heat until it is shimmering, almost smoking. Working in batches, without crowding, add the chicken to the pan and cook until golden brown on both sides, 3 to 4 minutes per side, turning the pieces with tongs or a spatula when the first side is done. When both sides are done, transfer the pieces to the paper-towel–lined plate to drain. Continue with the remaining chicken pieces, adding and heating the remaining ¼ cup of oil as necessary between batches to keep the pan from becoming too dry.

7. Arrange the chicken pieces on a large plate or platter and serve family style with lemon wedges.

Breaded Chicken with Vinegar Peppers

SERVES 4
PREP TIME: 15 MINUTES
COOK TIME: 40 MINUTES

The only place I ever ate this Italian-American classic was at my Auntie Anna's house. The recipe uses the brine of jarred, marinated peppers to flavor dark-meat chicken, the vinegar offsetting the richness of the bird. It's a brilliant use of a supermarket staple, and very inexpensive and easy to make. The best part might be the last few bites, when you end up with a little bread salad on the plate.

3 large eggs, beaten
2 tablespoons (½ ounce) finely grated
  Parmigiano-Reggiano
2 cups Homemade Breadcrumbs (page 295)
1½ pounds chicken drumsticks (4 to 6 pieces),
  trimmed of excess fat
1½ pounds chicken thighs (4 to 6 pieces),
  trimmed of excess fat
1 to 2 cups olive oil
1 jar (16 ounces) sweet red peppers packed in vinegar,
  such as B&G, strained, peppers and marinade
  reserved separately

1. Position a rack in the center of the oven. Preheat to 400°F. Position a wire rack over a baking dish.
2. Put the eggs and cheese in a wide, shallow bowl and whisk together. Put the breadcrumbs in another wide, shallow bowl.
3. Working with 1 piece at a time, dip the chicken pieces in the egg mixture, rolling it to coat all over. Lift from the mixture, letting any excess drip back into the bowl, then turn in the breadcrumbs to coat, pressing down gently to help the crumbs adhere to the chicken. As the pieces are prepared, place them in a single layer on the wire rack.
4. Pour the oil into a wide, deep, heavy skillet to a depth of ¼ inch and heat over medium heat until hot but not smoking.
5. Working in batches so as to not crowd the pan, place the chicken pieces in the oil and fry until golden brown all over, turning the chicken pieces with tongs or a slot-

ted spoon as the sides brown, about 2 minutes per side. (You do not have to cook them through, as they will finish in the oven.) As the pieces are done, transfer them to a 9-inch x 13-inch x 2-inch Pyrex or ceramic baking dish, or other dish that can accommodate the pieces in one layer without touching. Pour pepper marinade evenly over the chicken.

6. Bake for 10 minutes, then remove the pan from the oven, lower the temperature to 350°F, and carefully add the peppers to the pan, tucking them under and around the chicken. Return the dish to the oven and bake until the chicken is cooked through (when pierced with a sharp, thin-bladed knife, the juices should run clear and the meat should have no trace of pink), about 30 minutes.

7. Use the slotted spoon to transfer the chicken pieces to a platter and arrange the peppers over and around the chicken. Pour the pan juices over the chicken and serve.

Chicken Piccata

SERVES 4

PREP TIME: ABOUT 10 MINUTES

COOK TIME: ABOUT 12 MINUTES

This dish never fails to remind me of my father, because of the capers, which always bring up Sicily for me. This is one of those great, classic recipes that takes very little work but perfectly balances salty, acidic, and savory elements. It's also very quick and easy to make, a go-to preparation that everyone should have in their repertoire.

Kosher salt
1½ pounds thinly sliced chicken breast cutlets
½ cup all-purpose flour
2 to 3 tablespoons olive oil
3 to 4 tablespoons unsalted butter
½ cup dry white wine, such as Sauvignon Blanc
1 cup homemade Chicken Stock (page 303) or
*   low-sodium chicken broth*
2 small lemons, 1 juiced, 1 sliced into thin circles,
*   seeds removed and discarded*
2 tablespoons capers
¼ cup chopped flat-leaf parsley leaves
2 tablespoons finely grated Parmigiano-Reggiano

1. Lightly salt the chicken cutlets on both sides. Place the flour in a wide, shallow bowl, and dredge the chicken in the flour, gently shaking off any excess, then place the pieces on a plate.
2. Heat a large, heavy sauté pan over medium-high heat. Add the 2 tablespoons of oil and 1 tablespoon butter. When the butter melts and foams, add the cutlets in a single layer, working in batches if necessary to avoid crowding, and cook until browned on both sides, 2 to 3 minutes per side. (If working in batches, add an additional tablespoon of oil and butter between batches, and heat it before adding the chicken.) Transfer to a plate and cover loosely with foil to keep warm.
3. Pour the wine into the pan, turn the heat to high, and bring to a boil, stirring with a wooden spoon to loosen any flavorful bits on the bottom of the pan, continuing to cook until reduced by half, about 2 minutes. Pour in the stock and lemon juice, and stir in the lemon slices and capers. Boil and reduce, stirring, until slightly

reduced and nicely thickened (it should coat the back of a wooden spoon), 3 to 4 minutes. Season with salt, bearing in mind that the capers are salty, then swirl in the remaining 2 tablespoons butter and the parsley.

4. Divide the chicken among 4 plates and spoon some sauce over each piece. Top with the cheese and serve at once.

Roasted Rosemary Chicken

SERVES 4

PREP TIME: 15 MINUTES (NOT INCLUDING OVERNIGHT BRINING)

COOK TIME: ABOUT 1 HOUR 10 MINUTES

As good as this chicken is right out of the oven, I love having it around for leftovers; it makes great sandwiches and salads, and you can even shred it and add it to soups, like Minestrone (page 119). My mother made this dish all the time when my sisters and I were growing up; I intensify the flavors by marinating the chicken in garlic and rosemary overnight in the refrigerator.

1 small lemon, quartered

1 small Spanish onion, quartered

1 small head garlic, quartered, loose, papery skin discarded,
*   2 cloves broken off and set aside*

2 sprigs rosemary, chopped into 2-inch pieces

Kosher salt

Freshly ground black pepper

1 whole chicken, 3 to 3½ pounds

1 tablespoon unsalted butter, softened at room temperature

1 tablespoon coarsely chopped flat-leaf parsley leaves

1. The night before, put the lemon, onion, head of garlic, and all but 2 pieces of rosemary in a bowl and season with a generous pinch of salt and a few grinds of pepper. Stir until well blended, then stuff in the chicken's cavity. Put the 2 reserved garlic cloves in the neck cavity. Slip one piece each of rosemary under the skin on each breast. Sprinkle the entire outside of the chicken with a light coating of salt. Set the chicken on a baking dish or large plate, cover loosely with plastic wrap, and refrigerate overnight.

2. Remove the plastic from the chicken, pat off any lingering moisture with a paper towel, and let come to room temperature, about 20 minutes. Position a rack in the center of the oven and preheat the oven to 425°F.

3. Transfer the chicken to a cast iron skillet or roasting pan just large enough to hold the chicken snugly without crushing it, breast side up. Rub butter over the breast and season generously with salt.

4. Roast the chicken until the skin is burnished and an instant-read thermometer inserted in the thigh, without touching the bone, reads 165°F, 45 minutes to 1 hour.

5. Remove the pan from the oven and transfer the chicken to a wire rack or inverted plate. Let rest for 10 minutes. Tip the chicken over the pan to add any additional juices to the pan.
6. Carve the chicken, then place the pieces on a serving platter. Stir the parsley into the pan juices and pour over the chicken. Serve at once.

Mama's Chicken and Potatoes

SERVES 4 TO 6

PREP TIME: APPROXIMATELY 15 MINUTES

COOK TIME: 1 HOUR

Mama's chicken and potatoes was one of the recipes that were part of her weekly dinner lineup when my sisters and I were growing up. By roasting the potatoes and chicken in the same pan, the flavors really come together as the potatoes soak up the delicious chicken juices. This is another of those dishes that evolved over time: After my dad died, it's one of the things that my mom's housekeeper, Olga, learned to make, and her version is actually the best one in the family.

You can cut the potatoes to whatever size you like, just be sure all the pieces are about the same size, so that they cook at the same rate.

1½ pounds small-to-medium Idaho potatoes, peeled,
   halved lengthwise, and cut crosswise into large chunks
¼ cup olive oil
Kosher salt
Freshly ground black pepper
1 medium Spanish onion, thinly sliced lengthwise
4 large garlic cloves, thinly sliced
1 cup homemade Chicken Stock (page 303), low-sodium
   store-bought chicken stock, or water
6 chicken thigh/leg pieces, about 8 ounces each
2 teaspoons store-bought Italian seasoning,
   such as McCormick
1 can (28 ounces) whole, peeled tomatoes, crushed by
   hand, with their juice
1 cup defrosted frozen peas, or drained canned peas

1. Position a rack in the center of the oven. Preheat to 400°F.
2. Spread the potato pieces out over the surface of a roasting pan. Drizzle with 3 tablespoons olive oil and season with salt and pepper. Roast until they start to soften; a paring knife will slip easily into a potato piece or two, but encounter some resistance toward the center, 15 to 20 minutes.
3. Remove the pan from the oven and scatter the onions and garlic over the potatoes. Season with salt and pepper and drizzle the stock over the vegetables. Lay the

chicken pieces over the vegetables, gently pushing them down so they are nestled alongside the potatoes. It's all right if the onions are on top of the chicken pieces, but the potatoes should be alongside them, touching the bottom of the pan.

4. Drizzle some of the remaining 1 tablespoon of the olive oil over each piece of chicken, then season the chicken with salt and Italian seasoning. Bake for 30 minutes, then baste with the pan juices, spooning them from the bottom of the pan and over the chicken pieces. Turn the vegetables over and top with a scattering of the tomatoes and peas. Bake until the chicken is cooked through (when pierced with a sharp, thin-bladed knife, the juices should run clear and the meat should have no trace of pink), about 30 more minutes.

5. Transfer the chicken to a platter, stir the vegetables to coat well in juices, spoon over and around the chicken pieces, and serve.

Mozzarella-and-Sausage-Stuffed Chicken

SERVES 4 TO 6
PREP TIME: 20 MINUTES
COOK TIME: 15 TO 20 MINUTES

There's something really fun and decadent about these stuffed chicken breasts filled with spicy Italian sausage and gooey, melted mozzarella cheese. You can skip the tomato vinaigrette but I think it really adds another layer of flavor and helps cut the rich sausage-and-cheese filling.

2 tablespoons plus 1½ teaspoons olive oil, plus more
    for greasing baking dish
4 ounces hot Italian sausage, purchased loose or
    squeezed out of casings
2 tablespoons minced Spanish onion
2 tablespoons Homemade Breadcrumbs (page 295)
2 ounces fresh mozzarella, cut into small dice, or torn
    by hand into small pieces (about ¼ cup pieces)
6 boneless, skinless chicken breast halves, 8 to
    10 ounces each
Kosher salt
Freshly ground black pepper
½ cup dry white wine, such as Sauvignon Blanc
Juicy Tomato Vinaigrette (recipe follows)

1. Position a rack in the center of the oven. Preheat to 400°F.
2. Heat a small, heavy sauté pan over medium heat. Add 1½ teaspoons oil and warm it for about 1 minute. Add the sausage and cook, using the back of a wooden spoon or a fork to crumble it, and continue cooking until browned and cooked through, 5 to 7 minutes. Add the onion and cook, stirring, until softened, 1 to 2 minutes. Turn the contents of the pan, including all of the fat, into a heatproof bowl. Stir in the breadcrumbs and let cool, then stir in the mozzarella.
3. Cut slits into each chicken breast to create a pocket, taking care not to cut all the way through the chicken. Put ⅙ of the sausage-mozzarella mixture into each breast and seal each breast with 2 toothpicks.
4. Grease a 12 x 7½ x 2-inch baking dish or similar dish with olive oil.
5. Season the chicken with salt and pepper and arrange the breasts in the pan with-

out crowding. Rub 1 tablespoon of oil over each breast. Pour the wine around the chicken breasts into the pan. Bake just until the chicken is cooked through (when pierced with a sharp, thin-bladed knife, the juices should run clear and the meat should have no trace of pink), 25 to 30 minutes.

6. If you'd like to brown the tops of the chicken breasts, broil just until browned.

7. Remove the pan from the oven and let cool for 10 minutes. Transfer the breasts to a cutting board, remove the toothpicks, and slice diagonally into 1-inch slices. Arrange on 4 to 6 plates and spoon the tomato vinaigrette over slices. Serve at once.

Juicy Tomato Vinaigrette

MAKES ¾ CUP
PREP TIME: 10 MINUTES

2 small vine-ripened tomatoes
1 small shallot, minced
1 small garlic clove, minced
Pinch kosher salt
Pinch freshly ground black pepper
1 teaspoon sherry vinegar
½ teaspoon Dijon mustard
2 tablespoons basil chiffonade (see page 53)
½ cup extra-virgin olive oil

1. Bring a medium pot of water to a boil over high heat. Half fill a large bowl with ice water. Cut off and around the stem of the tomato and cut a shallow X into the bottom. Add the tomatoes to the boiling water and cook until the skin begins to peel away at the X, about 1 minute. Use tongs or a slotted spoon to transfer the tomatoes to the ice water to stop the cooking. When cool enough to handle, use a paring knife to remove the skin from the tomatoes; it should come right off. Seed (see page 30) and core the tomatoes and cut them into small dice.
2. Put the shallot, garlic, salt, pepper, vinegar, and mustard into a small mixing bowl and whisk. Fold in the tomatoes and basil and let rest for 10 minutes. Slowly add the oil in a thin stream, whisking, to form an emulsified vinaigrette.

Sausage-Stuffed Turkey Rollatini

SERVES 6
PREP TIME: 15 MINUTES
COOK TIME: 1½ HOURS

I came up with this recipe when I was looking for a new way to enjoy the flavors of turkey and stuffing without spending the whole day roasting and basting an entire bird: My inspiration was to make a quick sausage stuffing with onions, garlic, mushrooms, and breadcrumbs, and roll it up in a pounded-flat turkey breast. It worked better than I could have hoped and is a great, quick way to enjoy the flavors of Thanksgiving at any time of year with much less work and a much shorter cooking time.

You can also use this recipe for chicken breast, veal cutlet, or pork tenderloin. Serve it with wild rice and a mixed green salad.

¼ cup extra-virgin olive oil
1 cup finely diced Spanish onion
Kosher salt
2 large garlic cloves, finely chopped
12 ounces white button mushrooms, coarsely chopped
1 pound sweet Italian sausage, purchased loose or
*   squeezed from casings*
½ pound spinach, well washed in several changes
*   of cold water and spun dry*
1 boneless turkey breast half, about 3 pounds, with its skin
Freshly ground black pepper
1 cup Homemade Breadcrumbs (page 295)
2 tablespoons (½ ounce) finely grated Parmigiano-Reggiano
1 large egg, beaten
2 tablespoons unsalted butter, at room temperature
¼ cup dry white wine
1 large carrot, peeled and finely diced
1 large celery stalk, ends trimmed, finely diced
3 cups low-sodium chicken broth
3 tablespoons all-purpose flour

1. To make the stuffing: Heat a wide, heavy sauté pan over medium heat. Add 2 tablespoons olive oil and heat it until it is shimmering, almost smoking. Add ½

cup onions, season with a pinch of salt, and cook, stirring occasionally, until softened but not browned, about 5 minutes. Add the garlic and cook, stirring, until fragrant but not browned, about 1 more minute. Add the mushrooms and cook, stirring, until they release their liquid and begin to dry, 5 to 7 minutes. Stir in the sausage and cook, crumbling the sausage with a fork or the back of a wooden spoon, until all traces of pink are gone, 3 to 5 minutes. Stir in the spinach and cook until wilted but still nicely green, 2 to 3 more minutes. Transfer the mixture to a wide, heatproof bowl and let cool.

2. Meanwhile, use a heavy chef's knife to butterfly the turkey breast and open it so it lies flat. Put the butterflied breast between pieces of plastic wrap and pound with a meat mallet to make a wide, flat surface (one half will have skin, one will not). Season both sides with salt and pepper.

3. Once the sausage mixture has cooled, season with salt and pepper and stir in the breadcrumbs, Parmigiano-Reggiano, and egg.

4. Position a rack in the center of the oven. Preheat to 400°F.

5. Spread the stuffing evenly over the turkey, leaving a 1-inch border on all sides. Fold the long, skinless side over the stuffing to enclose, gently pressing on the stuffing, then roll up the breast, tucking in the sides as necessary, to make a neat, tight package, with the skin on the outside. Working with the seam side down to help keep it tightly closed, tie the rolled breast crosswise at 1-inch intervals with kitchen string, and once along its length.

6. Brush the turkey rollatini with softened butter and season with salt and pepper.

7. Heat a Dutch oven or other heavy pot wide enough to hold the rollatini over medium-high heat. Add the remaining 2 tablespoons of the olive oil and heat until it is shimmering, almost smoking. Add the turkey and brown on all sides, turning as it browns, 12 to 15 minutes total cooking time. Transfer the turkey to a plate. Pour the wine into the Dutch oven and bring to a boil, stirring to loosen any flavorful bits, and continue to boil until the wine is reduced by half, 3 to 4 minutes. Add the remaining diced onion, the carrots, and celery to the Dutch oven. Season with salt and cook, stirring, until the vegetables soften but do not brown, 7 to 8 minutes. Return the turkey to the Dutch oven, pour in 1 cup of the chicken broth, cover, put in the oven, and roast for 25 minutes. Remove the lid and roast for 15 more minutes.

8. Remove the pan from the oven and use tongs or a slotted spoon to transfer the turkey to a cutting board. Tent loosely with foil to keep warm. Let rest while you make the gravy.

9. To make the gravy: Return the Dutch oven to the stovetop over medium-high heat. In a small bowl, whisk the flour and 6 tablespoons of chicken broth, then slowly whisk the mixture into the turkey juices. Whisk in the remaining chicken

broth and bring the mixture to a boil. Lower the heat and simmer until the mixture has thickened considerably, about 5 minutes. Transfer the gravy to a sauceboat, straining it, if desired, or leaving the cooked vegetables in. Taste and add salt and pepper, if necessary.

10. Snip and remove the string from the rollatini, and slice crosswise into medallions (*roulades*). Arrange the roulades on a serving platter and serve with the gravy.

Perfect Pot Roast

SERVES 6
PREP TIME: ABOUT 15 MINUTES, NOT INCLUDING OVERNIGHT RESTING
COOK TIME: ABOUT 3½ TO 4 HOURS

This is another easier-than-it-seems recipe, which also happens to be my sister Madeline's favorite. The key to getting this to come out right is to braise it low and slow, keeping the liquid at a very gentle simmer all the way through the cooking. Do that and you'll end up with a fork-tender pot roast that will melt in your mouth.

If you're looking for a quick and easy accompaniment, this is delicious with, or over, egg noodles tossed with butter and parsley.

Note that you have to season the pot roast overnight.

Kosher salt
1 boneless chuck roast, 2½ to 3 pounds
2 tablespoons olive oil
8 ounces pancetta or slab bacon, cut into ¼-inch dice
    (about 1 cup dice)
1 medium Spanish onion, peeled and thinly sliced
    lengthwise
1 large stalk celery, ends trimmed and cut crosswise
    into 1-inch pieces
4 large garlic cloves, peeled and smashed with the side
    of a chef's knife
2 cups Chianti or other dry Italian red wine
About 1 cup homemade Chicken Stock (page 303) or
    low-sodium, store-bought chicken or beef stock or water
1 can (14½ ounces) diced tomatoes
Pinch sugar
½ tablespoon balsamic vinegar
Freshly ground black pepper
1 sprig rosemary
1 bunch slender carrots peeled and cut in half lengthwise,
    then crosswise
2 tablespoons coarsely chopped flat-leaf parsley leaves

1. Salt the roast on all sides, wrap in plastic, and refrigerate overnight. Let the meat come to room temperature before proceeding.
2. When ready to cook and serve the pot roast, position a rack in the center of the oven. Preheat to 300°F.
3. Heat a large, wide, heavy braising pan that has a tight-fitting lid, over medium-high heat. Add the oil and heat it until it is shimmering, almost smoking. Add the beef and sear until well-browned on all sides, 8 to 10 minutes per side, turning it with tongs as each side is browned. Use the tongs to transfer the meat to a plate and set aside.
4. Add the pancetta, onion, celery, and garlic to the pan. Season with a pinch of salt, and cook, stirring often, until the vegetables are softened but not browned, about 7 minutes. Pour in the wine, bring to a boil, and reduce by half, about 5 minutes, stirring to loosen any flavorful bits of beef cooked onto the pot. Stir in the stock, tomatoes, sugar, vinegar, a pinch of salt, and a few grinds of pepper. Bring to a simmer and continue to simmer, stirring occasionally, until the liquids are reduced by half, about 5 minutes. Stir in the rosemary and parsley.
5. Return the meat to the pot. The liquid should come at least halfway up its sides; if it doesn't, stir in more stock.
6. Cover the pot and braise the beef in the oven for 1 hour. During this time, the braising liquid should be barely simmering; if it's bubbling aggressively, lower the temperature by 25°F; if not simmering at all, raise it by 25°F. Maintaining a nice, gentle simmer is the key to the beef not becoming tough.
7. Remove the lid and turn the beef over, then replace the lid and braise for another hour. Add the carrots, submerging them in the liquid, replace the lid, and roast until the roast is very tender, 30 to 45 more minutes.
8. Transfer the meat to a cutting board, tent with foil, and let rest for 15 minutes.
9. Meanwhile, use a slotted spoon to remove the carrots, placing them in a small serving bowl.
10. Return the pot to the stovetop over high heat. Bring the liquid to a boil and continue to boil until the braising liquid thickens slightly, 5 to 7 minutes. Taste and add salt and/or pepper, if necessary. Stir in the parsley.
11. Slice the pot roast and arrange the slices on a serving platter. Serve the roast family style, passing the gravy and carrots.

Roast Prime Rib

SERVES 2 TO 4

PREP TIME: ABOUT 15 MINUTES (NOT INCLUDING OVERNIGHT MARINATING)

COOK TIME: ABOUT 1 HOUR (INCLUDING RESTING TIME)

This recipe is a perfect example of how family traditions can be born in the most casual, surprising ways. One Christmas season, my sales representative from the enormous food-service company Sysco gave me some beautiful, bone-in prime ribs. I wanted to do something memorable for the family, so I hit up Elias, the chef of Macaluso's, our family's favorite catering hall, for his recipe for roasted prime rib, which I've changed in some ways to make my own. He taught me how to coat the meat with a paste of garlic, onion, and herbs. By the time you get around to roasting the beef, it already smells like a winner, and when you serve it, it's positively bursting with flavor. Once you make this, you'll never go back to meeker prime rib recipes.

¼ cup coarsely chopped Spanish onion
4 large garlic cloves, coarsely chopped
2 tablespoons olive oil
1 tablespoon chopped rosemary leaves
1 tablespoon coarsely chopped flat-leaf parsley leaves
1 tablespoon coarsely ground black pepper
½ teaspoon crushed red-pepper flakes
1 bone-in prime rib, 2½ to 3 pounds, preferably
*   with nice fat cap (the fatty outside layer that partially*
*   rings the rib) at least ¼-inch thick*
About 1 tablespoon kosher salt

1. The night before you plan to cook and serve the prime rib, put the onion, garlic, 2 tablespoons oil, rosemary, parsley, black pepper, and red-pepper flakes in the bowl of a food processor fit with the steel blade and pulse to a paste. Season the prime rib all over with salt and rub it with the herb paste. Set in a baking dish, cover with plastic wrap, and refrigerate overnight. Remove the baking dish from the refrigerator, let the meat come to room temperature, and rub off as much of the paste as you can before proceeding.
2. Position a rack in the center of the oven. Preheat to 450°F.
3. Put the meat, bone side down, in a shallow roasting pan just large enough to hold the meat snugly without crushing it. Season the fat cap with salt and pepper.

4. Roast the prime rib in the oven for 20 minutes, then lower the heat to 325°F and continue to roast until an instant-read thermometer inserted into the thickest part of the meat reads 130°F for medium-rare; start checking after 15 minutes, although it should take 20 to 30 minutes. Cook a bit longer for well done.
5. Transfer the meat to a cutting board, tent with foil, and let rest for 15 minutes before slicing and serving. Pour the pan juices into a sauceboat.
6. Serve the sliced meat with the pan juices.

Steak alla Buddy

SERVES 4
PREP TIME: 10 MINUTES
COOK TIME: 20 MINUTES

The name of this recipe refers both to me and to my father, who was also named Buddy. Dad made a version of this dish that showed off his powers of improvisation with a quick oniony sauce. In time, as I began to cook and get comfortable winging it in the kitchen, I developed it a peppery red-wine sauce based on Dad's original recipe.

4 New York strip steaks, 10 to 12 inches each,
*   ideally cut 1-inch thick*
Kosher salt
1 tablespoon olive oil
1 tablespoon unsalted butter
1 large Spanish onion, thinly sliced lengthwise
2 teaspoons low-sodium soy sauce
1 teaspoon Worcestershire sauce
1 teaspoon coarsely cracked black pepper (page 71)
1 teaspoon dried thyme
¼ cup homemade Chicken Stock (page 303) or
*   low-sodium chicken stock or beef stock*
¼ cup dry red wine, such as Chianti

1. The night before you plan to cook and serve these steaks, season them with kosher salt, gather in a single layer on a plate, cover loosely with plastic wrap, and refrigerate overnight. Let come to room temperature before proceeding.
2. When ready to cook and serve the steaks, heat a wide, deep, heavy sauté pan over high heat. Add the oil and butter. When the butter melts and foams, add the steaks without crowding, and cook until browned on 1 side, 2 to 3 minutes. Turn the steaks over, brown on the other side, and continue cooking until cooked to desired doneness, 2 to 3 more minutes for medium rare, 4 to 5 minutes for medium, and 5 to 7 minutes for well done.
3. Transfer the steaks to a plate or platter and tent with foil.
4. Add the onions to the pan and stir to coat. Lower the heat to medium and cook,

stirring, until softened but not browned, about 5 minutes. Stir in the soy sauce, Worcestershire, pepper, and thyme, and cook, stirring, for about 30 seconds. Pour in the broth and the wine, raise the heat to high, and bring to a boil. Continue to boil, stirring, until reduced to a thick, syrupy consistency, 6 to 8 minutes.

5. Serve the steak on individual plates, spooning some onions on the side.

Steak Pizzaiola

SERVES 4

PREP TIME: ABOUT 20 MINUTES, NOT INCLUDING RESTING OVERNIGHT

COOK TIME: ABOUT 30 MINUTES

My father used to make this Sicilian dish, named for the pizza maker, because it's made with some of the most popular pizza ingredients: garlic, mushrooms, peppers, oregano, and parsley. To this day, I love making and cooking it: The peppers and spices get along with the meat like a match made in heaven and make a big impact. As an added bonus, the different colored peppers look very festive.

While you can make this dish with other cuts, such as a New York strip, to me it really needs to be made with a nice, fatty rib eye and served medium rare.

4 boneless rib-eye steaks, about 12 ounces each,
ideally 1½-inches thick
Kosher salt
3 large garlic cloves, minced
¼ cup plus 1 tablespoon olive oil
1 pound cremini mushrooms, wiped clean with a
damp cloth, trimmed and sliced thickly
1 medium red onion, thinly sliced lengthwise
1 large sweet red bell pepper, seeds and stems removed,
cut into ½-inch-thick slices
1 large yellow sweet bell pepper, seeds and stems removed,
cut into ½-inch-thick slices
½ cup dry white wine, such as Sauvignon Blanc
1 can (28 ounces) whole plum tomatoes with their juices,
crushed by hand
2 tablespoons coarsely chopped fresh oregano leaves
1 tablespoon chopped flat-leaf parsley leaves
Freshly ground black pepper
1 tablespoon unsalted butter

1. The night before you plan to cook, season the steaks with salt, rub with about a third of the garlic, and drizzle with 1 tablespoon of the olive oil. Put in a baking dish, cover with plastic wrap, and refrigerate overnight. Let the meat come to room temperature before proceeding.

2. Heat a wide, deep sauté pan over medium-high heat. Add 3 tablespoons of the oil and heat it until it is shimmering, almost smoking. Add the mushrooms and a pinch of salt, and cook, stirring with a wooden spoon, until the mushrooms are nicely seared and begin to give up their juices, about 3 minutes. Add the onions, red and yellow peppers, and a pinch of salt. Cook, stirring with a wooden spoon, until the peppers are lightly caramelized, 4 to 5 minutes.

3. Lower the heat and stir in another third of the garlic. Continue cooking and stirring until the peppers are tender, 4 to 5 more minutes.

4. Pour in the white wine, turn the heat to high, and bring the wine to a boil. Boil and reduce the wine until it's syrupy, 1 to 2 minutes. Pour in the tomatoes and their juices and cook, stirring, until the sauce reduces and is thick and flavorful, about 5 minutes. Remove the pan from the heat, stir in the remaining third of the garlic, the oregano, and the parsley. Season with salt and pepper. Cover the sauce and keep warm.

5. Heat a wide, deep, heavy sauté pan over high heat. Add 1 tablespoon of the oil and the butter. When the butter melts and foams, add the steaks without crowding and cook until browned on 1 side, 2 to 3 minutes. Turn the steaks over, brown on the other side, and continue cooking until cooked to desired doneness, 3 to 4 more minutes for medium rare, 5 to 6 minutes for medium, and 7 to 8 minutes for well done.

6. To serve, put 1 steak on each of 4 plates and smother with sauce, making sure you get a good mix of vegetables in each serving.

Stuffed Peppers

SERVES 4 TO 6
PREP TIME: ABOUT 20 MINUTES
COOK TIME: ABOUT 1 HOUR

Stuffed peppers remind me of a number of the women in my family: My wife, Lisa, and her mother, Gloria, both make a version of this dish, and they are one of my sister Grace's favorite meals. The secrets of its success are steaming the peppers before baking them to make them nice and soft, adding provolone to the sausage filling, and topping them with tomato sauce. All of those steps take what many Americans consider a plain, no-frills, home-cooked meal and make it exceptional.

Kosher salt
½ cup extra-long grain white rice
4 medium to large sweet bell peppers,
    ideally 2 red and 2 orange
1 tablespoon plus 1½ teaspoons olive oil
1 pound loose sweet Italian sausage
½ cup diced fennel
½ large Spanish onion, diced
1½ teaspoons coarsely chopped fresh oregano leaves
1½ cups provolone, grated on the large holes
    of a box grater
1¼ cups tomato sauce
Freshly ground black pepper
¼ cup plus 2 tablespoons Homemade Breadcrumbs
    (page 295)

1. Bring a small pot of salted water to a boil. Add the rice and parcook at a simmer for 7 minutes. Drain in a fine-mesh strainer, rinse with cold, running water to remove excess starch, and drain again. Set aside.
2. Cut the tops off the peppers and remove the seeds and stems.
3. Set a steamer basket over a pot of simmering water. Line a large plate with paper towels. Add the peppers to the steamer basket, cut sides down. Cover the pot and steam the peppers until slightly softened but not cooked through, about 5 minutes. Transfer to the paper-towel–lined plate to drain while you make the filling.
4. Position a rack in the center of the oven. Preheat to 350°F.

5. Heat a medium, heavy sauté pan over medium heat. Add 1½ teaspoons of the olive oil and heat it until warm. Add the sausage and cook, breaking it up with a wooden spoon or the back of a fork until crumbled and browned, about 7 minutes. Add the fennel and onion and cook, stirring, over medium-low heat, until softened and translucent, 4 to 5 minutes. Stir in the oregano, then transfer the mixture to a bowl and let cool, then stir in the rice, provolone, and ½ cup of the tomato sauce. Taste and add salt and/or pepper, if necessary.

6. Oil a 9-inch x 13-inch x 2-inch ceramic or glass baking dish with the remaining tablespoon of the olive oil. Spoon just enough of the remaining tomato sauce onto the bottom of the dish to coat it. Cut the peppers in half lengthwise and divide the filling evenly among the halves. Place the halves, open-side up, in the baking dish without crowding and top with the remaining tomato sauce and the breadcrumbs.

7. Bake until the filling is warmed through, about 30 minutes. Divide the pepper halves among 4 to 6 plates and serve.

Baked Sausages with Savory Onions

SERVES 4 TO 6

PREP TIME: ABOUT 15 MINUTES

COOK TIME: ABOUT 1 HOUR

This is another one of those recipes that always takes me back to the old days because my dad used to make it, and it was one of longtime Carlo's Bake Shop veteran Danny Dragone's favorites. Dad made his version by sautéing sausages with onions and adding a little soy sauce to the pan to pull the flavors together. My version leaves out the soy sauce, and adds fennel, brown sugar, and Dijon mustard. If you think of fennel as a strong-flavored vegetable, you might be amazed at how slowly cooking it down with onions really smooths and mellows it. This is an easy, homey recipe that will fill your home with terrific aromas, a perfect dish for family suppers, especially during the winter months.

6 fat links sweet Italian fennel sausage,
    about 2 pounds total weight
2 tablespoons olive oil
1 large fennel bulb, trimmed, halved, cored,
    and cut lengthwise into thin slices
2 medium Spanish onions, halved through the root,
    and thinly sliced lengthwise
2 large garlic cloves, minced
Leaves from 5 fresh thyme sprigs, plus more for garnish,
    if desired
1 teaspoon kosher salt, plus more as needed
1 tablespoon light brown sugar
¾ cup dry white wine, such as Sauvignon Blanc
1¼ cups homemade Chicken Stock (page 303)
    or low-sodium chicken broth
1 tablespoon Dijon mustard
Freshly ground black pepper

1. Position a rack in the center of the oven. Preheat to 400°F.
2. Prick each sausage several times with the tines of a fork to keep them from bursting when cooked. Heat a Dutch oven or other wide, deep, heavy ovenproof pot, large enough to accommodate the sausages in a single layer, over medium heat. Add 1

tablespoon of the oil and warm it. Add the sausages and brown them all over, turning them as they brown, 6 to 8 minutes total cooking time. (Do not worry about cooking them through.) Transfer to a plate.

3. Add the remaining tablespoon of the oil to the Dutch oven and heat it until it is shimmering, almost smoking. Add the fennel, onions, garlic, thyme, and salt to the pot. Stir, lower the heat to low-medium, and cook, stirring, until the vegetables are soft, translucent, and beginning to brown, 10 to 15 minutes. Stir in the brown sugar and cook for 30 seconds. Pour in the wine, raise the heat to high, bring to a boil, and continue to boil until reduced by half, 3 to 4 minutes. Stir in the stock, bring to a boil, and continue to boil, stirring occasionally, until reduced by half, about 10 more minutes.

4. Return the sausages to the pot, cover, and bake in the oven for 30 minutes. Remove the pot from the oven and transfer the sausages to a platter. Swirl the mustard into the sauce and taste the sauce. Adjust the seasoning with salt and/or pepper if necessary. Pour the sauce over the sausages, garnish with thyme sprigs if desired, and serve.

Fennel, Herb, and Garlic Roasted Pork

SERVES 4 TO 6
PREP TIME: 15 MINUTES
COOK TIME: ABOUT 1 HOUR

There's a simple perfection to roasted pork crusted with fennel and herbs. Not only is it delicious right out of the oven, but thin slices of leftovers can be used to top a salad or become the centerpiece of a great sandwich. For me, there are few things more satisfying to eat, especially when you consider how easy it is to cook: You lard (see note) a pork roast with garlic, sage, and rosemary and slather it with a quick grind of fennel and coriander seeds. (If you don't have a spice grinder, you can wipe out a coffee grinder and use that; just be sure to wipe it down before using it to grind coffee.)

The thing that makes this recipe my own is the butter and sage sauce that I make in the pan after roasting the pork. That is pure Buddy overkill, and really takes this dish over the top.

1 boneless center-cut pork roast, 2½ to 3 pounds,
*   with layer of fat on top*
4 large garlic cloves, 2 thinly sliced into 5 slivers each,
*   2 minced*
10 small or torn, large sage leaves (similar in size to
*   garlic slices), plus 8 whole leaves*
10 fresh rosemary leaves
1 tablespoon fennel seeds
1 teaspoon coriander seeds
1 teaspoon kosher salt
1 teaspoon cracked black pepper (page 71)
2 tablespoons olive oil
¼ cup dry white wine, such as Sauvignon Blanc
½ cup homemade Chicken Stock (page 303)
*   or low-sodium chicken broth*
2 tablespoons unsalted butter

1. Use a paring knife or other sharp, thin-bladed knife to cut 10 narrow slits, about 1-inch deep, in the top of the pork. Working in one slit at a time, place the knife edge in the slit and use it as a slide to push in 1 garlic sliver, 1 piece of sage, and 1

piece of rosemary. Remove the knife and use your index finger to push the ingredients in farther, so they don't fall out.

2. Grind the fennel seeds, coriander seeds, teaspoon of salt, and black pepper together in a spice mill. Spread the mixture over the surface of the pork.

3. Position a rack in the center of the oven. Preheat to 400°F.

4. Heat a large cast iron pan over medium-high heat. Add the olive oil and heat it until it is shimmering, almost smoking. Add the pork to the pan and sear it quickly on all sides, turning it as it sears, about 20 minutes total time.

5. Transfer the pan to the oven and roast until an instant-read thermometer inserted into the thickest part of the pork reads 130°F, 20 to 30 minutes.

6. Transfer the pork to a cutting board and tent with foil to keep it warm while you make the sauce.

7. Place the pan over medium heat. Stir in the minced garlic and the whole sage leaves, and cook for about 30 seconds. Pour in the white wine, bring to a boil over high heat, and boil until reduced by half about 1 minute. Pour in the stock, bring to a boil, and reduce by half, 3 to 5 minutes.

8. Remove the pan from the heat and swirl in the butter. Pour any accumulated juices from the pork into the sauce.

9. Slice the pork, arrange the slices on a platter, and serve family style. Pour the sauce into a sauceboat and pass.

Note: To *lard* means to cut little slits into a piece of meat and insert flavoring agents.

Rack of Lamb

SERVES 4 TO 6
PREP TIME: 15 MINUTES
COOK TIME: 25 MINUTES

My mother-in-law, Gloria, made so many meals for Lisa and me that, when the two of us got married, I wanted to cook her something special, and ended up making her rack of lamb. I'm not sure why, but a lot of home cooks I talk to are afraid of making rack of lamb. Maybe it's because it's a relatively expensive cut of meat, or because they're afraid of scorching it in the hot oven. Whatever the reason, don't you be afraid of rack of lamb: It's actually very easy to make, and really delicious. My version takes off on the classic French recipe, then I marinate it in garlic and oregano before coating it with mustard and breadcrumbs. Once you cook this, you might find yourself making it more and more often. It's that easy and delicious, and the Fresh Herb Salmoriglio sauce lightens what can sometimes be a gamy meat with lemon and herbs.

2 racks of lamb, about 1½ pounds each,
  Frenched by your butcher
4 large garlic cloves, smashed with the side
  of a chef's knife
6 sprigs fresh oregano, bruised with the back
  of a knife
2 teaspoons kosher salt
Freshly ground black pepper
1 tablespoon olive oil
1½ cups Homemade Breadcrumbs (page 295)
3 to 4 tablespoons Dijon mustard
Fresh Herb Salmoriglio sauce (recipe follows)

1. Rub smashed garlic and oregano all over the lamb racks, making sure to rub into all areas of the meat, bones and all. Season the racks with salt and pepper. Set the racks in a baking dish, cover loosely with plastic wrap, and refrigerate overnight. Let come to room temperature and remove the plastic before cooking the lamb.
2. Position a rack in the center of the oven. Preheat the oven to 400°F.
3. Heat a wide, deep sauté pan over medium-high heat. Add oil to the pan and heat it until it is shimmering, almost smoking. Add the lamb and sear on both sides, turning with tongs as the sides are seared, 3 to 4 minutes total cooking time.

4. Transfer the racks to a work surface. Spread the breadcrumbs out on a plate. When the racks are cool enough to handle, use the back of a spoon or a small offset spatula to spread mustard over the meat. Roll the racks in breadcrumbs, pressing down very gently to help the crumbs adhere to the mustard. Transfer the racks to a sheet pan, meat side up.

5. Roast the racks in the oven until an instant-read thermometer inserted into the thickest part reads, 130°F, about 25 minutes. Transfer the racks to a cutting board and tent with foil. Let rest 10 to 12 minutes to allow the juices to redistribute.

6. Carve the racks into individual chops and divide among 4 to 6 dinner plates. Serve with the Salmoriglio sauce alongside.

Fresh Herb Salmoriglio

MAKES ¾ CUP
PREP TIME: 12 MINUTES

This is a traditional Sicilian herb sauce that's used throughout the south of Italy as a dressing for cooked fish and meats, especially swordfish. Ask a Sicilian and he might tell you that the sauce has to be made with a little seawater, which is one of the best examples you'll ever find as to why sometimes those dishes you eat on vacation don't taste the same when you order them at a restaurant back home.

1 medium shallot, halved and shaved or
*   very thinly sliced lengthwise*
1 large garlic clove, minced
1 tablespoon balsamic vinegar
2 tablespoons freshly squeezed lemon juice
Kosher salt
¼ cup coarsely chopped flat-leaf parsley leaves
2 tablespoons chopped fresh oregano leaves
2 tablespoons coarsely chopped fresh mint leaves
About ½ cup extra-virgin olive oil
Freshly ground black pepper, if desired

Put the shallot, garlic, balsamic vinegar, lemon juice, and a pinch of salt in a bowl. Stir together and let marinate for 10 minutes. Add the parsley, oregano, and mint. Whisk in the olive oil. Taste the sauce and add salt and/or pepper, if necessary. To make it more pourable, you can also whisk in a little more oil.

Baby Lamb Chops with Lemon, Garlic, and Rosemary

SERVES 4

PREP TIME: 10 MINUTES PLUS PREHEATING TIME, DEPENDING UPON GRILL

COOK TIME: 8 MINUTES

When we visited my Grandma Grace's house, she'd usually cook for us, and this was one of the recipes she could make on a moment's notice, though it tasted like she had planned it for days: Small lamb chops marinated in an acidic marinade of oil, lemon juice and zest, garlic, and pepper. As soon as your grill is ready to go, you take the chops out of the marinade and throw them on. The zesty flavors—if you added a little vinegar and oregano you'd have a salad dressing—penetrate the meat and pair really well with the char from the grill.

I used to love sharing a plate of these chops with my grandmother; they're a quick, delicious dish that you can enjoy with your family.

16 baby lamb rib chops, cut from 2 racks of lamb,
*   about 3 pounds total weight*
Kosher salt
3 large lemons, zest removed from 1 lemon in strips
*   with a vegetable peeler, with no pith attached, and the lemon*
*   juiced; the other 2 halved across the equator*
4 large garlic cloves, pressed
2 pinches crushed red-pepper flakes
1 teaspoon cracked black pepper (page 71)
3 tablespoons coarsely chopped rosemary leaves
⅓ cup olive oil

1. Salt the chops on both sides.
2. Put the zest and juice of 1 lemon in a wide, shallow bowl or baking dish. Add the garlic, red-pepper flakes, black pepper, and rosemary. Whisk in the olive oil. Add the chops and turn to coat well with the marinade; leave in the marinade, but only for as long as it takes to preheat the grill.
3. Preheat a gas grill to high or light a charcoal grill, letting the coals burn down until covered with white ash.
4. Set the lemon halves on the grill, cut side down, and grill until they are caramel-

ized, 4 to 5 minutes, then transfer to a serving platter. Meanwhile, remove the lamb chops from the marinade, wiping off any solids, and place on the grill over direct heat. Grill the lamb chops until nicely marked and browned, 3 to 4 minutes, then use tongs to turn the chops and cook over indirect heat until nicely marked and browned on the other side, another 3 to 4 minutes.

5. Transfer the chops to the platter with the lemon halves and serve family style.

Roasted Leg of Lamb

SERVES 6 TO 8
PREP TIME: 25 MINUTES
COOK TIME: 2 HOURS

When I was growing up, my mother made only two roasts: beef and leg of lamb. Leg of lamb isn't an everyday dish, but it isn't difficult to make. The secret to the flavor here is larding the lamb (see Note, page 253). Usually, it's garlic slivers, which Mom used to do, but I also add bits of Parmigiano-Reggiano and chopped parsley. When the meat is roasted, those ingredients melt in and suffuse the meat, creating big, distinctly Italian flavors. (If you like, you can also add rosemary leaves along with the garlic and cheese.)

5-pound boneless leg of lamb roast, tied at 1-inch
intervals with kitchen twine (weighed without bone)
2 large garlic cloves, cut lengthwise into 5 slivers each
10 small chunks (¼-inch x ½-inch, 4 ounces)
Parmigiano-Reggiano
1 tablespoon coarsely chopped flat-leaf parsley leaves
Freshly ground black pepper
Kosher salt
¼ cup dry white wine, such as Sauvignon Blanc

1. Position a rack in the center of the oven. Preheat to 450°F.
2. Use a paring knife or other sharp, thin-bladed knife to cut 10 narrow slits, about 1-inch deep, in the top of the lamb. Place the knife edge in each slit, and use it as a slide to push in 1 garlic sliver, 1 piece of cheese, and some of the chopped parsley. Remove the knife and use your index finger to push the ingredients in further so that they don't fall out.
3. Set the lamb in a roasting pan with a rack and season liberally with salt and pepper.
4. Roast the lamb until the outside begins to sear, about 25 minutes.
5. Lower the oven temperature to 325°F and continue to roast until an instant-read thermometer inserted into the thickest part of the lamb reads 135°F for medium rare, about 90 minutes longer, or a bit longer for more well done.
6. Remove the pan from the oven, carefully transfer the lamb to a cutting board, and tent with foil to keep it warm. Let rest for 10 minutes to allow the juices to redistribute.
7. Meanwhile, put the roasting pan on the stovetop over 2 burners. Over medium-

high heat, pour in the white wine, bring it to a boil, and cook, stirring with a wooden spoon to loosen any flavorful bits cooked onto the pan. Once the wine has reduced slightly and the pan sauce is nicely thickened, about 1 minute, carefully pour or spoon it into a sauceboat or other serving vessel.

8. Slice the lamb crosswise into ¼-inch slices. Arrange them on a serving platter and serve family style, passing the sauce.

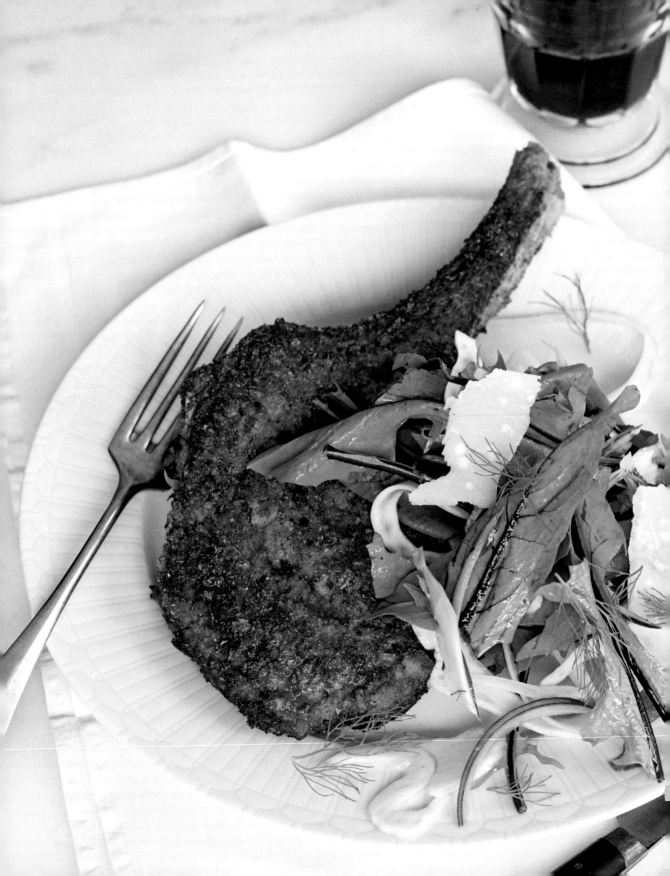

Veal Milanese

SERVES 4
PREP TIME: 30 MINUTES
COOK TIME: 30 MINUTES

I don't even need to take my first bite of veal Milanese in order to be happy. Just seeing that pounded out, bone-in, breaded chop, usually topped with some kind of a simple salad, puts a smile on my face. When you make this dish right, you don't even need a knife. You could probably top this with just about any salad in the book except the seafood salad, but I think the fennel and dandelion salad brings just the right mix of flavor and crunch to the plate.

4 bone-in veal chops, about 12 ounces each
2 cups all-purpose flour
4 large eggs, well beaten
3 cups Homemade Breadcrumbs (page 295)
Kosher salt
Freshly ground black pepper
¼ cup olive oil
2 tablespoons unsalted butter
Fennel and Dandelion Salad (recipe follows)
12 Parmigiano-Reggiano shards, shaved with a
*   vegetable peeler (about 1 ounce total)*

1. Position a rack in the center of the oven. Preheat to 300°F.
2. Working with 1 veal chop at a time, sandwich it between large pieces of plastic wrap. Use a meat mallet or the bottom of a heavy pan to gently pound them to a uniform thickness of ¼ inch.
3. Put the flour in a wide, shallow bowl, the eggs in another, and the breadcrumbs in a third. Season the veal chops generously with salt and pepper. One by one, dredge the chops in the flour, gently shaking off any excess, then the egg, letting any excess run back into the bowl, then coat in the breadcrumbs, pressing gently to help the crumbs adhere to the meat.
4. Heat a wide, deep skillet over medium high heat. Add 2 tablespoons olive oil and 1 tablespoon butter. When the butter melts and is foamy, add 1 chop and cook until golden-brown on both sides, 5 to 7 minutes per side. As the chops are done,

transfer them to a baking sheet and keep warm in the oven. Add more oil and butter between batches as necessary.

5. To serve, put 1 veal chop on each of 4 dinner plates, top with some of the fennel and dandelion salad and 3 cheese shavings. Serve at once.

Fennel and Dandelion Salad

SALAD TO TOP 4 SERVINGS OF FRIED, BREADED MEAT OR POULTRY
PREP TIME: 15 MINUTES

The only thing I use this salad for is as a topping to veal Milanese, but you can top other breaded, fried meats and poultry with it. Ideally, the vegetables should be shaved on a mandoline, but they can also be very thinly sliced with a heavy chef's knife and a steady hand.

Juice of one large lemon
Pinch kosher salt
½ cup extra-virgin olive oil
½ medium red onion, very thinly sliced
1 medium bulb fennel, fronds trimmed and finely chopped,
    fennel cored, and very thinly sliced
2 loosely packed cups hand-torn tender dandelion leaves
Few grinds of black pepper

Put the lemon juice and salt in a mixing bowl large enough to hold all the ingredients. Whisk in the oil, then add the onion and fennel and gently toss to coat them with the dressing. Let the salad rest for 10 minutes. Add the dandelion leaves and a few grinds of black pepper.

Veal Saltimbocca

SERVES 4
PREP TIME: 10 MINUTES
COOK TIME: 10 MINUTES

I remember eating veal saltimbocca in restaurants as a kid and, when I started to learn how to cook, it's one of the first things I wanted to make because it seemed special and a little fancy to me. The name means "jump in the mouth," and that's no joke: It's another one of those dishes that really show off how little you need to do with the all-stars of Italian ingredients to make something memorable. Little stacks of veal, mozzarella, prosciutto, and sage are seared in a pan, then a quick sauce of white wine, stock, and butter is made and poured over the veal. That's it! It takes just a few minutes, but when those flavors melt together, it's magic.

1 pound milk-fed veal, cut for scaloppine,
*   cut into 8 slices*
Kosher salt
4 ounces fresh mozzarella, cut into 8 thin slices
8 large fresh sage leaves
4 ounces prosciutto, cut into 8 thin slices
2 tablespoons olive oil
3 tablespoons unsalted butter
1 tablespoon all-purpose flour
½ cup dry white wine, such as Sauvignon Blanc
½ cup homemade Chicken Stock (page 303)
*   or low-sodium chicken broth*

1. One by one, put the pieces of veal between pieces of plastic wrap and lightly pound with a meat mallet or the bottom of a heavy pan to a thickness of ⅛-inch.
2. Season the veal on both sides with salt. Lay a piece of mozzarella on top of each piece of veal, top with a sage leaf, then a slice of prosciutto. Weave a toothpick in and out to secure the prosciutto and other ingredients to the veal.
3. Heat a wide, deep, heavy sauté pan over medium heat. Add the oil and 2 tablespoons butter. When the butter has melted and is foamy, add 4 pieces of the veal, prosciutto-side down. Raise the heat to high and cook until browned, about 1 minute. Use tongs or a spatula to turn the pieces over and brown on the other

side, about 1 minute. Transfer the veal to a platter and repeat with the remaining prepared veal.

4. When all the veal has been cooked and removed from the pan, add the flour to the pan and stir until it comes together with the fat in a tan mixture. Pour in the wine and bring to a boil, stirring, over high heat. Continue to boil until reduced by half, 1 to 2 minutes, continuing to stir to loosen up any flavorful bits cooked on to the bottom of the pan. Add the stock to the pan, bring to a boil, and continue to boil until reduced by half, 1 to 2 minutes. Remove the pan from the heat and whisk in the remaining tablespoon of butter.

5. Remove the toothpicks from the veal and pour the sauce over the veal. Serve family style.

Osso Buco

SERVES 6

PREP TIME: 15 MINUTES, NOT INCLUDING RESTING OVERNIGHT

COOK TIME: ABOUT 3 HOURS

Not all of my favorite Italian dishes come from Sicily. When it's made right, osso buco ("hole in the bone"), a specialty of Milan, knocks my socks off every time. Crosscuts of meaty veal shanks are braised ever-so-gently in a white braising liquid until they are literally falling off the bone and ready to melt in your mouth. I came to love osso buco at a restaurant called Tutto a Modo Mio (the name means "everything my way") in Ridgefield, New Jersey, but my wife, Lisa, makes a version that is even better: I think it's the lemon zest and leek in the base which lighten the braising liquid and give the dish a real lift.

There's only one way to serve osso buco: topped with a pinch of gremolata and set atop a mound of saffron risotto (page 189) to complement its flavors and soak up the juices.

6 meaty veal osso buco shanks, ideally 1½ inch thick,
    about 12 to 14 ounces each
Kosher salt
2 tablespoons olive oil
2 tablespoons unsalted butter
1 medium Spanish onion, cut into large dice
2 medium carrots, peeled and cut into large dice
2 medium stalks celery, ends trimmed and cut into medium dice
1 medium leek, white and pale green parts only, well washed
    under cold running water, quartered lengthwise, and diced
2 tablespoons tomato paste
1 cup dry white wine, such as Sauvignon Blanc
2 cups homemade Chicken Stock (page 303) or high-quality,
    store-bought veal stock
1 can (14½ ounces) whole canned plum tomatoes in their juices,
    crushed by hand
2 small sprigs rosemary
4 sprigs thyme
2 strips lemon zest, removed with a vegetable peeler,
    with no pith attached
Gremolata (recipe follows)

1. The night before you plan to cook and serve the osso buco, season the shanks with salt, place in a baking dish, cover loosely with plastic wrap, and refrigerate overnight. Let come to room temperature before proceeding.
2. Position a rack in the center of the oven. Preheat to 350°F.
3. Heat a Dutch oven or other heavy braising vessel that has a tight-fitting lid over medium-high heat. Add the oil and butter. When the butter melts and is foamy, lower the heat to medium, add the shanks to the Dutch oven, and brown slowly and thoroughly on all sides, turning with tongs as each side browns, 15 to 20 minutes total cooking time. Once the shanks are browned all over, use the tongs to transfer them to a plate and set them aside.
4. Add the onions, carrots, celery, leeks, and a pinch of salt to the Dutch oven and cook, stirring often, until they are tender, about 7 minutes. Stir in the tomato paste and keep stirring until the vegetables are coated with the paste. Pour in the wine, raise the heat to high, bring it to a boil, and reduce by half, about 5 minutes. Pour in the stock and add the tomatoes, rosemary, thyme, and lemon zest. Bring the liquid to a boil.
5. Return the shanks to the Dutch oven, submerging them in the liquid. Put the lid on the Dutch oven and braise in the oven until the meat is tender, 2 to 2½ hours. During this time, the braising liquid should be barely simmering; if it's bubbling aggressively, lower the temperature by 25°F; if not simmering at all, raise it by 25°F. Maintaining a nice, gentle simmer is the key to the veal not becoming tough.
6. Use tongs or a slotted spoon to transfer 1 shank to each of 6 wide, shallow bowls. Spoon some vegetables alongside and some sauce over and around the shank in each bowl. Garnish each serving with some gremolata and serve.

Gremolata

GARNISH FOR 6 SERVINGS OF OSSO BUCO (2 TABLESPOONS)
PREP TIME: LESS THAN 5 MINUTES

This is the classic topping for osso buco, a condiment of lemon zest, parsley, and garlic. Though you will probably never see it served over anything else in a restaurant, you can top other braised meats, such as lamb shanks, with it. You can also play with the flavors, making it with, say, orange zest, instead of lemon zest.

Finely grated zest of 2 lemons
¼ cup coarsely chopped flat-leaf parsley leaves
2 large garlic cloves, minced
Pinch kosher salt
1 tablespoon olive oil, optional

Put the lemon zest, parsley, garlic, salt, and olive oil, if using, in a small bowl and stir together.

Sides

Side dishes, or *contorni,* are an important part of the Italian-American table, adding to the sense of conviviality and community as everybody passes the dishes around, taking what they like and as much as they'd like, and leaving the rest to others. They also offer incredible flexibility to the cook, allowing him or her to adjust the daily menu to use what's on hand or looked especially fresh and delicious at the market that day.

There are really no hard and fast rules for what side dishes to pair with what main courses, or how many dishes to offer with a meal, although my general feeling—as you might imagine—is "the more the merrier," especially because leftovers of almost all these dishes, with the notable exception of the Italian-Spiced Oven Fries (page 285), can be served hot or cold the following day. That said, at a minimum you will probably want to serve at least one green vegetable and one potato dish with any meal.

Many of these recipes can also be part of an antipasti spread, especially the Roasted Asparagus with Crispy Breadcrumbs (page 276), Broccoli Rabe with Sausage (page 277), Sautéed Spicy Peppers (page 284), and Sautéed Mushrooms (page 289).

Roasted Asparagus
with Crispy Breadcrumbs

SERVES 4

PREP TIME: 10 MINUTES

COOK TIME: 10 MINUTES

If you want to get your kids to eat asparagus, make them this way, with my wife, Lisa's, recipe: The asparagus are tossed with olive oil, topped with breadcrumbs, roasted until fork tender, then showered with Parmigiano-Reggiano cheese. For crispier breadcrumbs, finish under the broiler for one minute.

1 pound medium-thick asparagus stalks, rinsed in cold
   running water and patted dry, ends trimmed about
   2 inches from the bottom
About 2 tablespoons olive oil
Kosher salt
¼ cup Homemade Breadcrumbs (page 295)
2 tablespoons (½ ounce) finely grated Parmigiano-Reggiano

1. Position a rack in the center of the oven. Preheat to 450°F.
2. Put the asparagus in a wide bowl and drizzle with just enough olive oil to coat them. Add a generous amount of salt and gently toss to season the stalks evenly and coat them with oil.
3. Spread the stalks in a heatproof baking vessel, nice enough to serve from, and large enough to hold the spears in a single layer. Sprinkle the breadcrumbs evenly over the spears. Roast the asparagus until fork tender and the breadcrumbs are golden brown, 7 to 10 minutes.
4. Remove the dish from the oven, top with the cheese, and serve.

Broccoli Rabe
with Sausage

SERVES 4 TO 6
PREP TIME: 5 MINUTES
COOK TIME: 20 TO 25 MINUTES

Every holiday season, I make broccoli rabe and sausage for the crew at the bakery. It's also a favorite dish at my house, where Lisa loves it. The slightly bitter broccoli flavor (actually, broccoli rabe, or cima di rapa as it's called in Italy, is a member of the turnip family) matches really well with the sausage.

Broccoli rabe and sausage is also a classic combination with the ear-shaped pasta called orecchiette: if you choose to toss this with pasta, cook the pasta in the same water you used for the broccoli, and the pasta will take on some of its flavor. Be sure to slice the sausage into bite-size pieces if serving with pasta.

1 large bunch broccoli rabe (rapini), about 1 pound
¼ cup olive oil
3 large garlic cloves, thinly sliced
1 pound link sweet or hot Italian sausage,
*   preferably thin sausages (about 2 ounces each)*
Kosher salt

1. Bring a large pot of water to a boil. Half fill a large bowl with ice water.
2. Wash and drain the broccoli rabe. Trim the stem ends, thick stems, and yellowed or discolored leaves. Blanch the broccoli rabe in the boiling water for about 2 minutes. Drain in a colander and shock in the ice water to stop the cooking and preserve the vibrant color. Drain, pat dry gently with paper towels, and set aside.
3. Heat a wide, deep, heavy sauté pan over medium heat. Add 2 tablespoons of the oil and heat it until it is shimmering, almost smoking. Add half the garlic and cook, stirring, just until it turns golden, about 30 seconds. Add half the sausage and stir it into the garlic to stop the garlic from burning. Brown the sausages, turning to cook evenly all over, turning as needed and monitoring the heat level, until seared all over and cooked through, 10 to 12 minutes. Add half the broccoli rabe to the pan, season with salt, and cook, stirring as you cook, until slightly

darkened and cooked through, 3 to 5 minutes. Transfer the broccoli and sausage to a wide, deep serving bowl. Repeat with the remaining oil, garlic, sausage, and broccoli. You can also slice the sausage into bite-sized pieces, add to the rabe, and toss before serving.

Buddy's Swiss Chard

SERVES 4 TO 6
PREP TIME: ABOUT 10 MINUTES
COOK TIME: ABOUT 15 MINUTES

Believe it or not, Swiss chard was my favorite vegetable as a kid, because my mother made it in a quick tomato sauce that turned it into a kind of veggie stew. Like I always say, if you want kids to eat their vegetables, it's really not that difficult: Just make them taste great!

Kosher salt
3 bunches Swiss chard, all white or all red,
    not rainbow, about 3 pounds total weight,
    well washed, stems trimmed
¼ cup olive oil
3 large garlic cloves, thinly sliced
1 can (15 ounces) plum tomatoes, drained of juice,
    mashed with a potato masher
Freshly ground black pepper

1. Bring a large pot of salted water to a boil. Half fill a large bowl with ice water.
2. Blanch the chard in the boiling water for 30 to 60 seconds, then drain it in a colander and quickly transfer it to the ice water to stop the cooking and preserve its color. When cool enough to handle, drain again, squeeze out the excess liquid by hand, transfer to a cutting board, and coarsely chop.
3. Heat a wide, deep, heavy sauté pan over medium heat. Add the oil and heat it until hot and almost shimmering. Lower the heat, add the garlic, and cook over low heat to infuse the oil for 1 to 2 minutes. Stir in the tomatoes, and season with salt and pepper. Cook, stirring occasionally, for 5 minutes. Stir in the chard, season again, and cook, stirring, until soft and heated through, 5 to 6 minutes.
4. Transfer the chard to a bowl and serve.

Sautéed Escarole
with Garlic and Tomato

SERVES 4
PREP TIME: 10 MINUTES
COOK TIME: 10 MINUTES

This crunchy side dish was often served at my Aunt Nina's house. It's especially good with poultry and fish.

¼ cup olive oil
3 large garlic cloves, thinly sliced
Pinch crushed red-pepper flakes
1 large head, or 2 small heads, escarole, about 1 pound
    total weight, well washed, cored, and cut into small pieces
Pinch kosher salt
1 can (14½ ounces) plum tomatoes, drained of their
    liquid and crushed by hand

1. Heat a large sauté pan over medium heat. Add the olive oil and heat it until it is shimmering, almost smoking. Add the garlic and pepper flakes and cook, stirring, just until the garlic turns golden, about 1 minute. Stir in the escarole and salt and cook, turning with tongs, until wilted, 7 to 10 minutes. Stir in the tomatoes and cook until their juice starts to cook off and the escarole and tomatoes are nicely tangled and the mixture is still moist but not soupy, about 3 minutes.
2. Transfer to a bowl and serve immediately.

Sautéed Spicy Peppers

SERVES 4
PREP TIME: 10 MINUTES
COOK TIME: 15 TO 20 MINUTES

These spicy peppers can be served as a side dish with grilled meats and sausages, and the leftovers can be chopped up and used as a relish for subs and heroes. You can use just one type of pepper, but the variety of colors really gives this some visual excitement. For a less spicy version, leave out or use less of the crushed red-pepper flakes and serrano chili. This makes a terrific topping for crusty bread.

¼ cup olive oil
1 teaspoon crushed red-pepper flakes, or to taste
1 medium red onion, halved and thinly sliced
2 large red bell peppers, seeded and sliced ¼-inch thick
1 large yellow bell pepper, seeded and sliced ¼-inch thick
2 large banana peppers, seeded and sliced ¼-inch thick
1 serrano chili, seeded and coarsely chopped
Kosher salt
2 large garlic cloves, pressed
1 tablespoon coarsely chopped flat-leaf parsley leaves
1 tablespoon white balsamic vinegar

1. Heat a wide cast iron pan, or heavy stainless steel pan, over medium heat. Add the oil and crushed red pepper and cook until the oil starts to shimmer and the pepper is fragrant, 1 to 2 minutes.
2. Add the onions; the red, yellow, and banana peppers; and the chili to the pan and season generously with salt. Lower the heat to medium low and sauté, stirring occasionally, until soft and beginning to brown, about 15 minutes.
3. Add the garlic and sauté until fragrant, about 30 seconds. Remove the pan from the heat and stir in the parsley and vinegar. Let cool for 5 minutes, then transfer to a shallow bowl and serve.

Italian-Spiced Oven Fries
with Homemade Ketchup

SERVES 4

PREP TIME: 5 MINUTES FOR FRIES, 10 MINUTES FOR KETCHUP

COOK TIME: 25 TO 30 MINUTES FOR KETCHUP, 25 TO 30 MINUTES FOR FRIES

I came up with this recipe for two reasons: One was to find a way to bake rather than fry French fries for a relatively healthful alternative. The other was to make my own ketchup, which is something I'd wanted to do for a long time. The two make a perfect pairing: What the fries lose by not frying them is made up for by the fresh, vibrant flavor of the ketchup.

FOR THE KETCHUP

2 tablespoons olive oil
¾ cup finely chopped onion
1½ teaspoons minced garlic
½ cup red wine vinegar
½ cup apple cider vinegar
1 cup dark brown sugar
1 teaspoon kosher salt
½ teaspoon Dijon mustard
Pinch of ground allspice
1 can (28 ounces) crushed tomatoes with their juice

1. Heat a large, heavy saucepan over medium heat. Add the olive oil and heat it until it is shimmering, almost smoking. Add the onions and garlic and cook until softened but not browned, 4 to 5 minutes. Pour the red wine and apple cider vinegars into the pan and stir in the brown sugar, salt, mustard, and allspice. Bring to a boil, then stir in the tomatoes. Continue to cook until the liquid has reduced by half, 20 to 25 minutes. Remove the pot from the heat and let cool, 10 to 15 minutes.
2. Transfer the mixture to the bowl of a food processor fitted with the steel blade and process until very smooth. Use the ketchup right away or refrigerate it in an airtight container for up to 3 weeks.

FOR THE FRIES

4 russet potatoes, about 14 ounces each
3 tablespoons olive oil
1 teaspoon kosher salt, plus more for serving
1 teaspoon freshly ground black pepper
½ teaspoon dried oregano
½ teaspoon dried basil
½ teaspoon garlic powder
¼ teaspoon ground coriander seed

1. Position a rack in the center of the oven. Preheat to 400°F.
2. Line a baking sheet with aluminum foil and coat with 1 tablespoon olive oil.
3. Peel the potatoes and cut them into ¼-inch fries. Arrange the potatoes on the baking sheet in a single layer. Drizzle with remaining 2 tablespoons oil.
4. Put the salt, pepper, oregano, basil, garlic powder, and coriander in a small bowl and stir together. Sprinkle the mixture over the potatoes and toss to coat evenly.
5. Bake the potatoes until golden brown, about 25 to 30 minutes, using tongs or a spatula to turn once during baking.
6. When the fries are done, sprinkle with salt, and serve immediately with the ketchup.

Sautéed Mushrooms

SERVES 4 TO 6
PREP TIME: 5 MINUTES
COOK TIME: 15 MINUTES

Sautéed mushrooms are one of those things that too many cooks take for granted because simply sautéing them in olive oil and/or butter tastes so good. But, if you go a little further, adding some white wine, as I do here, it pays big dividends, because mushrooms are one of those rare ingredients that have great flavors of their own, and can also take on other flavors really well.

You can play around with the mix of mushrooms here; even white button mushrooms will be delicious.

¼ cup olive oil
3 large garlic cloves, minced
1½ pounds mixed mushrooms, such as cremini,
    oyster, and/or shiitake, ends trimmed, thinly sliced
Kosher salt
¼ cup crisp white wine, such as Pinot Grigio
1 tablespoon unsalted butter
¼ cup coarsely chopped flat-leaf parsley

1. Heat a large sauté pan over high heat. Add the oil and heat it until it is shimmering, almost smoking. Add garlic and cook for 30 seconds, then stir in the mushrooms and a pinch of salt and cook, stirring with a wooden spoon, until the mushrooms begin to give off their juices, are tender, and have taken on some color, 10 to 12 minutes. Pour in the wine, bring it to a boil, and let reduce until syrupy, about 3 minutes. Remove the pan from heat, swirl in the butter, and stir in the parsley. Taste and add salt and/or pepper, if necessary.
2. Transfer the mushrooms to a serving dish and serve family style.

Buddy's Favorite Roast Potatoes

SERVES 4
PREP TIME: ABOUT 15 MINUTES
COOK TIME: ABOUT 40 MINUTES

This sweet and savory combination of russet and sweet potatoes, tossed with onions, garlic, olive oil, and oregano, was something that my mother's housekeeper, Olga, used to make for us at the holidays, and it really showed off how well she'd assimilated our family's collective palate, as well as her ability to come up with something distinctly her own that still felt Italian-American.

1 pound russet potatoes, cut in half lengthwise and
    sliced crosswise into ½-inch-thick slices
1 pound Garnet sweet potatoes, cut in half lengthwise
    and sliced crosswise into ½-inch-thick slices
1 large Spanish onion, thinly sliced
1 teaspoon dried oregano
2 large cloves garlic, coarsely chopped
3 tablespoons olive oil
Kosher salt
Freshly ground black pepper

1. Position a rack in the center of the oven. Preheat to 375°F.
2. Put the potatoes, onion, oregano, garlic, and oil in a bowl, season with salt and pepper, and toss gently to coat the vegetables with the oil and seasonings. Spread the potatoes out in a baking vessel wide and deep enough to hold them in a single layer.
3. Roast the potatoes until a sharp, thin-bladed knife slides easily to the center, about 30 minutes. Turn the oven to broil and broil the potatoes until crispy and browned on top, 5 to 10 minutes.
4. Transfer the potatoes to a serving dish and serve family style.

Buddy Basics

Homemade Breadcrumbs

This is an old family recipe for breadcrumbs that we use to add extra flavor to a wide range of recipes. I present two versions here: the first is made with dried herbs and can be held in an airtight container for a long time; the second uses fresh garlic and herbs, produces a smaller quantity, and should be used right away.

Make-Ahead Breadcrumbs

MAKES ABOUT 8 CUPS;
CAN BE STORED IN AN AIRTIGHT CONTAINER FOR UP TO 5 DAYS
PREP TIME: 5 MINUTES
COOK TIME: 5 MINUTES

If you like, in order to add some freshness, stir in a clove of minced garlic just before using.

2 loaves rustic Italian bread, such as Pugliese
1 cup (4 ounces) finely grated pecorino Romano or
*   Parmigiano-Reggiano*
2 tablespoons dried Italian herbs
3 tablespoons dried parsley flakes
½ tablespoon fine sea salt

1. A day or two before you plan to make breadcrumbs, slice the bread into ½-inch slices. Place the slices on cake racks or baking sheets and let dry for 1 to 2 days.
2. Working in batches, crumble or tear the bread slices into the bowl of a food processor fitted with the steel blade. Pulse the pieces to fine crumbs. The crumbs may not process uniformly; you may leave as is for a rustic finished texture, or sift the larger pieces though a mesh sieve.
3. Gather the crumbs in a large, wide bowl and stir in the cheese, Italian herbs, parsley, and salt. Store crumbs you do not use right away in an airtight container at room temperature for up to 5 days, or freeze in freezer bags for up to 1 month.

Fresh Breadcrumbs

1 12-inch loaf rustic Italian bread,
preferably one day old
1 large garlic clove, finely chopped
1 tablespoon finely chopped flat-leaf parsley
1 tablespoon finely chopped fresh oregano
2 tablespoons finely grated pecorino Romano
Kosher salt
Freshly ground black pepper

1. The day before you plan to make breadcrumbs, slice the bread crosswise into ½-inch slices. Place the slices on a cake rack or baking sheet to dry overnight.
2. In batches, crumble or tear bread slices into the bowl of a food processor fit with the steel blade. Pulse to fine crumbs. The crumbs may not process uniformly; you can leave some larger than others for a rustic effect, or sift the larger pieces through a mesh sieve.
3. Put the breadcrumbs in a bowl and add the garlic, parsley, oregano, and cheese. Season with salt and pepper.

Pesto alla Genovese

MAKES ABOUT ¾ CUP
PREP TIME: 20 MINUTES

This traditional Ligurian condiment is a bit looser than the pesto you might be used to, but its basil flavor is truly spectacular. Use it in recipes that call for pesto, toss it with hot pasta, or spread it on grilled bread.

3 cups small, tender basil leaves, stems trimmed
Heaping tablespoon pine nuts
½ cup (2 ounces) finely grated pecorino Romano
Pinch kosher salt
3 small garlic cloves
½ cup extra-virgin olive oil

Put the basil leaves in the bowl of a food processor fitted with the steel blade. Add the pine nuts, pecorino, and salt. With the motor running, drop the garlic into the processor's tube, then add the oil in a thin stream and keep processing until it is blended. Stop the motor and use a rubber spatula to scrape any pesto from the sides, then replace the lid and pulse a few more times.

Caponata

MAKES 4 CUPS
PREP TIME: 20 MINUTES
COOK TIME: ABOUT 30 MINUTES

This Sicilian eggplant-and-caper condiment is delicious on grilled bread or even on crackers. As wonderful as it is freshly made, it's even more tasty after a day or two in the fridge, because the flavors intensify.

¼ cup plus 2 tablespoons extra-virgin olive oil
1 medium eggplant, cut into ½-inch dice
Kosher salt
1 medium Spanish onion, cut into small dice
1 large stalk celery, ends trimmed, cut into small dice
2 large garlic cloves, minced
½ teaspoon crushed red-pepper flakes, plus more to taste
1 can (14 ounces) Italian cherry tomatoes
2 teaspoons sherry vinegar
1 tablespoon sugar
¼ cup golden raisins
1 tablespoon capers, soaked for 20 minutes in warm water,
*   rinsed, and drained*
2 tablespoons toasted pine nuts (see page 69)
⅓ cup coarsely chopped flat-leaf parsley

1. Heat a large, heavy skillet over medium-high heat. Add ¼ cup olive oil to the pan and heat it until it is shimmering, almost smoking. Add the eggplant and a pinch of salt, stir, and cook, stirring occasionally, until softened and browned, 5 to 10 minutes. Transfer the eggplant to a bowl.
2. Add the remaining 2 tablespoons of oil to the pan and heat it. Add the onion, celery, and a pinch of salt and cook, stirring, until softened but not browned, about 5 minutes. Stir in the garlic and red-pepper flakes, and cook, stirring, just until fragrant, about 30 seconds. Stir in the tomatoes, vinegar, sugar, raisins, and capers, then stir in the cooked eggplant. Cook at a low simmer, stirring occasionally and mashing the cherry tomatoes a bit with the back of your spoon, until richly flavored, 15 to 20 minutes. Remove the pan from the heat and fold in the pine nuts and parsley. Taste and adjust the seasoning with salt, if necessary.
3. Let the caponata cool and serve at room temperature, or chill and serve cold.

Homemade Stocks

If you've never made your own stocks, you may never go back to canned versions; the depth of flavor a homemade stock adds to sauces, soups, and risottos just can't be beat.

Fish Stock

MAKES 2½ QUARTS
PREP TIME: 10 MINUTES
COOK TIME: ABOUT 40 MINUTES

3 pounds fish bones (from halibut, snapper, or grouper)
3 quarts water
1 large Spanish onion, thinly sliced
2 stalks celery, thinly sliced
1 medium leek, white and light green part only,
*   thinly sliced and well rinsed to remove any dirt*
6 to 8 sprigs flat-leaf parsley
1 to 2 teaspoons kosher salt

1. Put the fish bones and water in a stock pot or other deep pot. Set the pot over medium-high heat and bring to a boil, skimming off the foam and impurities from the stock as it begins to boil.
2. Lower the heat, so that the liquid slows to a simmer. Add the onion, celery, leek, parsley, and salt. Simmer for 30 minutes.
3. Remove the pot from the heat. Use tongs or a slotted spoon to fish out and discard some of the bones and other solids to make straining easier, then strain the stock and discard the solids.
4. Use the stock right away, refrigerate in airtight containers for 2 to 3 days, or freeze for up to 1 month.

Chicken Stock

MAKES 2 TO 3 QUARTS
PREP TIME: 5 MINUTES
COOK TIME: ABOUT 3 HOURS

5 pounds chicken bones
5 quarts water
2 medium Spanish onions, coarsely chopped
4 large stalks celery, coarsely chopped
3 medium carrots, coarsely chopped
6 to 8 fresh parsley stems
Kosher salt

1. Put the chicken bones in a large stockpot and pour the water over them. Bring the water to a boil over medium-high heat, skimming off the foam and impurities from the stock as it begins to boil.
2. Add the onions, celery, carrots, parsley, and 1 tablespoon salt, lower the heat, and simmer for 2½ hours, adding more water during that time, if necessary, to keep the bones submerged.
3. Check seasoning; add salt, if needed.
4. Use tongs or a slotted spoon to fish out and discard some of the bones and other solids to make straining easier, then strain the stock and discard the solids.
5. Use the stock right away, refrigerate in airtight containers for 2 to 3 days, or freeze for up to 1 month.

Fresh Pasta Sheets

PREP TIME: ABOUT 30 MINUTES

If there's a good specialty-foods store in your area, you can probably purchase high-quality, fresh pasta sheets there, but making them yourself is a satisfying project at home and especially fun with kids.

You will need a pasta machine; there's just no other way to produce uniformly thin sheets.

3 cups all-purpose flour, plus more
for dusting work surface
3 large eggs, lightly beaten
1 teaspoon kosher salt
2 to 3 tablespoons water

1. In a food processor, blend the flour, eggs, salt, and 2 tablespoons water until the mixture comes together in a ball. If the dough looks dry, add a little more water.
2. Remove the dough from the processor, wrap in plastic wrap, and let rest at room temperature for 30 minutes.
3. Set the rollers on a pasta machine to the widest setting.
4. Divide the dough into 6 or 8 pieces and flatten each piece into a rectangle. Keep the pieces you are not working with covered with plastic wrap or a clean dish towel, so that they don't dry out.
5. Lightly dust 1 pasta rectangle with flour and pass it through the machine. Continue to pass it back through the machine, lowering the settings each time, until you have a uniformly thin sheet. Repeat with the remaining portions of dough, keeping the rolled sheets covered with plastic to prevent them from drying out.
6. Pasta sheets may be used whole for ravioli or lasagna, or cut into desired shapes with a pizza cutter.

Desserts

With a bakery at my disposal 24/7, I never really have to make dessert at home, and neither does anybody else in my family: We can grab anything from a box of cannoli to a platter of assorted cookies to a pie or cake on our way out the door at the end of the day.

But, just as we love cooking savory foods at home, we also love making dessert. I'll be honest: We don't bake much at home, unless we're having some fun with our kids, because that's how we spend our working days. The result is that we've built up a repertoire of relatively easy-to-make desserts that any home cook can prepare. In fact, given how complex many of our theme cakes are, you might be surprised at the simplicity of what's here, but I believe that, in a home setting, dessert should be uncomplicated for both cook and diner. After making a full meal, the person in the kitchen is ready to relax, and after a meal of big flavors, most diners want something straightforward to end with, as well.

All of these desserts put one or two flavors front and center, such as the lemon in a granita, the strawberries and chocolate in the tuxedo strawberries, or the vanilla and espresso in the affogato.

My general advice is that, if you're eating a light meal, you can serve a relatively rich dessert; while after a rich meal, a lighter, fresher dessert is often what people crave. But you really can't go wrong with any of these: If you can't make up your mind, make a few, give people a choice, and you'll have leftovers the next day.

Lemon Granita

SERVES 4 TO 6

PREP TIME: 5 MINUTES

COOK TIME: 3 TO 4 HOURS, INCLUDING FREEZING TIME

Here in the United States, lemon ices are a popular dessert among Italian-Americans; it is scooped from huge tubs in ice-cream freezers at pizzerias and sandwich shops. When I went to Sicily with my father, I discovered a different, more refined version of an ice: *granita*. It's made by preparing a simple syrup flavored with whatever you like, usually a citrus or fruit juice, then freezing it and scraping it with a fork every so often to create crystals. When made right, granita is downright fluffy, with an intense flavor you just don't get in an ice.

I make my lemon granita with rosemary added to the syrup; the herbaceous flavor is surprising and never fails to make people happy.

This is a very tart granita; you can add 1 to 2 tablespoons of sugar to make it sweeter.

Long strips of zest from one lemon
1 cup fresh lemon juice (from about 4 lemons)
2 cups water
⅔ cup sugar or more, to taste
2 small rosemary sprigs, bruised with the back
    of a knife

1. Put all the ingredients in a heavy saucepan and bring to a boil over high heat. Lower the heat and simmer, stirring occasionally until the sugar has dissolved, 3 to 4 minutes. Remove the pan from the heat and let cool 15 minutes. Transfer the pan to the refrigerator and chill the mixture completely.

2. Strain the mixture into a shallow, rimmed, scratch-proof and temperature-proof vessel and freeze for 2 to 3 hours, scraping it with a fork every 30 minutes until the mixture is a frozen, fluffy ice. Divide the granita among 4 to 6 small bowls and serve.

Rockin' Rice Pudding

SERVES 4

PREP TIME: 5 MINUTES

COOK TIME: ABOUT 2 HOURS, INCLUDING CHILLING TIME

This creamy rice pudding never fails to remind me of my Aunt Franny, who used to make it for me and my sisters when my parents went on their annual vacation to Acapulco. Franny made her rice pudding with Arborio rice, the same short-grain rice used in risotto; it was a brilliant choice because it really soaks up all the flavors: sugar, vanilla, and orange zest. This is a supercharged dessert that will become a family favorite.

½ cup Arborio rice
4 cups whole milk
¼ cup sugar
Strip orange zest, removed from the fruit
    with a vegetable peeler
Pinch kosher salt
½ vanilla bean, cut lengthwise with
    its seeds intact
2 large egg yolks

1. Put the rice, milk, sugar, orange zest, and salt in a deep, heavy saucepan. Use a paring knife to scrape the seeds of the vanilla bean into the pot, then add the bean as well. Set the pot over medium-high heat and bring the milk to a boil, stirring constantly. Lower the heat and cook at a simmer until the rice is tender and the mixture has thickened, 30 to 40 minutes.
2. Whisk the egg yolks in a heatproof bowl and ladle in about ½ cup of the rice pudding, whisking, to temper the eggs. Pour the egg-pudding mixture into the pot, stirring constantly until the mixture is beautifully creamy, about 15 minutes. Remove the pot from the heat and use tongs or a slotted spoon to fish out and discard the vanilla pod and orange zest. Use a ladle to divide the rice pudding evenly among 4 serving bowls and let cool, and serve, or chill for at least 1 hour in the refrigerator.
3. Serve chilled or at room temperature.

Tuxedo Strawberries

SERVES 2

PREP TIME: ABOUT 5 MINUTES

COOK TIME: ABOUT 10 MINUTES (20 TO 30 WITH OPTIONAL PIPING)

This is a simple, elegant dessert to make for somebody you love. They're so perfect for a romantic occasion that this recipe serves just two, but it multiplies well. With the chocolate front and center as it is here, you really need a good-quality chocolate; if you can find it, I suggest Callebaut, which is one of my go-to brands.

6 to 8 big, beautiful, ripe strawberries with stems,
rinsed and patted dry, at room temperature
8 ounces bittersweet or semisweet chocolate chips
6 ounces white chocolate chips

1. Line a small plate or cookie sheet with wax paper, parchment paper, or foil.
2. Pour about an inch of water into each of 2 small pots and bring to a simmer over medium-high heat. Put the dark chocolate chips in a stainless steel bowl, or double boiler sized to fit over the pots. Put the white chocolate chips in another. Set the bowls over the simmering water and melt the chocolate, stirring it occasionally with separate implements, to keep the two chocolates distinct.
3. Pick up 1 strawberry by the stem end or leafy crown. Dip and turn it in the white chocolate to coat it. Give the berry a quick twist to allow excess to drip back into the bowl, and place the berry on the lined plate. Repeat with the remaining berries and chocolate.
4. Put the plate in the refrigerator and let the chocolate harden for ten minutes, then dip in the dark chocolate, leaving a cuff of white chocolate showing toward the top. (See box for instructions on optional tuxedo piping.) Return the berries to the lined plate and let the chocolate harden in the refrigerator for 10 minutes.
5. The strawberries are best eaten the day you prepare them.

Piping a Bow Tie and Buttons

If you want the full tuxedo effect, follow these steps.

1. Make a parchment triangle: Cut a 12-inch-square piece of parchment paper diagonally in half, either with scissors, or by laying it on a cutting board or work station and slicing through it with the tip of a very sharp knife, to create two triangles. You will only use one triangle; save the other for the next time you need a parchment pencil.
2. Make a parchment cone: With one hand, hold the triangle in front of you with the point facing down. Use your other hand to wrap the paper around itself into a cone, coming around twice to use all the paper.
3. Tighten the cone: Pinch the wide, open end of the cone with your thumb and forefinger and rub your fingers together repeatedly to tighten the cone. It should still be wide at the open end, and tighten into a firm, conical shape.
4. When dipping the strawberry in dark chocolate, wipe a small portion of the berry against the rim of the pot to leave a "V" of white showing, simulating the black jacket and white shirt of a tuxedo.
5. Fill the cone. Use a tablespoon or small rubber spatula to fill the cone about two-thirds with melted chocolate. Hold the cone securely so that it doesn't unravel and the tip doesn't become wider than you want it to be.
6. Close the top. Roll the top closed over the chocolate, pressing down to pack the chocolate in tightly all the way to the bottom.
7. Cut the bottom. Use scissors to snip off the bottom of the cone and approximate the effect of a pastry tip.
8. Pipe a bowtie and buttons onto the white "V" on the strawberry.
9. Let the chocolate harden in the refrigerator for at least 10 minutes.

Funnel Cakes

SERVES 4

PREP TIME: 5 MINUTES

COOK TIME: 2 MINUTES

Anybody who's ever lived in or near an Italian-American neighborhood and attended a street fair has seen funnel cakes: hot discs of fried dough, crunchy on the outside and soft and warm inside. Powdered sugar is the most popular finishing touch, but I prefer to top them with cinnamon sugar. Whichever you choose, be sure to hit the funnel cakes with it the moment they come out of the oil, so that the sugar melts onto the pastry.

1¼ cups packaged pancake mix, such as Hungry Jack
⅔ cup milk
2 tablespoons canola oil, or other neutral oil, plus about
    3 cups for frying
1 large egg plus one large egg yolk
1 teaspoon pure vanilla extract
½ cup confectioner's sugar, or cinnamon sugar
    (¼ cup granulated sugar stirred together with
    2 tablespoons ground cinnamon)

1. Put the pancake mix in a bowl. In another bowl, whisk the milk, 2 tablespoons of the oil, the egg, yolk, and vanilla. Pour this mixture over the pancake mix and stir to combine well. Put the batter in a measuring cup with a spout or similar vessel, such as a small pitcher.
2. Line a plate with paper towels. Pour oil into a cast iron skillet to a depth of about ½ inch. Heat the oil over medium heat to a temperature of 325°F to 350°F.
3. Hold a funnel over the oil, a couple of inches from the surface.
4. Working very carefully to avoid splashing hot oil, pour about one-quarter of the batter into the funnel and, working from the center, drizzle a web of batter over and around to create a disk approximately 6 inches in diameter. It's desirable to have some gaps or holes in the disk, but it should be whole enough to facilitate turning it over.
5. When the bottom of the funnel cake is lightly browned, about 1 minute, turn the cake over, moving it away from you, and cook until golden on the other side, about 1 more minute.

6. Transfer the funnel cake to the paper-towel–lined plate and dust immediately with sugar.

7. Repeat with the remaining batter, letting the oil reheat between cakes, and serve immediately.

Sautéed Peaches with Sweetened Ricotta and Mascarpone

SERVES 6
PREP TIME: 10 MINUTES
COOK TIME: 20 MINUTES

This simple and elegant dessert cooks peaches in butter and the Italian sparkling wine, Prosecco, then serves them atop a sweetened mixture of cool, creamy ricotta and mascarpone cheeses enlivened with citrus and vanilla. The two components are united by the peaches' cooking syrup. Prosecco doesn't keep for very long once you've popped its cork, so I suggest serving ice-cold glasses of it alongside this dessert for a festive and celebratory conclusion to any meal.

2 tablespoons unsalted butter
4 cups thin peach slices (from 2 to 3 large fresh peaches
    or measured from a bag of frozen peach slices;
    if using frozen peaches, defrost them)
¼ cup plus 2 tablespoons sugar
¼ cup Prosecco
1 cup ricotta
1 cup mascarpone
Finely grated zest and juice of 1 medium orange
½ teaspoon pure vanilla extract

1. Heat a wide, deep, heavy sauté pan over medium heat. Add the butter and let it melt, then add the peaches and sauté until slightly softened but still holding their shape, 3 to 5 minutes. Sprinkle with 2 tablespoons of the sugar and continue to cook, stirring the peaches gently, until the sugar dissolves. Pour in the Prosecco, bring to a simmer, and let simmer, until nicely reduced, and the butter and Prosecco have come together in a syrup, 3 to 5 minutes. Remove the pan from the heat and let cool to room temperature or, to speed the process, chill over an ice bath or transfer to a mixing bowl and chill in the refrigerator, but do not allow it to become too cold.

2. Meanwhile, put the ricotta and mascarpone in a mixing bowl. Add the remaining 4 tablespoons of sugar, the orange juice and zest, and the vanilla. Stir with a rubber spatula just until the ingredients are well mixed and the sugar has dissolved.

3. Divide the ricotta-mascarpone mixture evenly among 6 dessert glasses or small bowls. Spoon some peaches over the mixture, and spoon some syrup over and around the peaches and cheese. Serve at once.

Zabaglione

SERVES 4
PREP TIME: ABOUT 10 MINUTES
COOK TIME: ABOUT 20 MINUTES

Zabaglione is an Italian custard that my dad used to make when we had dinner parties. It was one of the few things he made where I saw a direct line between what we did at the bakery and what we served at home: Constant whipping produces a light as air, dreamy custard that goes great over any fresh berries.

The key to any zabaglione is to keep moving the pot you're whipping it in on and off the heat to keep from scrambling the eggs. The two tricks to our family version are adding some sweet Marsala and a little of the berry juice to pull all the flavors together.

1 pint beautiful strawberries, trimmed and sliced lengthwise,
*   plus 4 beautiful strawberries, fanned for garnish*
½ cup plus 1 tablespoon sugar
¼ cup sweet Marsala
8 large egg yolks, preferably organic
1 pint heavy cream, whipped to soft peaks

1. Put the strawberries and 2 tablespoons of the sugar in a medium saucepan. Set the pan over medium heat and cook the berries, stirring gently, until they give off their juices and begin to soften, 2 to 3 minutes. Pour in 3 tablespoons of the Marsala, raise the heat to high, bring to a boil, and let boil until slightly reduced, 1 to 2 minutes. There should be a nice combination of berries and juices in the pan and the strawberries should still be holding their shape. Set the pan aside while you make the zabaglione.

2. Bring a pot with about 2 inches of water to a low simmer over moderate heat.

3. Off the heat, put the egg yolks and ¼ cup plus 2 tablespoons of the sugar in a stainless steel pot sized to fit over the pot of simmering water or the top of a double boiler, and whisk with a balloon whisk until well emulsified and beginning to lighten in color. Set the bowl over the simmering water and continue to whip the eggs continuously as they begin to froth and further lighten in color. Slowly pour in the remaining tablespoon of the Marsala as you continue to whip. Ladle in 1 tablespoon of the juices from the strawberries and the remaining 1 tablespoon of sugar, to infuse the mixture with berry flavor.

4. Keep whisking, moving the pot off and on the heat to keep the eggs from scrambling, until the mixture is thick and silken and falls in ribbons from the whisk, 7 to 10 minutes total.

5. Set the bowl on the counter and whisk gently for a moment to help it cool. Fold in some of the whipped cream to lighten the mixture, then fold in the remaining whipped cream.

6. Divide the strawberries and their juices among 4 wine or coupe glasses. Spoon zabaglione over the berries in each dish and garnish with a whole, fanned strawberry. Serve.

Apple Snacking Cake

MAKES ONE 9-INCH X 13-INCH CAKE
PREP TIME: ABOUT 15 MINUTES
COOK TIME: 45 MINUTES, PLUS COOLING TIME

This cobblerlike recipe is one that my family turns to when we need to use up a surplus of fruit after a fall apple-picking expedition. Relative to how delicious it is, the recipe is almost unbelievably easy; the apples and spices do all the work for you!

Unsalted butter, for greasing baking pan
2 cups all-purpose flour
1 cup plus 1½ tablespoons sugar
½ cup light or dark brown sugar
1¼ teaspoons baking soda
½ teaspoon fine sea salt
2½ teaspoons ground cinnamon
¼ teaspoon ground nutmeg
¼ teaspoon ground allspice
¼ cup canola oil or other neutral oil
Scant ½ cup natural applesauce
2 large eggs
1 medium Granny Smith apple, peeled, cored,
*   and cut into medium dice*
2 medium Gala apples, peeled, cored,
*   and cut into medium dice*
½ cup chopped toasted walnuts (see page 69
*   for toasting instructions)*

1. Position a rack in the center of the oven and preheat to 350°F. Grease a straight-sided 9-inch x 13-inch baking pan.
2. Put the flour, 1 cup of the sugar, brown sugar, baking soda, salt, 1 teaspoon cinnamon, nutmeg, and allspice in a large bowl and whisk.
3. Put the oil, applesauce, and eggs in another bowl and whisk.
4. Add the wet ingredients, the apples, and the walnuts to the dry ingredients, folding in with a spatula until everything is moistened and well mixed. The mixture will be chunky with what might seem a large amount of apples in proportion to batter.

5. Spread the mixture out evenly in the prepared pan.
6. Put the remaining 1½ tablespoons of sugar and remaining 1½ teaspoons of cinnamon in a bowl and stir together. Sprinkle the cinnamon-sugar evenly over the batter.
7. Bake until the cake is set and a toothpick inserted into the center comes out clean, 40 to 45 minutes.
8. Remove the pan from the oven and let the cake cool before slicing and serving.

Banana Cream Pie

MAKES ONE 9-INCH PIE.
PREP TIME: ABOUT 90 MINUTES (INCLUDING CUSTARD CHILLING TIME;
DOES NOT INCLUDE PIE CRUST PREP TIME)
COOK TIME: ABOUT 2 HOURS (INCLUDES 1 HOUR COOLING TIME)

Today, we make a number of American desserts at Carlo's Bake Shop, but banana cream pie was among the very first we ever offered, all the way back when my father first bought the bakery. I'm including the recipe in this book because it's such an easy, satisfying dessert to make: You don't have to make your own pie shell, but I recommend it, because it's easier than it might seem, and is really the only cooking required here.

2½ cups whole milk
1 tablespoon pure vanilla extract
5 extra-large egg yolks
1½ cups sugar
⅔ cup cake flour, sifted
2 teaspoons unsalted butter
3 cups heavy cream
1 9-inch pie shell, blind baked and cooled (recipe follows),
   or a store-bought shell
3 large bananas
Juice of 1 large lemon
1 large strawberry, optional

1. Make a custard: Pour the milk and vanilla into a deep, heavy saucepan, bring to a simmer over medium-high heat, then turn off heat. Put the eggs in a mixing bowl and whisk 1 cup of the sugar into the eggs. Pour the cake flour into the eggs while whisking well to incorporate. Ladle about ¼ cup of hot milk into the egg mixture, whisking to incorporate it. Repeat with another ladle of hot milk.

2. Pour the egg mixture into the milk in the saucepan, using a wooden spoon or spatula to scrape all of the mixture into the pan. Set over medium-low heat and cook, whisking continuously, taking care to scrape the bottom and sides of the pan. The mixture should thicken within 1 minute. After it does, continue to whisk another 30 seconds. Whisk in the butter, then lower heat and whisk until quite thick, another minute or two. Remove the pan from heat and let the custard cool. Transfer to a bowl, cover loosely with plastic wrap, and chill for at least 1 hour.

3. Make whipped cream: Put the cream and remaining ½ cup of sugar in a bowl and

whip with a hand mixer fitted with the blending attachments on high speed until a whipped cream is formed; do not overwhip or you'll end up with butter. You should have about 2½ cups of whipped cream.

4. Put the custard in a mixing bowl, whisk to smooth it, and use a rubber spatula to fold in half the whipped cream, making a French cream.

5. Peel 2 of the bananas and slice them crosswise over the French cream, so the slices fall into the cream.

6. Transfer the banana cream to the shell, using a rubber spatula to scrape as much cream out of the bowl as possible and then to level it off in the pie, or mound it high to use all the filling.

7. Transfer the remaining whipped cream to a pastry bag fit with the #7 star tip and pipe bits of cream all over the pie. Peel the remaining banana and slice it crosswise on an angle into 8 pieces. Put the pieces in a bowl and toss with the lemon juice to prevent them from oxidizing. Arrange the banana slices at even intervals around the edge of the pie.

8. If using the strawberry, position it in the center of the pie.

How to Hide Oxidized Bananas

The lemon juice in this recipe will keep the bananas from oxidizing, but for good measure (and more flavor), consider topping the pie with chocolate cake crumbs or processed chocolate cookies, or grating a few ounces of semisweet chocolate over it.

How to Blind Bake

If you need to bake the crust with no filling, fill the pie with dry beans or rice, or set another pie pan in the well, invert, and bake on the center rack of an oven pre-heated to 350°F until the crust is firm and golden, approximately 25 minutes.

Pie Crust

MAKES ONE 9-INCH PIE CRUST
PREP TIME: ABOUT 1 HOUR
COOK TIME: ABOUT 30 MINUTES

This all-purpose pie crust is a terrific recipe to have in your arsenal. While you can buy a quality pie crust at most supermarkets these days, it's easy to make your own, and there's nothing like the smell of a homemade crust baking in the oven. I'm a professional baker, and even I get a big smile on my face when I see a just-baked pie crust, golden-brown and piping hot, resting on a kitchen counter.

> *2 cups all-purpose flour, plus more for dusting work surface*
> *¾ cup vegetable shortening*
> *1 tablespoon granulated sugar*
> *1 teaspoon fine sea salt*
> *7 tablespoons ice-cold water (if making in the summer,*
> *   use 6 tablespoons to allow for increased humidity*
> *   affecting the moisture content of the flour)*

1. Put the flour, shortening, sugar, and salt in the bowl of a stand mixer fitted with the paddle attachment and paddle at lowest speed just until the mixture holds together, approximately 30 seconds. (If you don't have a stand mixer, you can put the ingredients in a bowl and blend with a hand mixer.) Add 6 or 7 tablespoons of water, and paddle until absorbed, approximately 30 seconds.

2. Remove the dough from the bowl, wrap with plastic wrap, and refrigerate for 30 to 60 minutes.

3. Lightly flour a work surface, and roll out the dough in a circle, about 14 inches in diameter and about ¼-inch thick. Roll it up onto the rolling pin and transfer to a 9-inch pie pan, unrolling it over the top. Tap the pan gently on the counter and the dough will fall into place. Put your hands at the 2 o'clock and 10 o'clock positions on the side of the pan, and rotate the pan from just under the lip to cause the excess dough to fall away. (If molded to an aluminum pie pan, the dough can be wrapped in plastic and frozen for up to 2 months. Let thaw to room temperature before filling and baking.)

Cocoa-Hazelnut Cream with Berries

SERVES 4
PREP TIME: ABOUT 10 MINUTES
COOK TIME: ABOUT 10 MINUTES

Here's another cream-and-berry combination that shows how many different results you can get with a similar technique. A cocoa-hazelnut cream served over mixed berries produces a rich, complex result. Where the zabaglione is terrific for just about any occasion, I save this one for more formal, momentous occasions, such as New Year's Eve.

1 cup heavy whipping cream
1½ tablespoons Dutch cocoa
2 tablespoons sugar
½ teaspoon pure vanilla extract
¼ cup Frangelico liqueur
2 cups mixed berries (½ pint each of blackberries, raspberries, and blueberries)
Dark chocolate, for garnish
Crisp cookies such as amaretti, vanilla wafers, or biscotti

1. In the bowl of a stand mixer fitted with the whip attachment, whip together the cream, cocoa, sugar, vanilla, and Frangelico at medium-high speed for 4 minutes. (This may also be done in a stainless-steel mixing bowl using a hand mixer; you may need to mix for about 1 minute longer.) Remove the bowl from the mixer, cover with plastic wrap, and refrigerate for 1 hour.
2. Divide the berries among 4 dessert glasses, being sure to include a good mix of berries in each glass. Top with some of the whipped, flavored cream and shave dark chocolate over each serving. Serve with crispy cookies.

Affogato

SERVES 4

PREP TIME: 10 MINUTES

My maternal grandfather used to make this Italian ice cream float, which pours freshly pulled espresso over vanilla ice cream (*affogato* means "drowned"). Grandpa's espresso could be a little muddy because he cooked it forever. These days, with all the great espresso makers and high-quality ice creams out there, you can make this into a gourmet treat with even less work than it used to take.

1 pint heavy cream
1 tablespoon sugar
2 pints excellent-quality vanilla-bean gelato
     or ice cream
4 shots freshly pulled espresso
2 tablespoons crumbled amaretti, pizzelle,
     or biscotti, for garnish

1. Put the cream and sugar in a mixing bowl and whip with a hand mixer until soft peaks form.
2. Scoop 3 small scoops of gelato into each of 4 parfait or Irish coffee glasses. Pour 1 shot of espresso over each serving. Crumble some cookie pieces over the ice cream. Top with a dollop of whipped cream and more crushed cookies.

Joe's Chocolate Mousse

SERVES 6
PREP TIME: 5 MINUTES
COOK TIME: 5 TO 7 MINUTES

It's not often that the Valastros take their hats off to another person's dessert, but Joe Park Casino was such a terrific chef that we had to give it up even for the sweet stuff he served at his catering hall. This chocolate mousse was part of all the Venetian Hours, when a dessert buffet was served, at the Park Casino. When we were kids, my cousin Frankie and I used to run around eating as many servings as we could get our hands on. It's hard to believe it's made with plain old Hershey's syrup, but it really is a heavenly mousse with the chocolate and cream in perfect balance.

2 cups heavy cream
2 tablespoons sugar
½ cup Hershey's syrup
1 tablespoon sifted cocoa powder
1 tablespoon crème de cacao

1. In a chilled bowl, whip the heavy cream and sugar with a hand mixer until stiff peaks form. Use a rubber spatula to fold in the chocolate syrup, cocoa powder, and crème de cacao. Divide among 6 glass bowls and chill for 1 hour, or up to 4 hours, to let the cream set.
2. Serve chilled.

Nina's Ricotta Cheesecake

MAKES ONE 9-INCH CAKE

PREP TIME: 5 MINUTES

BAKE TIME: 1 HOUR 15 MINUTES PLUS 4 HOURS COOLING AND CHILLING TIME

A perfect reflection of our family's heritage, my Aunt Nina's ricotta cheesecake is a mix of Italian and American cheesecakes. It uses the ricotta cheese you find in most Italian recipes, but unlike those cakes, which can come out dry, this is a moist and smooth cake. It's a real one-of-a-kind creation that's a true original in our family.

Unsalted butter, for greasing cake pan
3 pounds whole-milk ricotta
1 cup sugar
4 large eggs, separated
Finely grated zest of 1 large lemon
1 teaspoon pure vanilla extract
1 tablespoon Strega liqueur (Cointreau or
*   Triple Sec may be substituted)*

1. Position a rack in the center of the oven. Preheat to 400°F. Butter a 9-inch spring-form pan and place on a baking sheet.
2. In a stand mixer fit with the paddle, beat the cheese, sugar, egg yolks, lemon zest, vanilla, and liqueur on medium until very smooth, about 4 minutes. Transfer the mixture to a mixing bowl and wipe out the mixer bowl.
3. Put the egg whites in the mixer bowl and whip until soft peaks form. Fold the whites by thirds into the cheese mixture. Pour mixture into the prepared baking pan and level it.
4. Put the cake in the oven and immediately lower the heat to 350°F. Bake until the cake has risen higher on the sides than in the middle and is set but jiggling in the center, 1 hour to 1 hour, 10 minutes. Turn off the oven and prop the door open; a wine cork is a good tool for propping the door open just enough. (Be careful not to let it fall into the oven.) Let the cake cool completely in the oven for 1 hour, then cover the cake with plastic wrap and refrigerate it for at least 3 hours or overnight before removing the springform sides, slicing, and serving.

Orange Angel Food Cake
with Orange-Cinnamon Glaze

SERVES 8

PREP TIME: 20 MINUTES

COOK TIME: 40 MINUTES, PLUS 60 TO 90 MINUTES COOLING TIME

I love the spongy texture of angel food cake and, as a baker, appreciate the simplicity of its preparation. The sweet, white cake is also a wonderful foil for any number of complementary flavors; here, a simple drizzle of orange-cinnamon glaze changes the entire flavor profile of the dessert.

2 cups sugar

1⅓ cups sifted cake flour (not self-rising)

1½ cups egg whites (from 10 to 12 large eggs),
*   at room temperature (see Note, page 76,*
*   for instructions on separating eggs)*

¾ teaspoon kosher salt

1½ teaspoons cream of tartar

¾ teaspoon pure vanilla extract

1½ teaspoons grated orange zest (from 1 large orange),
*   plus 2 to 3 tablespoons freshly squeezed orange juice*

1 cup confectioner's sugar

¼ teaspoon cinnamon

1. Preheat the oven to 350°F.
2. Put ½ cup sugar and the flour in a bowl, and sift together 4 times, or pulse together in a food processor fitted with the steel blade. Set aside.
3. Put the egg whites, salt, and cream of tartar in the bowl of an stand mixer fitted with a whisk attachment and beat on high speed until there are medium-firm peaks, about 1 minute. With the mixer on medium speed, add the remaining 1½ cups of sugar by sprinkling it over the beaten egg whites in a constant stream. Beat for a few minutes until thick and shiny. Beat in the vanilla and orange zest and continue to whisk until very thick, about 1 more minute. Sift about ¼ of the flour mixture over the egg whites and fold it into the batter with a rubber spatula. Continue adding the flour by fourths, by sifting and folding until all the flour is incorporated.

4. Pour the batter into an ungreased 10-inch tube pan, smooth the top, and bake until it springs back to the touch, and a toothpick inserted into the center comes out clean, about 40 to 45 minutes. Remove the cake from the oven and invert the pan on a cooling rack until cool, 1 to 1½ hours.

5. While the cake is cooling, make the glaze by putting the confectioner's sugar and orange juice in a bowl and stirring together until the sugar is dissolved and a thin, syrupy consistency is attained. Stir in the cinnamon.

6. Once cooled, unmold the cake from the pan and drizzle the glaze over the top, using the tines of a fork.

Sofia's Sweet Pizza

MAKES ONE 9- TO 10-INCH PIZZA
PREP TIME: ABOUT 15 MINUTES (NOT INCLUDING PIZZA DOUGH)
COOK TIME: ABOUT 10 MINUTES

My father-in-law, Mauro, an accomplished pizza maker, and I, came up with this dessert pizza especially for my daughter, Sofia, to satisfy her love of Nutella. With bananas and strawberries taking the place of other toppings, and chocolate sauce instead of cheese, it's a great dessert that kids find amusing and delicious.

One-third Pizza Dough recipe (page 95)
¼ cup sugar
1 teaspoon ground cinnamon
1 tablespoon unsalted butter, melted
½ cup Nutella
1 firm ripe banana, sliced crosswise
½ cup sliced strawberries
¼ cup Chocolate Sauce (recipe follows)

1. Position a rack in the bottom of the oven and put a pizza stone on the rack. (See page 90.) Preheat the oven to its highest setting, ideally 450°F to 500°F.
2. Flour a pizza peel.
3. Pat, stretch, and/or roll out the dough to a 9- to 10-inch circle and, in one swift movement, drag it onto the floured peel.
4. Put the sugar and cinnamon in a small bowl and stir.
5. Brush the pizza dough with the melted butter, leaving a ½-inch border. Prick the buttered portion of the dough all over with a fork. Sprinkle the cinnamon sugar evenly over the butter.
6. Slide the pizza onto the pizza stone and bake until the dough is cooked through and browned in spots, 5 to 7 minutes. Remove the pizza from the oven. Use a rubber spatula to spread with the Nutella, and top decoratively with bananas and strawberries. Drizzle with the chocolate sauce, slice into individual slices, and serve.

Chocolate Sauce

MAKES ABOUT 2 CUPS
PREP TIME: 5 MINUTES
COOK TIME: ABOUT 10 MINUTES

1 cup Hershey's semisweet chips
¾ cup heavy cream
1 tablespoon unsalted butter
1 teaspoon pure vanilla extract

Put the chips and cream in a small, heavy saucepan and set over low-medium heat. Cook, stirring, until the chips have melted and the chocolate and cream have come together in a uniform mixture. Remove the pan from the heat and stir in the butter and vanilla.

Dark Chocolate Bread Pudding

SERVES 8

PREP TIME: 15 MINUTES

COOK TIME: 45 TO 50 MINUTES

This decadent chocolate bread pudding is a great choice when feeding a large group, because it serves eight people and can be made in advance, saving you another trip to the kitchen at the end of the meal. Be sure to use good-quality chocolate and cocoa, so that this packs the proper punch.

Unsalted butter for greasing pan
1 day-old country-style loaf, cut into 2-inch chunks
    (about 6 to 8 cups)
8 ounces bittersweet chocolate, cut into chunks
4 cups half and half
¾ cup granulated sugar
¼ cup unsweetened cocoa powder
Pinch kosher salt
8 large eggs
2 teaspoons pure vanilla extract
1 tablespoon coarse sugar

1. Grease a 9-inch x 13-inch x 2-inch (deep) baking pan with butter. Arrange the bread cubes in the pan. Tuck half the chocolate chunks among the bread cubes.
2. Put 1½ cups of the half and half, the remaining chocolate chunks, the granulated sugar, cocoa, and a pinch of salt in a heavy saucepan and set over medium-low heat. Cook, whisking occasionally, until the sugar has dissolved and the mixture is smooth, 8 to 10 minutes. Remove from the heat.
3. In a large bowl, whisk the remaining 2½ cups half and half, the eggs, and the vanilla. Whisk in the warm chocolate mixture and pour over the bread and chocolate. Let soak at room temperature for 1 hour, occasionally poking the bread down into the mixture with a spoon. Sprinkle the coarse sugar over the top.
4. Position a rack in the center of the oven. Preheat to 325°F.
5. Set the baking pan inside a slightly larger pan and fill the larger pan with warm water halfway up the sides of the baking pan.

6. Bake just until the center of the bread pudding is firm but jiggles, 45 minutes to 1 hour. Carefully remove the baking pan from the water bath and let cool on a wire rack.
7. The bread pudding can be covered loosely with plastic wrap and refrigerated for up to 3 days.

Ice Cream Parfaits
with Warm Berry Sauce

SERVES 4 TO 6
PREP TIME: 10 MINUTES
COOK TIME: 10 MINUTES

This is a very easy dessert that layers a quick cooked berry sauce with vanilla ice cream and crushed cookies for a layered sundae. It's best in the summertime when you can get fresh berries but, because they're cooked, you can get away with making it just about any time of year that you crave those sweet, explosive flavors; in a pinch, you could even use defrosted, frozen berries.

2 cups fresh blueberries
2 cups fresh strawberries, cored and quartered
2 tablespoons sugar
⅛ teaspoon kosher salt
⅛ teaspoon cinnamon
2 tablespoons water
½ teaspoon cornstarch
1 teaspoon freshly squeezed lemon juice
1 cup crushed biscotti or other hard cookie
2 pints vanilla ice cream

1. Put the blueberries, strawberries, sugar, salt, cinnamon, and water in a medium, heavy saucepan. Bring the mixture to a boil over medium heat, then lower the heat and simmer, uncovered, until the mixture thickens and the berries have begun to burst, 3 to 5 minutes.
2. Put the cornstarch and lemon juice in a small bowl and stir until smooth, then stir into the berry mixture. Simmer until the mixture thickens, 1 to 2 more minutes. Remove from the heat.
3. Divide one-third of the crushed cookies among the bottoms of 4 glasses. Place a scoop of ice cream in each glass and top with some warm fruit sauce. Sprinkle another third of the crushed cookies into glasses. Top with another scoop of vanilla ice cream, the remaining fruit sauce, and the remaining third of the crushed cookies. Serve immediately.

Acknowledgments

As always, I give all my thanks to the following people for their help with this book, and in producing my various shows:

My immediate family: My wife, Lisa. My four incredible kids: Sofia, Buddy, Marco, and Carlo. My mother, Mary Valastro. And, as always, the memory of my father, Buddy Valastro, the original Cake Boss.

My four sisters: Grace, Madeline, Mary, and Lisa, and my brothers-in-law: Mauro, Joey, and Joe.

The crew at the bakery, especially Frankie, Danny, and Leo.

Adam Bourcier for continuing to manage this empire's growth.

My personal assistant, Nikki O'Connell.

Tony Guglielmelli, who tested the recipes for this book.

The book jacket photographer and photographer for the beautiful shots of the food inside the book: Miki Duisterhof. And Miki's incredible team, Paul Grimes, food stylist; food stylist assistants John Bjostad, Monica Pierini, and Chelsea Zimmer; Cindy DiPrima, prop stylist; photography assistant Tiffany Howe; and digital tech Steven Boljonis.

The team at my publisher, Free Press: my editor, Leslie Meredith; Publisher Martha Levin; Associate Editor Donna Loffredo; Senior Publicist Meg Cassidy; Director of Publicity Carisa Hays; Editor-in-Chief Dominick Anfuso; and Associate Publisher Suzanne Donahue.

Jon Rosen and the team at William Morris Endeavor Entertainment, especially literary agent Eric Lupfer.

My extended family—my aunts and uncles, cousins and second cousins—and to all my friends: Sorry, guys, there are too many of you to name!

My creative family at TLC and Discovery: President and CEO David Zaslav, Discovery Communications; Group President Eileen O'Neill, Discovery & TLC Networks; President, Advertising Sales Joe Abruzzese, Discovery; Executive Vice President Nancy Daniels, Production & Development, Discovery Channel; Senior Vice President, Production & Development Howard Lee, TLC; Vice President, Communications Dustin Smith, TLC; Director, Licensing Sue Perez-Jackson, Discovery Communications; Group Chief Operating Officer Edward Sabin, Discovery & TLC Networks; Senior Vice President Jen Williams, Talent Management & Strategy, Discovery & TLC Networks; and Director of Production Jim Kowats, TLC.

God, for giving me more than any man could ever expect in life.

And, as always, to the customers of Carlo's Bake Shop, and to the fans of my show. Without you guys, we wouldn't be who we are or where we are. Thanks for visiting the bakery, watching the show, coming to the live performances, and buying my books. You're the ones we do it for. I love you and promise to keep it coming!

Index

Page numbers in *italics* refer to illustrations.

ABOUT THE AUTHOR

Buddy Valastro is the author of the *New York Times* bestsellers *Cake Boss* and *Baking with the Cake Boss,* and star of the hit TLC series *Cake Boss* and *Next Great Baker*. He lives in New Jersey with his wife and four children.